D0848916

Composition and Copyright

Composition & Copyright

Perspectives on Teaching, Text-making, and Fair Use

EDITED AND WITH AN INTRODUCTION BY
STEVE WESTBROOK

Published by
STATE UNIVERSITY OF NEW YORK PRESS
ALBANY

© 2009 State University of New York

For information, address
State University of New York Press,
90 State Stree, Suite 700, Albany, NY 12207

Production by Marilyn P. Semerad
Marketing by Michael Campochiaro

Library of Congress Cataloging-in-Publication Data

Composition and copyright : perspectives on teaching, text-making, and fair use / edited and with an introduction by Steve Westbrook.
    p. cm.
  Includes bibliographical references and index.
  ISBN 978-1-4384-2591-7 (hardcover : alk. paper)
  1. Fair use (Copyright)—United States.   2. Copyright—United States.
I. Westbrook, Steve, 1973-
  KF3020.C66 2009
  346.7304'82—dc22   2008024280

10 9 8 7 6 5 4 3 2 1

CONTENTS

Introduction

STEVE WESTBROOK

Five years ago and fresh out of graduate school, I accepted my first tenure-track job at a small university. I had been trained in composition pedagogy. I had completed a dissertation that focused, in part at least, on the ways that new media texts challenged print culture's conventions of genre and contested perceived divisions between the academic enterprises of composition-rhetoric and creative writing. On the side, I had become proficient with programs like iMovie, PowerPoint, and Photoshop, which I used to compose new media texts that combined my own writings with appropriations of the sounds and images of others. In theory, I was prepared to teach new media composition and to take on one of the major tasks of my new job: to help create a writing program that blurred the boundaries between rhetoric and poetics, print and digital composition. Like most new professors, I quickly experienced the shock of experientially understanding the distinction between *learning about* teaching writing and designing writing programs and *actually doing so*. Although I mainly experienced what might be called the disillusionment of an ordinary grad-school idealism, I found myself positively deficient in at least one area. Despite my training, I was woefully naïve about intellectual property and copyright law; quite simply, I did not know how recent legal developments could affect my own and my students' freedom to produce and circulate new media compositions.

I became quickly aware of this problem when Sara, a student enrolled in one of my classes, was prohibited from posting a digital text she had designed in class on her own website. In short, she had created a feminist counter-ad (akin to the sorts produced by Adbusters) that relied on images appropriated from an original Maybelline advertisement. Maybelline's parent company, L'Oreal, refused requests for permission and claimed ownership to Sara's text under copyright law's provision of rights to derivative works; in fact, L'Oreal's legal representative responded to my own inquiry by, first, claiming they had a blanket policy of rejecting permissions for what they called "viral ads" and, second, suggesting that I contact an attorney should I choose to pursue the matter further. I have narrated this experience at length elsewhere (see "Visual Rhetoric in a Culture of Fear," *College English* 68.5 [2006]: 457–80) and relate it here only briefly to reveal the shock of my sudden awareness about a matter for which I had not been prepared. Through this experience, I came to understand the discrepancy between, legally speaking, what might be done in the classroom and what might be done in the public sphere and, perhaps more generally, what I needed to know about copyright law as a teacher of writing in the twenty-first century.

I begin with this anecdote for another reason as well: the story is not exclusively my own. That is, as the technology of writing changes at an unprecedented pace and as legislation struggles to keep up with these changes, most of us who teach text-making find ourselves facing the subject of composition and copyright in one capacity or another, whether we are concerned with tracking down permissions for our publications, wondering who may claim legal ownership to the work we produce for our employing institutions or agencies, or deciding how to advise students when they want to appropriate images or lyrics from the Internet. In fact, as the nascent but growing body of scholarship on the subject suggests, copyright law's effect on composition has become a rather exigent matter in our professional lives.

While the amount of scholarship addressing the subject is far from adequate for the current demand, it has been developing quickly since the founding of the Conference on College Composition and Communication's Caucus on Intellectual Property (CCCC-IP) in 1994. Martha Woodmansee and Peter Jaszi's "The Law of Texts: Copyright in the Academy" (1995) and Andrea Lunsford and Susan West's "Intellectual Property and Composition Studies" (1996) offered early calls for an increased awareness of how developments in copyright and intellectual property laws threatened to affect the practices of students, scholars, artists, and teachers. Since the publication of these two seminal essays, the scholarship has been diverse in form and varied in subject.

In 1998, Laura Gurak and Johndan Johnson-Eilola edited a themed issue of *Computers and Composition* devoted entirely to matters of intellectual property. After the publication of this collection, a number of notable articles appeared in composition journals, including the CCCC-IP's "Use Your Fair Use: Strategies Toward Action" (2000), Charles Lowe's "Copyright, Access, and Digital Texts" (2003), Jessica Reyman's "Copyright, Distance Education, and the TEACH Act" (2006), and, most recently, Martine Courant Rife's "The Fair Use Doctrine: History, Application, and Implications for (New Media) Writing Teachers" (2007). Two book-length studies have also addressed the intersections of composition and copyright: TyAnna K. Herrington's *Controlling Voices: Intellectual Property, Humanistic Studies, and the Internet* (2001) and John Logie's *Peers, Pirates, and Persuasion: Rhetoric in the Peer-to-Peer Debates* (2006). Of course, in addition to appearing in print, the scholarship on the subject has taken the form of numerous conference presentations, including, perhaps most notably, attorney Lawrence Lessig's featured presentation at the 2005 Conference on College Composition and Communication.

In this book, contributors who have been active participants in the CCCC-IP and instrumental in developing the body of scholarship on composition and copyright now expand this ongoing conversation. They bring with them a rich diversity of perspectives. Many, like me, were trained in composition and came to the subject of copyright law somewhat circuitously through the practical demands of their teaching and research experience. Some, like Brian Ballentine, approach the subject from the perspective of professional writers who inform their composition teaching and scholarship with an industry perspective on the complications of intellectual property. Others, like Clancy Ratliff and Martine Courant Rife, hold degrees in jurisprudence and composition; they bring with them useful backgrounds as both practicing lawyers and composition teachers. Predictably, then, the work of the contributors offers less a consensus on defining what are or should be considered legal composing behaviors and more a collective of divergent arguments and understandings. In other words, the essays do not provide any sort of final word on legality; rather, they offer analyses useful for readers who seek to investigate the theoretical premises underlying copyright law and its practical application to both the writing classroom and the larger field of composition-rhetoric.

For purposes of practical organization, I have arranged the contributors' essays into three sections. The first section, Defining Cases and Contexts: Copyright, Digital Ethics, and Composition Studies, offers an introduction to the larger cultural debates over copyright law; here, contributors examine recent developments in legislation, case law, and writing technologies in relation to the field of composition-rhetoric. In the first chapter, "Property, Theft, Piracy: Rhetoric and Regulation in *MGM Studios v. Grokster*," Jessica Reyman provides an introduction to the debates over peer-to-peer file sharing and its implications for rhetoric and writing scholars by examining one of the most recent copyright cases to reach the Supreme Court. In chapter 2, "Fair Use and the Vulnerability of Criticism on the Internet," Sohui Lee discusses problems the Digital Millennium Copyright Act (DMCA) poses to e-rhetoricians, whose critical commentary relies on multimedia sampling practices. She recommends that we join together as compositionists to avoid potential censorship by developing an internal set of guidelines modeled in part on the Documentary Filmmakers' Statement of Best Practices in Fair Use. Clancy Ratliff presents the results of her study of blogging in chapter 3, "'Some Rights Reserved': Weblogs with Creative Commons Licenses." She reveals a growing tendency for bloggers to reject standard "All Rights Reserved" copyright licenses in favor of an alternative "Some Rights Reserved" licensing system that enables more writerly freedom and contributes to the realization of the Web as an intellectual commons. Offering a counterbalance to some ideological strains of the open source movement, Brian D. Ballentine draws on his own experience as a medical software engineer to argue for the value of restricted access and proprietary rights in chapter 4, "In Defense of Obfuscation: Questioning Open Source and a New Perspective on Teaching Digital Literacy in the Writing Classroom." Further, he recommends that teachers of professional writing adopt a balanced perspective on the debate over copyright and intellectual property by encouraging students to apply a particular code of ethics to problems of ownership they may encounter in their careers.

The second section of *Composition and Copyright* focuses more pointedly on the law's influence on classroom teaching and composition pedagogy. In chapter 5, "A Refrain of Costly Fires: Visual Rhetoric, Writing Pedagogy, and Copyright Law," I examine the ways in which visual rhetoric textbooks frame discussions of copyright and contrast these discussions with the norms of the publishing and entertainment industries. In chapter 6, "Beyond the Wake-up Call: Learning What Students Know about Copyright," Lisa Dush relies on interview data to survey students' attitudes about copyright law and, further, offers strategies for using the classroom to discuss students' decisions to consciously follow or subvert proprietary conventions. In chapter 7, "Ideas Toward a Fair Use Heuristic: Visual Rhetoric and Composition," Martine Courant Rife explores the differences between students' alphabetic and visual composition under the current norms of copyright law. After surveying a number of relevant cases concerned with appropriations of visual material, she offers a fair use heuristic that instructors might consider adopting in courses that involve new media and visual composition. TyAnna K. Herrington returns to the subject of weblogs in chapter 8, "Blogging Down: Copyright Law and Blogs in the Classroom." Focusing on the ownership of blogs used within the setting of a writing class, Herrington argues that because students may claim copyright control over the content of their blogs (according to statutory and case law), composition teachers making use of this technology should understand not only the concept of fair use but also the implications of Sections 101 and 106 of the Copyright Act.

Contributors to the third and final section, Concluding Polemics: Changing the Future of Composition and Copyright, offer activist arguments for rethinking our understandings of the key terms of this collection—*composition* and *copyright*—and the relationship between them. In chapter 9, "The (Re) Birth of the Composer," John Logie expands on the work of Roland Barthes to discuss the problem of authorship in relation to copyright and digital culture. In his argument, he reveals why our field should replace the rather antiquated term *author* with *composer* so that, in our discourse, we more accurately name the appropriative and transformative practices of student-writers and other contemporary text-makers. In chapter 10, "Own Your Rights: Know When Your University Can Claim Ownership of Your Work," Jeffrey R. Galin reveals an increasing trend among American universities to attempt to claim ownership of the research- and teaching-related intellectual property created by individual faculty members under their employ. Advocating actions that might impede this trend, Galin provides readers strategies for negotiating the copyright to the scholarship they produce.

PART I

Defining Cases and Concepts

Copyright, Digital Ethics, and Composition Studies

CHAPTER 1

Property, Theft, Piracy

Rhetoric and Regulation in
MGM *Studios v. Grokster*

JESSICA REYMAN

In recent years we have witnessed a rising tension between the open architecture of the Internet and legal restrictions for online activities. Digital recording technologies and distributed file sharing systems have forever changed the
expectations of everyday users with regard to digital information. At the same
time, however, legal developments, particularly in copyright law, show a decided
trend toward more restrictions over what we are able to do with digital materials. The Digital Millennium Copyright Act (DMCA),[1] codified in 1998, asserts
new "anticircumvention" provisions that make illegal any attempt to defeat
anti-piracy protections added to copyrighted works and ban circumvention
technologies used for that purpose. In 2002, the ruling in the *Eldred v. Ashcroft*
case upheld the constitutionality of the Sonny Bono Copyright Term Extension
Act,[2] which extended copyright ownership an additional twenty years from the
1976 Act. And, in the past several years, we have seen the content industries win
cases against peer-to-peer file sharing services (*A&M Records v. Napster*, 2002),
file lawsuits against individual users of the networks, and challenge the legality
of the technologies themselves (*MGM Studios v. Grokster*, 2005).

This chapter analyzes the public and legal rhetoric at work in the most recent copyright case to reach the U.S. Supreme Court: *MGM Studios v. Grokster*. This case was brought in 2001 by twenty-eight of the largest entertainment companies against the makers of Grokster and StreamCast software products. The case raised the issue of whether a distributor of a technology that may be used for copyright infringement should be held liable for contributing to the unlawful activities of its end users. Intellectual property as it is exchanged on peer-to-peer networks blurs the boundaries of discrete packages of intellectual property—the basis for current copyright law—and encourages certain types of nontraditional composing, even certain forms of unlawful copying. Peer-to-peer networks allow users to bypass an intermediary, centralizing content controller and exchange content directly with other users in a client-to-client fashion. They operate on individual computers that connect directly with others' individual computers, meaning that peer-to-peer networks cannot operate without this type of peer-to-peer interaction. Further, peer-to-peer networks grow larger and stronger, not weaker, through the increased activity of users. These characteristics—distributed architecture, decentralized control, and facilitation of sharing—challenge a property-based model of copyright law. In this way, the balance formulated by copyright law between creativity and distribution becomes ill-fitting: the very structure of the balance no longer works the way it did in a print-based culture. While print- and analog- based intellectual and creative works required a publisher's stewardship (and, subsequently, incentives for publisher involvement), on peer-to-peer networks these products are created and circulate in the public sphere without this stewardship.

Nevertheless, in *MGM Studios v. Grokster*, the Supreme Court ruled in favor of the entertainment industry by assigning potential liability to Grokster and StreamCast Networks. This ruling set a precedent for the regulation of information and innovation in our culture. Establishing where the line should be drawn between copyright protection and innovation, this case reveals the tensions between several interested parties: artists and creators, users of copyrighted works (including students, researchers, and instructors), content industries, and technologists. A glance at the history of copyright law in the United States shows us that these tensions are not new: technological development has both presented challenges to and opened new outlets for the creation and distribution of copyrighted works. From the Gutenberg printing press to the player piano to the Xerox machine to the VCR to the CD burner, new technologies have upset the balance between copyright protection and innovation. What makes *MGM Studios v. Grokster* significant, however, is that it is situated within a culture marked by increasingly centralized markets for content and a proliferation of legal restrictions for online activity that run counter to the values brought forth by Internet technologies, which are built on new, digital models of collaboration, sharing, and composition. As Lawrence Lessig notes in his most recent book, *Free Culture*, "*Never in our history have fewer had a legal right to control more of the development of our culture than now*" (170, italics in original).

What follows is a case study, based on rhetorical analysis, of the public and legal discourse surrounding the *Grokster* case. Through analysis of the discourse of the content owner petitioners and their supporters, including the petitioners' legal briefs and the entertainment companies' public websites, press releases, and consumer awareness campaigns, I demonstrate that the rhetoric of property stewardship, as used by supporters of MGM Studios, normalizes ownership-based structures for copyright regulation and identifies particular uses of the new technology as its natural, inevitable, and legal purpose. This discourse, while failing to take into account the unique characteristics of digital composition and creativity, gains strength by suggesting a coherence with legal history and defining property, exclusivity, and originality as foundational principles in copyright law.

OVERVIEW OF THE CASE: *MGM STUDIOS V. GROKSTER*

The roots of *MGM Studios v. Grokster* can be traced back to 1999, when college student Shawn Fanning developed a technology called Napster, which was one of the first file sharing applications released on the Internet. The service garnered a large following of music fans that liberally traded copyrighted music files on the network. The recording industry did not approve of such activity, and in 2001 a federal judge forced Napster to shut down (*A&M Records v. Napster*).[3] Not long after the *Napster* decision, a second generation of peer-to-peer file sharing technologies emerged to take Napster's place. What separated this second generation of file-swapping services from Napster was a technological tweak that had major legal implications.

Napster allowed users to browse each other's computers and share copyrighted songs with one another, but it routed all of those transactions through its own centralized servers, maintaining an ability to monitor users and a level of control over how people used its network. That control was Napster's downfall. The judge ruled that since Napster had the ability to prevent copyright infringement, it had a responsibility to do so. The developers of the new services learned from Napster's mistake. Their software abandoned centralized servers, allowing users to connect directly with each other. In October 2001, the major music and movie companies sued developers of two of these new peer-to-peer file sharing applications, Grokster and StreamCast Networks, for contributing to the theft of millions of copyrighted music and movie files. In 2004, the Ninth Circuit Court of Appeals upheld a lower court ruling that file sharing software could be used for legitimate purposes, and as such was protected under the 1984 *Betamax* ruling (*Sony v. Universal Studios*). The Supreme Court agreed to hear the case in December of 2004, and on June 27, 2005, the court reached the decision that the developers of peer-to-peer file sharing technologies can be held liable for inducing the infringing activities of their users. This ruling was, in effect, in favor of the content industry, and soon motivated Grokster to shut down their peer-to-peer file sharing services.[4] Figure 1.1 shows the home page displayed on the Grokster website within months of the ruling. This page presents the misleading message that all use of peer-to-peer technologies is unlawful. You can see here the threatening language supporting this perception: "Your IP address has been logged. Don't think you can't get caught. You are not anonymous."[5] At the bottom of the page are links to websites presented by the content owners, the Recording Industry Association of America (MusicUnited.org [RIAA]) and the Motion Picture Association of America (RespectCopyrights.com [MPAA]).

While the Supreme Court ruling does not explicitly rule that peer-to-peer networks, in general, are unlawful, this is clearly the message being communicated by the entertainment industry. The implications of this case are important for rhetoric and writing studies because, as shown in other

FIGURE 1. Grokster Homepage. Available at http://grokster.com/ (March 2006)

chapters in this collection, the field has had a long-standing interest in cultural and legal understandings of the relationship between authors (writers, artists, musicians, moviemakers, on the production side) and users (readers, listeners, viewers, on the consumption side), particularly as affected by the introduction of new technologies. This case offers an ideal site for rhetorical study, as it addresses these issues in the context of a Supreme Court battle around which a very high-profile online debate about copyright emerged. A closer look at the rhetoric at work in the debate reveals the prevalence of the destructive language of "property stewardship," and shows how such rhetoric supports a particular print- and analog-based model of copyright over other possible digital models.

THE RHETORIC OF PROPERTY STEWARDSHIP:
A CASE STUDY ANALYSIS

The rhetoric of property stewardship surrounding the *MGM Studios v. Grokster* debate identifies a conflict between victimized businesses and predatory technology developers and their opportunistic consumers. According to this model of intellectual property regulation, the U.S. system of copyright law protects the interests of content owners from those who would otherwise exploit copyrighted works through unauthorized reproduction and distribution. Such protections are necessary because they give creators economic rewards for their efforts and incentives to continue to create. According to this discourse, organizations such as the RIAA and the MPAA play the role of stewards, who ensure a "healthy environment" for creativity through proper management of and sustained market value for intellectual and creative goods. A conflict arises with the introduction of peer-to-peer technologies, which threaten the sustenance of the established management system by enabling users to bypass the property stewards and exchange, reproduce, and distribute content directly with other users. According to this rhetoric, in order to restore the proper, healthy state of copyright management, technology, including peer-to-peer networks, needs to be highly regulated.

Interestingly, the terminology of stewardship has been used in debates concerning intellectual property regulation from both supporters of increasingly regulatory copyright protections and proponents of less restrictive copyright protections. I demonstrate later in this chapter that the content owners in *Grokster* used this term to show the necessity of their role as "protectors" of a public interest (rather than, for example, as "guardians" of property, which places the emphasis on disciplinary action based on private interest). But this same language of stewardship has also appeared in academic scholarship on the relationship between the notion of a "public trust," which restricts the state's ability to privatize public resources and turn them over to private parties, and intellectual property (see James Boyle's "Second Enclosure Movement" and Molly van Houweling's "Cultivating Open Information Platforms: A Land Trust Model"). In the context of *Grokster*, however, the role of stewardship was most widely adopted by content owners, who attempted to demonstrate their protective role in support of a public good, rather than a role of property owner or guardian, which may suggest models based on control and punishment.

Within the discourse of property stewardship, a comparison is made between intellectual property and physical property, where value is assigned according to market forces and economic worth. Treating intellectual property as property serves to give the intangible, nonrivalrous resource[6] of intellectual property, for which the cost of creating works is often high and the cost of reproducing them is low, a marketable value. While protecting authors from those who may pilfer their works may be the *effect* of recent applications of copyright law, it is not the *reason* that copyright law exists. As stated in the U.S. Constitution's intellectual property clause, the fundamental purpose of copyright is to "Promote the progress of Science and useful Arts."[7] This constitutional language raises more questions than it answers, however, about why copyright exists: What is "progress"? How is it best promoted? The operation of the rhetoric of property within discourse about intellectual property has assumed that "progress" includes individualized creation of original works of authorship and that it is best promoted through economic incentives for authors and publishers. Such a model requires that copyright law create exclusivity (limits on copying and distribution), which enables an economic value in intangible intellectual and creative works that, in turn, provides incentives for future production. A threat, then, is introduced when modern technology threatens this exclusivity by making works widely and freely available. It is in this way that peer-to-peer technology disrupts the normalized context and creates a conflict. In order to return to the healthy, proper, and legal state of affairs, according to the rhetoric of property stewardship, uses of peer-to-peer technology need to be highly regulated to ensure the exclusivity of copyrighted materials.

In the months preceding the Supreme Court decision for *MGM Studios v. Grokster*, many supporters of the movie and music industries relied on the rhetoric of property stewardship in their responses to the perceived threat posed by peer-to-peer technologies. The most adamant proponents of the discourse of property were the petitioners, who told their story within the specialized discourse of legal briefs, and two representative organizations, the RIAA and the MPAA, who told their stories publicly on the Internet, through press releases, updated website content, and "educational" campaigns about how intellectual property should be managed.

The Motion Picture Studio and Recording Company (one of two groups of petitioners) filed a brief with the Supreme Court on January 25, 2005. In a section of the brief entitled "Statement of the Case," they offered this version of what happened:

> Respondents Grokster and StreamCast operate Internet-based services that contribute to copyright infringement on a "mind-boggling" scale. Their services make it possible for millions of users to reproduce and distribute copyrighted sound recordings and motion pictures without permission—and without paying for them. Virtually all those who use Grokster and StreamCast are committing unlawful copyright infringement, and they commit millions of acts of infringement each day. Grokster and StreamCast exploit this massive infringement for profit, and petitioners are suffering extreme harms as a consequence. The question is whether Grokster and StreamCast will be held responsible for their conduct under well-established principles of copyright liability, or whether they have a perpetual free pass to inflict these harms because a tiny fraction of the material available on their services may not be infringing.[. . .]
>
> *Sony-Betamax* calls for a balance between "effective—and not merely symbolic—protection" of copyright, and "the rights of others freely to engage in substantially unrelated areas of commerce." Ignoring the need for balance, the Ninth Circuit denied petitioners any possibility of "effective protection" of their copyrighted works in the digital era, while shielding enterprises that profit directly from brazen expropriation of the value of those works. (Motion Picture Studio and Recording Company Br. 1–2)

The first point of interest in the story as it is presented here is the cast of characters. The conflict presented is between entertainment companies and technology developers. Creators and users of copyrighted works are only indirectly implicated: they do not demonstrate agency within this context, but remain unaware, helpless, and passive. Later in the content owners' legal brief, the creators are circumstantial victims ("[C]reators of the copyrighted material must stand by helplessly as the value of their copyrighted works vanishes" [Motion Picture Studio and Recording Company Br. 50]) and users of peer-to-peer networks are unaware of how they are being manipulated by the technology companies ("Users whose computers are commandeered for this purpose are almost never aware of the role they have been conscripted to play" [Motion Picture Studio and Recording Company Br. 10]). This cast of characters makes the role of property stewards—as played by the RIAA and MPAA—rather than the role of the artist or creator, of primary interest. In the past, the role of the corporate copyright owner was more well defined and necessary to make possible the availability of materials from writer/creator to reader/public. In the age of print, copyright law provided publishers and distributors with incentives for investing in finding authors/creators and printing, publishing, marketing, and distributing their works. In recent times, however, the role of the publisher in cultural production has become uncertain. In the digital age, the cost of copying and distributing intellectual property can be minimal. The ease of distribution directly to users on a peer-to-peer network makes the very presence of a publisher or content owner unnecessary. The cast of characters in this passage includes publishers and entertainment companies opposing technology developers and fails to attribute to authors and consumers a central role. In this way, the rhetoric defines the issue in the debate as one to be resolved between owners and distributors of content, and falls short in acknowledging the challenges of modern technology to the customary role of the property stewards themselves.

Outside of the context of this legal brief, users of copyrighted works (or "consumers" in the property stewardship rhetoric) do not appear as so passively implicated. In the high-profile online debate occurring on the Internet, users of peer-to-peer networks are not "unaware of the role they have been conscripted to play," but actually become conscious, active contributors to a crime. A new character is introduced in this context: the pirate, criminal, or thief. The RIAA's public website includes perhaps the most pejorative statement about file sharers:

> No black flags with skull and crossbones, no cutlasses, cannons, or daggers identify today's pirates. You can't see them coming; there's no warning shot across your bow. Yet rest assured the pirates are out there because today there is plenty of gold (and platinum and diamonds) to be had.[. . .] The pirate's credo is still the same—why pay for it when it's so easy to steal? The credo is as wrong as it ever was. Stealing is still illegal, unethical, and all too frequent in today's digital age. ("Anti-piracy")

The introduction of the character of the "pirate" into public discourse attempts to raise the stakes in the debate by assigning an intention of harm to the file sharer, and thus frames the activity of file sharing as a moral issue (not to be confused with authors' "moral rights"[8]). The user of the peer-to-peer network is no longer an innocent pawn, but a thief with criminal intent. Without the protection of an outside party (i.e., the movie and recording industry), copyrighted works are exposed to uncharted waters (i.e., peer-to-peer networks), and are subject to hijacking (copying by users). The MPAA, known for its use of hyperbolic rhetoric and the fight against piracy,[9] joined the RIAA in announcing its own round of lawsuits filed against individual file sharers on November 16, 2004. At this time, president and CEO Dan Glickman stated in a press release, "These initiatives are part of our efforts to ensure the Digital Age does not get commandeered by thieves who see it as an open grab bag" ("Studios File First Wave of Suits"). With this statement, Glickman presents the character of the thief, a robber who "commandeers," or takes arbitrarily by force, property that does not belong to him or her. The public discourse of the entertainment industry assigns blame to the users of the Grokster and StreamCast technologies, thus implicating its own consumers in the high-profile public debate. Though this strategy may have questionable market effects on music and movie sales, it adds force to the message from petitioners as they attempt to ward off file sharing on two fronts: the activity of technology developers and the behaviors of technology users. Despite the differences in who carries the blame for the infringement claim, litigants and public messengers supporting petitioners agree that new digital technologies pose a threat to the established and appropriate system for the regulation of cultural production. This casting of blame creates a conflict between the "good" businesses and the "bad" pirates who use technologies for destructive purposes, presenting a misleading dichotomy between copyright law and technology.

In addition to its cast of characters, the discourse of property stewardship presents what appears to be a "natural order" for cultural production, based on the stewardship of cultural goods and regulation of technology to sustain current markets for copyrighted works. This healthy state of copyright regulation is based on assertion of both a legal and natural right to authors. First, in the aforementioned "Statement of the Case," we see the reasoning for legal recourse based on "well-established principles of copyright liability," including the precedent set in the *Betamax* case. The statement bases a claim for legal relief on violations of specific legal rules and obligations, the identified "foundational principles of copyright law," and case precedent. The brief goes on to argue, "reversing the Ninth Circuit [the lower court decision that did not hold technology companies liable for contributing to the infringing

activities of users] is necessary to preser[ve] the 'economic incentive to create
and disseminate ideas,' and ensur[e] that copyright remains the 'engine of free
expression' the Framers' intended" (Motion Picture Studio and Recording
Company Br. 20–21). Such a system of economic incentive is enabled by the
involvement of property stewards, organizations like the Stationer's Company
of the past and like the RIAA and MPAA today. Further, the brief argues,
"permitting businesses to profit from products or services used primarily for
infringement undermines the fundamental purpose of copyright protection
without a countervailing benefit of any legitimate area of commerce" (31).
Because what defines a "legitimate area of commerce" for copyrighted works
is based on structures that create exclusivity and economic reward, this statement suggests that the only uses of peer-to-peer technologies that may be
permitted are those that participate in established economic markets. Based
on the fundamental purpose of copyright law, the petitioners' claim is out-
lined by the Framers of the Constitution, as well as the legal duty to case
precedent, but the language here presents a normalized state in which exclusivity in intellectual products is the natural order of things, and progress in
copyright law must regulate and sustain established economic markets. This
normalized state asserts a permanent, intrinsic right of intellectual property
as "property" to owners of copyrighted materials. In this way, the property
model for intellectual property regulation becomes absolute, despite its incon-
sistencies with models proposed for cultural production by peer-to-peer file
sharing technology.

   In addition, a natural right to authors appears in the rhetoric of property
stewardship, as presented on the RIAA's MusicUnited.org and the MPAA's
RespectCopyrights.com websites. The MusicUnited.org website makes the
point that downloading music is "wrong" because it deprives creators of their
natural right to the fruits of their labor. To humanize the effects of consumers' supposed lack of respect for this natural right, the website adds details
about the labor-intensive process of creating music. It states, "Music doesn't
just happen. It's made, note by note, beat by beat, by people who work hard
to get it right" ("Why You Shouldn't Do It"). It goes further to point out that
the people who contribute to the intellectual or creative work deserve economic reward ("It's about putting food on the table and covering the rent")
for their intrinsic qualities of "imagination, soul, and courage." Probably the
most convincing claims on the site come from artists themselves. On a page
dedicated to accounts from artists about peer-to-peer file sharing appears this
quotation from James Grundler, singer/songwriter and member of the band
Paloalto: "I live with my drummer and guitarist and we have no money. Our

survival is based solely on the purchase of our music. Music is not free. Even the street performer gets a dime in his box" ("What the Artists and Songwriters Have to Say"). This language clearly follows from a foundational principle of absolute and intrinsic rights to property, in particular John Locke's idea that an individual "person" is his own property, and, as such, has a natural right to what results from his labor. In this case, that right is the right to an economic reward for an intellectual work. In the well-known passage from his chapter on property, Locke gives a defense of the right of unilateral appropriation:

> Though the Earth [. . .] be common to all Men, yet every Man has a Property in his own Person. This no Body has any Right to but himself. The Labour of his Body, and the Work of his Hands, we may say, are properly his. Whatsoever then he removes out of the State that Nature hath provided, and left it in, he hath mixed his Labour with, and joyned to it something that is his own, and thereby makes it his Property. It being by him removed from the common state Nature placed it in, it hath by this labour something annexed to it, that excludes the common right of other Men. (*Second Treatise of Government*, chap. II, par. 27)

It is this natural right to "exclu[sion from] the common right of other Men" that the RIAA and MPAA defend through their services. The MPAA's RespectCopyrights.com website shows the relevance of this argument today:

> Copyrights allow the people who create movies, music, art, dance, software and books—and other creative and expressive works—to be paid and to earn a living from their jobs, just like a clerk at a store and a businesswoman behind a desk. Without the protection of copyrights, creators would not be able to survive by doing what they do best, and they would be forced out of their creative fields to find other jobs. Eventually, there would be fewer and fewer new works for all of us to enjoy. (RespectCopyrights.com)

In a contemporary context, Locke's description of "the Labour of his Body and the Work of his Hands" becomes the work of the clerk, the businesswoman, and the "people who create movies, music, art, dance, software, and books."

The notion of *natural rights* for authors employed by petitioners in the *Grokster* case has strong historical basis in the metaphor of authorial property. The metaphor of property is a central tenet to the origin of the legal rights of the author: according to a Western view of authorship on which copyright was

designed, texts are objects of appropriation and authors the solitary, natural owners of the textual objects they create. Providing historical accounts of the evolu-
tion of legal protections for works of authorship over time, copyright scholars
emphasize that copyright law relies on the identification and sustenance of the
individualized author as singular and proprietary owner of a commodified text
(see Patterson and Lindberg; Rose; Woodmansee; Woodmansee and Jaszi). They
show that proprietary authorship, while seemingly a natural right, emerged by
the late seventeenth and early eighteenth centuries when the London bookselling
trade flourished and gained a monopoly over printing privileges.

In Mark Rose, in his 1993 study of literary authorship in the eighteenth century, notes that the discourse of intellectual works as property arose at a time
when the liberal discourse of property and the literary discourse of original
genius came together in the context of a legal battle over perpetual copyright
(see *Tonson v. Collins* [1761], *Millar v. Taylor* [1769], and *Donaldson v. Becket*
[1774]). Rose argues that it was at this time that intellectual property rights
came to be seen as natural rights, fueled by the discourse of property rights
promulgated by John Locke's *Second Treatise on Government*. Rose writes, "The
key to John Locke's thought was the axiom that an individual 'person' was his
[*sic*] own property. From this it could be demonstrated that through labor an
individual might convert raw materials of nature into private property" (5).
An individual's right to what results from her or his labor, such as the land
she or he has cultivated, was a natural right, and this right had to be protected
by legal order. When applied to intellectual property, this right became an
author's rights to the fruits of her or his labor, a copyrighted work that had
to be protected. Such protections came in the form of commercialized ownership of copyrighted works: they were largely assigned to booksellers, not
authors, who were in the practice of selling their works outright to the booksellers for printing and distribution.

In addition to this discourse of property rights, proprietary authorship
also relied on the concept of *original genius*. Law professor Peter Jaszi collaborated with Martha Woodmansee in the introduction to their edited collection
The Construction of Authorship to offer a historical look at authorship in the
Romantic period. They write, "the modern regime of authorship, far from
being timeless and universal, is a relatively recent formation—the result of a
quite radical reconceptualization of the creative process that culminated less
than 200 years ago in the heroic self-presentation of the Romantic poets"
(2–3). This "relatively recent formation," they note, draws heavily on the
notion of authorship as "originary": an intellectual work "results not in a vari-
ation, an imitation, or an adaptation [. . .] but in an utterly new, unique—in

a word, 'original'—work which, accordingly, may be said to be the property of its creator" (3). According to Rose, it was the combination of this discourse of property rights coupled with the Romantic notion of the individual genius that shaped the construction of the foundational principle of property owner-ship in intellectual property law.

The RIAA and MPAA rely on an appeal to this natural, absolute right of a copyright owner to support the concept of "theft" that pervades their discourse. The moral of their story seems simple: "don't steal." The RIAA's MusicUnited. org website compares downloading the recorded songs of popular artists to the petty theft of items from a friend: "Most of us would never even consider steal-ing something—say, a picture or a piece of clothing—from a friend's house. Our sense of right and wrong keeps most of us from doing something so selfish and antisocial" ("Who Really Cares?"). In this way, the RIAA relies on a les-son in morality that music listeners have been taught from a young age: taking what's not yours is wrong. Like their music industry counterpart, the MPAA presents analogies between theft and movie piracy. Part of their educational campaign is a forty-seven-second film titled *Piracy—It's a Crime* that has been shown widely on the big screen during previews of Hollywood films. This short film presents a series of excerpts in which criminals are stealing others' property: a car, a handbag, a cell phone. The analogy is clear: movie piracy, like these other acts, is the same as theft of physical goods. The text of the film reads as follows, coupled with the images of the crime, like stealing a car:

> You wouldn't steal a car.
> You wouldn't steal a handbag.
> You wouldn't steal a mobile phone.
> You wouldn't steal a DVD.
> Buying pirated films is stealing.
> Piracy. It's a crime. (RespectCopyrights.com)

While this film's focus is on buying pirated copies of films, rather than on downloading and distributing copies on peer-to-peer networks, the message appears the same in both contexts: the copies are to be considered private property and taking them is the same as stealing someone's privately owned property. This language of theft relies on three questionable assumptions. First, it assumes that intellectual property is "property" and thus belongs to a private owner. This assumption, as shown earlier, neglects the distinctions of rivalrous and nonrivalrous resources and suggests that intellectual property has an intrinsic, absolute value as a commodified "good." Second, it assumes

that a creator has an individualized, absolute, natural right to his or her creations, which neglects the notion that the author is a cultural and historical
construct. Third, the language of theft does not clearly identify its victim. In
the peer-to-peer file sharing debate, public discourse often suggests that the
victims are the creators of copyrighted works. However, the victims in the
discourse of property stewardship are actually the content owners who resist
adapting to the unique conditions of digital music and movie distribution.

The content owners argue further that peer-to-peer file sharing technologies, in contributing to the infringement of the natural rights of copyright owners, disrupt not only established markets for copyrighted works,
but also the very democratic ideals of our society. On one level, the danger
appears to be the threat of a breakdown of copyright law into the "law-
less" free-for-all of digital networks. The petitioners' legal brief identifies
this danger: "Their [Grokster and StreamCast] services breed a culture of
contempt for intellectual property, and for the right of others generally, in
cyberspace" (Motion Picture Studio and Music Publisher Br. 13). In addition
to "erod[ing] respect for the very foundations of copyright law in the digital
age" (14), peer-to-peer file sharing technologies present the even larger threat
of a breakdown of the fundamental democratic right to property. Creating a
sense of fear of the effects of such lawlessness, the entertainment companies
suggest connections between criminals of much more dangerous crimes and
participation on peer-to-peer file sharing networks. In two print advertisements circulated by the RIAA, they attempt to create a sense of terror. One
advertisement presents a hand holding a computer mouse, highlighted by an
ominous glow and dark shadows: the positioning of the mouse looks much
like a dangerous weapon. And another advertisement creates a connection
between inappropriate (perhaps violent or sexual) content on the Internet and
peer-to-peer file sharing activity by offering the following message in bold,
red letters: "PARENTAL GUIDANCE SUGGESTED" and "Illegal Downloading: Inappropriate for All Ages." The advertisement plays on the fear par-
ents may have of the dangers of pornography, child predators, and other more
threatening dangers children and teenagers face on the Internet. These images
suggest that file sharing does more than rob artists of their paychecks; it poses
a risk to the order of society by subjecting innocent people, even children, to
immanent dangers. The images suggest that technology itself is dangerous (a
weapon) and that peer-to-peer file sharing networks must be regulated for the
very safety and well-being of society.

When the opinion for *MGM Studios v. Grokster* was announced on June
27, 2005, the decision was viewed by the RIAA and MPAA as a clear victory

or the content industries. In a flurry of media coverage of the case in the days following the decision, 2005, the content industry released public statements and participated in interviews offering responses to the ruling. Dan Glickman, the president and CEO of the MPAA, in a statement about the ruling, said, "This case speaks to the values we hold dear as a nation. It is wrong to promote stealing. Grokster promotes stealing, and it ought to be held responsible for its actions "(Press Release). Invoking another contemporary court ruling involving display of the Ten Commandments, Mitch Bainwol, head of the Recording Industry Association of America, said the court affirmed the notion that "thou shalt not steal" (Krim). And in the official "RIAA Statement on *MGM v. Grokster* Supreme Court Ruling," he added:

> With this unanimous decision, the Supreme Court has addressed a significant threat to the U.S. economy and moved to protect the livelihoods of the more than 11 million Americans employed by the copyright industries. The Supreme Court has helped to power the digital future for legitimate online businesses—including legal file sharing networks—by holding accountable those who promote and profit from theft.

From the entertainment companies' perspective, peer-to-peer technologies present dangers larger than the disruption of legitimate business models; they threaten the moral fabric of our society. These companies assert it is "wrong"—in both the legal and moral sense—to share files. According to the petitioners, then, the natural state of copyright regulation was properly restored in the *Grokster* case. By supporting the regulation of the use of new technologies, the ruling goes further to restore our society's respect for the fundamental value of private property.

In showing the ways in which file sharing both threatens the foundations of copyright law (breaks down "exclusivity") and is morally wrong ("file sharing is stealing"), petitioners establish both the natural order of the property stewardship model of copyright regulation and the conflict posed to that natural order by the use of peer-to-peer technologies. While what is defined as "legal" is not based on an absolute truth about the way intellectual property should be regulated, it does reflect what has been established as the natural or normal system of regulation by a particular society's set of beliefs and mores about appropriate conduct. In making a claim for regulating peer-to-peer networks to support established economic markets, litigants and observers highlight one set of uses and meanings as the natural, inevitable purpose of copyright law. Here, that set of uses involves maintaining the exclusivity of intellectual property in order for it to retain its economic value as property. Such uses require regulation of users' activities and pay-per-download models that more directly map to current methods for buying and selling individualized copies. Because the peer-to-peer file sharing technologies of Grokster and StreamCast relied on an alternative value of distribution, they did not even appear on the "grid" of contemporary copyright law and, thus, could only be viewed as deviant.

CONCLUSIONS

It is not within the scope of this chapter to explore whether the content industry's use of the rhetoric of property stewardship has effectively shaped their target audience's perception of file sharing.[10] However, we can look at the ways in which this discourse gains legitimacy in the peer-to-peer file sharing debate, that is, how it operates to constitute a particular understanding of the role of technology during a contentious time in the legal history of copyright. Examining the rhetoric of property stewardship in *Grokster* reveals that the use of property-based rhetoric in contemporary discourse about intellectual property establishes a normalized state of copyright enforcement in which technology must be regulated to sustain current economic markets for intellectual property. In doing so, the value of cultural production is defined in terms of exclusivity and competition in markets for packaged, transmittable intellectual and creative goods. This view of cultural production gains force based on its asserted alignment with the foundational principles of property and exclusivity in copyright law. It allows a sense of coherence with legal history within new contexts, rather than giving in to a state of "lawlessness" and social chaos on the Internet. In addition, it also demonstrates consistency with the foundational principle of private property in our democratic society by equating file sharing with theft.

Relying exclusively on a property rights approach to copyright emphasizes the individual benefit of economic reward and advancement and the natural right of the author, perhaps at the expense of the community. While a property rights model of copyright does call on us to respect and reward the contributions of individuals, it fails to highlight the relatedness of intellectual and creative activity—the inherently collaborative nature of composition, a sense of communal responsibility, and the common good of sharing access to information. The "proper state" of copyright law in property stewardship rhetoric appears as the natural and inevitable structure for regulating peer-to-peer technologies, but it is only one of many possible structures.

Peer-to-peer technologies themselves have many applications in many contexts, and while our culture has until now relied on a stewardship system for the exchange of intellectual works, there are other forms of content creation and exchange that may serve just as well—or better—for these activities in a digital age. In the past decade, technology developments have made visible the fact that the current regime of intellectual property does not work well in practice, and other models that are not supposed to work are facilitating creative and intellectual activity. From an intellectual standpoint, if there is nothing to anchor intellectual property rights where they are except utilitarianism (the idea that a property-based model of intellectual property produces more good than any other possible structure), it would no longer be so. As James Porter and Dànielle DeVoss point out, this utilitarian justification for contemporary copyright law has recently come under considerable scrutiny (3–4). They cite James Boyle, who recently noted the fallacy in the assertion from the "copyright maximalists" that "the more intellectual property rights we create, the more innovation" ("Deconstructing Stupidity"). Boyle uses Europe's Database Directive as an example, showing how its model of providing strong copyright protection over databases has not helped Europe compete with the U.S. information industry. Although strong copyright protections can lead to short-term benefits for established industries, such protectionism does not demonstrate a strong correlation with increased development and creativity. To the contrary, there is evidence that alternative models of copyright may actually heighten economic development. Lawrence Lessig notes one example, the free software movement in Brazil, which has helped to increase its wealth and develop the potential of its technology industry (Koman).

The current model of copyright cannot be justified based on a purely utilitarian argument. So, why does the property-based model of copyright persist in rulings like *MGM Studios v. Grokster*? The property stewardship model likely retains its privileged position because it is based on more deeply embedded cultural values of private property and economic reward for individual labor. While a system of authorial property recognizes authorship as individual and authored works as discrete and privately owned, these values are clearly neither necessary nor inevitable. New models of copyright introduced by peer-to-peer file sharing technologies faced an overwhelming challenge because they required more than a demonstration of file sharing as economically advantageous; they required a fundamental shift in the notion of property rights from a value in exclusivity to a value in distribution. Rather than reinforcing the notion that creativity is supported by limiting distribution, peer-to-peer networks could be used to support distribution that, in turn, leads to increased access and more creativity. The RIAA and MPAA fear Grokster and StreamCast, not because of the advancement of technology (after all, they too have benefited from advancement in digital technology), but because of the conceptual shift that the technology represents. They are fearful that alternative models for cultural production based on distribution rather than on exclusivity will threaten their very existence. Therefore, in the wake of the development of peer-to-peer file sharing networks, the entertainment industry had to show that the technology presents a threat large enough to justify legal regulation. In a social and political context that, for the most part, values technological advancement for the sake of efficiency and competence within institutional structures, this required a rhetorical move that revealed that this particular type of technological development was economically unsound and, further, destructive to the public good. The entertainment industry was largely successful in this effort, and the *Grokster* decision cut short one experiment with a distribution model of cultural production.

TOWARD A NEW RHETORIC OF INTELLECTUAL PROPERTY

If rhetoric and composition instructors and researchers want to resist the destructive rhetoric of property, theft, and piracy, we need to find our own ways of talking and thinking about intellectual property. Such a discourse cannot arise from legal experts, academics, or lobbyists; rather, it needs to come from the writers, users, and creators that work with digital technology themselves. We would do well to conduct research that seeks to better understand the range of activities based on copying, reusing, and repurposing digital works that are acceptable and fruitful within particular contexts, according to the norms of particular settings and characteristic of particular genres. For example, in professional writing settings, the use of boilerplates and templates for web pages and PowerPoint presentations, ghostwriting, and honorary authorship in scientific research are just a few examples of how certain types of copying and reuse are appropriate within a given setting. We need to uncover through research the practices that govern what can be copied, by whom, and with what attribution, and how they vary depending on context. But it is only by talking to creators, composers, and authors who rely on digital technologies that we can better understand the need to move beyond considering seemingly universal rule of "do not steal" to more context-contingent applications of norms.

Finally, writing instructors and researchers should move to discuss issues not only in terms of the "rules" for legal behaviors but also in terms of how rhetoric and discourse shape those rules. It is up to us, based on the analysis presented in this chapter and in others in this collection, to focus our work on the constructive and ethical uses of peer-to-peer networks and other digital technologies as *copyright activists* rather than passive users who allow copyright to be defined for us. As a result, we can move the intellectual property debate from a small number of legal experts and technology gurus to include the voices of those who create and use copyrighted materials in their everyday experiences. By promoting new ways for talking and thinking about writing that emphasize collaboration, sharing, and interaction, we can begin to challenge the discourse of property stewardship that pervades the current legal debate about intellectual property.

NOTES

1. Pub. L. No. 105–304, 112 Stat. 2860 (1998).

2. 17 U.S.C. Sec. 505–508. (1998).

3. Napster has since relaunched under different ownership as a pay-per-use service.

4. While the decision in *Grokster* was technically unanimous, the justices' perspectives on the issue were more diverse than the 9–0 vote would suggest. The justices split themselves equally in number across a majority opinion and two concurring opinions, each signed by three justices.

5. Users of this website should not be scared off by this message. Individuals cannot easily be traced by the IP addresses assigned to their computers. IP addresses are usually assigned to an Internet service provider, a university, or a company. They don't usually lead to a single computer, but rather are assigned to a network of computers that share the address.

6. The rivalrous versus nonrivalrous distinction in intellectual property scholarship can be traced back to economic terminology. See Paul Samuelson's 1954 article, in which he develops of theory of public goods, "The Pure Theory of Public Expenditure." Samuelson argues that a public good, which intellectual property arguably is, is a nonrivalrous resource: an unlimited number of people may "consume" the work without depleting it.

7. U.S. Constitution, Article I, Section 8.

8. While the concept of *moral rights* is not formally recognized as part of U.S. copyright law, it is recognized in other countries, such as France and Germany. The notion of *moral rights* for an author does not refer to morality as in ethics or religion, but rather the ability of authors to control the fate of their works. Such protections

include preventing the tarnishing of an author's reputation by determining when credit is given (or denied) for the work, preventing the work from being altered, or deciding where it may be displayed. In the United States, the only moral rights that exist explicitly for authors are those assigned to works of visual art. The Visual Artists Rights Act (VARA) of 1990 (17 U.S.C. Sec. 106a) established the rights of attribution and integrity to prevent destruction or alteration of visual works existing in small numbers or a single copy.

9. Former MPAA president Jack Valenti's rhetoric is now infamous among those who follow copyright debates. Beginning with the perceived threat of an early technology, the VCR, to the movie industry, Valenti sought rhetorical strategies to criminalize the technologies themselves. In 1983, Valenti proclaimed that the VCR "is to the American film producer and the American public as the Boston Strangler is to the woman home alone." More recently in 2002, he declared war on peer-to-peer file sharing technologies: "We're fighting our own terrorist war," he reported to the *New York Times* (Harmon). For more on Jack Valenti's rhetoric in the peer-to-peer file sharing debate, see John Logie's "A Copyright Cold War?"

10. Having said that, it is not difficult to see that the efforts of the two consumer awareness campaigns fail miserably on many counts at making connections with their target audience, presumably teenagers and young adults. For instance, on the Music United.org website, despite its images of young, hip people listening to music, the use of outdated slang terms and headings like "It's a Drag!" in a prominent location on the site (http://www.musicunited.org/1_whocares.html) shows that the contributors to the site are not up to date with current trends. The error of using slang incorrectly is no doubt one of the quickest ways to appear "uncool" to young consumers.

WORKS CITED

A&M Records, Inc. v. Napster, *Inc.*, 239 F.3d 1004 (Ninth Circuit 2001).

"Anti-piracy." Recording Industry Association of America. 7 Aug. 2005 <http://www.riaa.com/issues/piracy/default.asp>.

Boyle, James. "Deconstructing Stupidity." *Financial Times* 21 Apr. 2005. 9 Apr. 2006 <http://news.ft.com/cms/s/39b697dc-b25e-11d9-bcc6-00000e2511c8.html>.

———. "The Second Enclosure Movement and the Construction of the Public Domain." *Law and Contemporary Problems* 66 (Winter/Spring 2003): 33–74. 6 Apr. 2006 <http://www.law.duke.edu/journals/lcp/articles/lcp66dWinterSpring2003 p33.htm>.

CCCC Caucus on Intellectual Property. "Use Your Fair Use: Strategies toward Action." *College Composition and Communication* 51.3 (2000): 485–88.

Donaldson v. Becket. 4 Burr 2408, 98 Eng. Rep. 257 (1774).

Eldred v. Ashcroft, 537 U.S. 186 S.Ct. (2003).

Grokster home page. 20 Mar. 2006 <http://grokster.com/>.

Harmon, Amy. "Black Hawk Download: Pirated Videos Thrive Online." *New York Times*. 17 Jan. 2002. 10 June 2005 <http://www.nytimes.com/2002/01/17/technology/circuits/17VIDE.html>.

Koman, Richard. "Remixing Culture: An Interview with Lawrence Lessig." O'Reilly Policy Development Center. 24 Feb. 2005. 10 Apr. 2006 <http://www.oreilly net.com/pub/a/policy/2005/02/24/lessig.html>.

Krim, Jonathan. "File Sharing Firms Can Be Held Liable: Ruling Aids Entertainment Industry." *Washington Post*. 28 Jan. 2005: A01.

Lessig, Lawrence. *Free Culture: How Big Media Uses Technology and the Law to Lock Down Culture and Control Creativity*. New York: Penguin, 2004.

———. "Who Owns Culture?" Introduction to a lecture with Jeff Tweedy. New York University Library. 7 Apr. 2005. 11 May 2006 <http://www.videobomb.com/posts/show/2121>.

Locke, John. *Second Treatise of Government*. 1690. 10 Apr. 2006 <http://www.constitution.org/jl/2ndtreat.htm>.

Logie, John. "A Copyright Cold War? The Polarized Rhetoric of the Peer-to-peer Debates." *First Monday*. 8.7: 2003. 9 Apr. 2006 <http://www.firstmonday.org/issues/issue8_7/logie/>.

MGM Studios, Inc v. Grokster, Ltd., 545 U.S. 125 S.Ct. 2764 (2005) (Ginsburg, R., concurring, Breyer, S., concurring).

Millar v. Taylor, 4 Burr. 2303, 98 Eng. Rep. 201 (1769).

Motion Picture Studio and Recording Company Br. *MGM Studios, Inc. v. Grokster, Ltd.*, 545 U.S., 125 S.Ct. 2764 (2005).

Motion Picture Studio and Recording Company' Reply Br. *MGM Studios, Inc. v. Grokster, Ltd.*, 545 U.S., 125 S.Ct. 2764 (2005).

MusicUnited.org. Recording Industry Association of America. 7 Aug. 2005 <http://www.musicunited.org/>.

Patterson, L. Ray, and Stanley W. Lindberg. *Copyright in Historical Perspective*. Nashville, TN: Vanderbilt UP, 1968.

Porter, James E., and Dànielle Nicole DeVoss. "Rethinking Plagiarism in the Digital Age: Remixing as a Means of Economic Development?" Paper presented at WIDE Research Center 2006 Conference. 24 Apr. 2006 <http://www.wide.msu.edu/conference/wdk_plagiarism_FINAL.doc>.

Porter, James E., and Martine Courant Rife. "*MGM v. Grokster*: Implications for Educators and Writing Teachers." Wide Research Center. 28 June 2005. Michigan State University. 10 Apr. 2006 <http://www.wide.msu.edu/widepapers/grokster/>.

Press Release. Motion Picture Association of America. 29 June 2005. 7 Aug. 2005 <www.mpaa.org/MPAAPress/2005/2005_03_29.doc>.

RespectCopyrights.com. Motion Picture Association of America. 7 Aug. 2005 <http://respectcopyrights.com/content.html>.

"RIAA Statement on *MGM v. Grokster* Supreme Court Ruling," Recording Industry of America. 27 June 2005. 7 Aug. 2005 <http://www.riaa.com/news/newsletter/062705.asp>.

Rose, Mark. *Authors and Owners: The Invention of Copyright*. Cambridge: Harvard UP, 1993.

Samuelson, Paul A. "The Pure Theory of Public Expenditure." *Review of Economics and Statistics* 36 (1954): 387–89.

Sony Corp. of America v. Universal City Studios, Inc., 464 U.S., S.Ct. 417 (1984).

"Studios File First Wave of Suits Against Online Illegal File Traders." Motion Picture Association of America. 16 Nov. 2004. 7 Aug. 2005.<http://www.respect copyrights.org/11–16–04_Lawsuit_Press_Release.pdf >.

Tonson v. Collins, 96 Eng. Rep. 169, 188 (1761).

Valenti, Jack. "Home Recordings of Copyrighted Works Hearings Before the Subcommittee on Courts, Civil Liberties, and the Administration of Justice of the Committee of the Judiciary, House of Representatives." 12 Apr. 1983. 10 June 2005 <http://cryptome.org/hrcw-hear.htm>.

van Houweling, Molly. "Cultivating Open Information Platforms: A Land Trust Model." *Journal of Telecommunications and High Technology Law* 1 (2002): 309–23.

"What the Artists and Songwriters Have to Say." MusicUnited.org. 7 Aug. 2005 <http://www.musicunited.org/3_artists.html>.

"Who Really Cares?" MusicUnited.org. 7 Aug. 2005 <http://www.musicunited.org/1_whocares.html>.

"Why You Shouldn't Do It." MusicUnited.org. 7 Aug. 2005 <http://www.music united.org/4_shouldntdoit.html>.

Woodmansee, Martha. "The Genius and the Copyright: Economic and Legal Conditions of the Emergence of the 'Author.'" *Eighteenth-Century Studies* 17.4 (1984): 425–48.

Woodmansee, Martha, and Peter Jaszi. Introduction. *The Construction of Authorship: Textual Appropriation in Law and Literature*. Ed. Martha Woodmansee and Peter Jaszi. Durham: Duke UP, 1994. 1–14.

CHAPTER 2

Fair Use and the Vulnerability of Criticism on the Internet

SOHUI LEE

In 1995, English professor Martha Woodmansee and Law professor Peter Jaszi published "The Law of Texts: Copyright in the Academy," a clarion call for readers of *College English* and scholars in composition and communication to be alert to potential tectonic changes in the U.S. copyright system that would directly impact their pedagogy and practice. Three years later, the passage of the Digital Millennium Copyright Act (1998) reaffirmed Woodmansee and Jaszi's apprehensions of the bias in court and legislative decisions toward copyright holders in cases dealing with Internet technology. There are two central reasons why we as composition scholars should be concerned about the DMCA. Although widespread misunderstanding of fair use and copyright law among university and college teachers has been a major deterrent to our exercise of fair use, the DMCA, first, further complicates our practice in the way it impacts how we transform, criticize, or study copyrighted works for academic purposes and, second, affects whether we can circulate our scholarly work online.

While composition scholars have variously addressed the urgent need for teachers to be aware of how copyright laws like the DMCA regulate our classroom pedagogy, this chapter joins that discussion by calling on an important aspect of our professional identity that is being shaped by the DMCA: scholarship and criticism, particularly those belonging to e-rhetoricians. E-rhetoricians are an emergent group of scholars of rhetoric and composition whose subject matter deals with the rhetoric of electronic technologies or Internet media culture and, for these reasons, regularly publish their scholarship on the World Wide Web. Because of the DMCA and changing attitudes toward fair use, foundational fair use provisions in the Copyright Act—particularly that of criticism—may become compromised as steady shifts in the norms of Internet fair use practice and increased censorship restrict our ability to consider and employ noninfringing use of copyrighted material. Moreover, this chapter recommends a creation of detailed guidelines for fair use that is specific to the demands of our own field practices and puts forward the Documentary Filmmakers' Statement of Best Practices in Fair Use (2005) as a model. Such guidelines, created in consultation with legal experts and in conversation with the greater public, could shed light on misinformation about fair use, make our case more sympathetic, and carve out best practice solutions for composition scholars that are consistent with the copyright laws contained in Title 17 of the U.S. Code. To be clear, what is at stake for scholars and the academic community is self-determination: rather than accepting current developments in which copyright holders define fair use standards according to their industry interests and commercial goals, our best practice policy on fair use can carry out the intended goals of the Constitution to further public interest and knowledge, as well as ensure that the fair use doctrine continues to benefit research and teaching.

FAIR USE HISTORY: FROM THE
CONSTITUTIONAL CLAUSE TO CASE LAW

Fair use, as defined by the U.S. Code, is a doctrine that permits the free use of portions of copyrighted work "for purposes such as criticism, comment, news reporting, teaching (including multiple copies for classroom use), scholarship, or research" (17 U.S.C. Sec. 107). While the fair use doctrine was codified in 1976 and is often discussed in terms of a legal defense for copyright infringement, scholars of copyright law note the long- standing and central role of fair use principles in the U.S. copyright system by pointing to the Constitutional provision called the copyright clause, or the intellectual property clause. This clause describes, among Congress's other powers, the task to "promote the progress of science and useful arts, by securing for limited times to authors and inventors the exclusive right to their respective writings and discoveries" (U.S. Constitution, Article 1, Section 8). While the Constitution confers Congress with the powers to present copyright holders with economic incentives by granting them an "exclusive right to their respective writings and discoveries," their works are provided copyright protection for "limited times." Many legal scholars have read this crucial exception in the passage to verify the importance of public access to copyrighted material. Fair use, Dan Thu Thi Phan argues, plays an important function in the copyright system because it not only balances social good with copyright holders' economic interests, but also "ensure[s] that the creator's limited monopoly in currently copyrighted works does not stifle innovation or the promotion of knowledge" (198). Phan's interpretation of the constitutional standing of fair use for public good is reinforced by others. Mark Gimbel points out, "[Copyright] must be limited because the primary purpose of copyright, as it is *constitutionally conceived*, is not to secure a return to authors but to advance the public good" (1680, my italics). Kenneth Crews also argues, "The *framers of the U.S. Constitution* clearly intended that the law of copyright—including fair use—would be tailored to serve the advancement of knowledge" (3, my italics).

This public-minded concept of fair use of copyrighted material has been not only an expressed part of judicial decisions since 1841, but also linked fundamentally with the activities of criticism and scholarship. In *Folsom v. Marsh*, Circuit Justice Joseph Story raised the issue of how to consider fair use of copyrighted material when weighing the charge of literary piracy held against Reverend Charles W. Upham, the author of *Life of Washington*. The plaintiff Jared Sparks, former editor of the prominent literary journal *North American Review*, published *Writings of President Washington*, a twelve-volume collection consisting primarily of George Washington's private and official letters. The case before Justice Story was the issue of whether Upham's appropriation of Washington's letters from Spark's collection was permissible under fair use. Unlike Sparks's collection, Upham's work related the narrative of Washington's life; however, a third of Upham's two-volume book incorporated letters of Washington that were copied "verbatim" from Sparks's collection. Acknowledging an already existing practice of fair use in the United States, Story specifically referred to the example of criticism and scholarship as a case for fair use:

> [N]o one can doubt that a reviewer may fairly cite largely from the original work, if his design be really and truly to use the passages *for the purposes of fair and reasonable criticism*. On the other hand, it is as clear, that if he thus cites the most important parts of the work, with a view, not

to criticise, but to supersede the use of the original work, and substitute the review for it, such a use will be deemed in law a piracy. (*Folsom v. March* 1841, my italics)

A landmark case, *Folsom v. Marsh* provided a common law precedent for fair use practice and eventually laid the foundation for an explicit statutory description of fair use factors in the Copyright Act of 1976. The real controversy of the case, Judge Story argued, was whether the defendant had the "right to abridge and select, and use the materials which they have taken for their work" because they were producing "original and new work." While a third of Upham's work included letters from Sparks's copyrighted volume, Story noted that infringement did not "necessarily depend on the quantity taken" but also whether

the value of the original is sensibly diminished, or the labors of the original author are substantially to an injurious extent appropriated by another. [. . .] In short, we must often, in deciding questions of this sort, look to the nature and objects of the selections made, the quantity and value of the materials used, and the degree in which the use may prejudice the sale, or diminish the profits, or supersede the objects, of the original work. (*Folsom v. March* 1841)

In other words, he identified three factors for determining fair use:

1. The "nature" of copyright infringement (how was the copyrighted material selected to be used?),
2. the "quantity and value" of the appropriation (how much of it was used and was it the most vital part of the original work?), and
3. the "degree in which the use may prejudice the sale" (how much is the copyright holder economically hurt by the infringing work?).

The updated fair use factors enacted by Congress through the Copyright Act of 1976 demonstrate how Story's standards of fair use remain the basis for our copyright system:

1. The purpose and character of the use, including whether such use is of a commercial nature or is for nonprofit educational purposes;
2. the nature of the copyrighted work;

3. the amount and substantiality of the portion used in relation to the copyrighted work as a whole; and

4. the effect of the use upon the potential market for or value of the copyrighted work. (17 U.S.C. Sec. 107)

The essential difference between Story's factors and the fair use factors listed in the U.S. Code is the clarification of Story's point on the "nature and objects of the selections made." The U.S. Code breaks this point into two key identifying factors of the copyrighted and infringing piece: the first criterion ascertains the "purpose" and "character" of the new infringing work (whether it is commercial or nonprofit and how the copyrighted material was used); the second pinpoints the "nature of the copyrighted work." For us, the first factor s the most salient, as it registers the degree by which copyrighted materials ire "transformed" in new works as part of other creative pieces or framed in scholarship, criticisms, and parodies.

The history of fair use is important for scholars of composition and communication to understand because it reinforces the evolutionary and theoretical trajectory of the fair use doctrine from its implicit role as a copyright provision in the Constitution to common law precedent beginning 1841, and finally its formal statutory codification in 1976. It confirms the dominant view of legal scholars who have argued that fair use, especially in the form of criticism and scholarship, is an important provision to the U.S. copyright system that ultimately supports the interest of the public good: the primary reason for permitting the free use of copyrighted material is to allow for the "free flow of ideas and information" (Phan 170). As Peter Jaszi declared in testimony to the House of Representatives in 2005, fair use is more than a "mere affirmative defense" against copyright infringement, but rather "an important entitlement for students, artists, teachers, librarians, writers, entrepreneurs, musicians, programmers, and ordinary consumers" (quoted in United States). Nonetheless, despite the history of fair use protection afforded to criticism and scholarship and the public interest in such expressions, recent legislations and court rulings indicate a trend away from the traditional practice of fair use and toward a contrary fair use practice, which ultimately strengthens copyright holders' privileges.

THE DMCA AND CENSORSHIP

When, in 2000, the CCCC Caucus on Intellectual Property released their statement "Use Your Fair Use: Strategies toward Action" in *College Composition and Communication*, the article offered to clarify "contradictory advice circulating throughout academia" regarding fair use of copyrighted material (485). The article identified three reasons why teachers did not exercise their fair use rights: 1. confusion over traditional standards of fair use as it applied to print medium and its new application to electronic discourse; 2.the chilling effect on practice due to two court cases dealing with the copying of material for classroom use; and 3. restrictive CONFU guidelines for exercising fair use in the classroom. The statement concluded by encouraging teachers and college administrators to "make informed decisions about their own practices" as fair use is decided on a case by case basis (486).

Undoubtedly, a better understanding of copyright law and fair use written in the U.S. Code would enable scholars and teachers to make better fair use decisions; however, as I have begun to suggest, fair use in new media compositions is becoming a restricted option for individuals. Despite the history of fair use defense in our legal system, recent legislations and court rulings has made fair use more difficult to carry out due to what Lunsford and West call a "trend in copyright, a shift toward expanded rights for creators and publishers at the expense of information users—like teachers and students" (384). Legal scholar Jane Ginsburg describes this shift in fair use as a "new legal calibration," adjusted to take into account digital technologies and copyright issues on the Internet (1614). However, congressional lawmakers who defend this "tilt" or legal calibration often argue that the DMCA was created to correct piracy and that fair use only justifies "theft" (United States, H.R. Committee on Energy and Commerce 4). In such an anti–fair use climate conditioned by copyright laws like the DMCA, digital academic works that use copyrighted material are vulnerable to two types of censorship: the first, asserted by the copyright holder; the second, by Internet Service Providers (ISPs).

Censorship by Copyright Holders

One of the important ways the DMCA undermines fair use is the requirement for authorized access to technologically restricted material, which gives copyright holders the power to decide on the fair use of their product. Though the DMCA appears only to be concerned with copyright infringing technologies, it also bans the use of such technologies to circumvent copyright protection through "unauthorized *access* to a copyrighted work and unauthorized *copying* of a copyrighted work." (U.S. Copyright Office, "Digital Millennium Copyright Act" 3–4). Although the DMCA cannot prohibit the act of unauthorized copying if the copying represents fair use of the material, "since the fair use doctrine is not a defense to the act of gaining unauthorized access to a work, the act of circumventing a technological measure in order to *gain access* is prohibited" (4, my italics). This prohibition in the DMCA transforms copyright holders into de facto gatekeepers of fair use, since they can control the copying of digital data by barring access. Pamela Samuelson, codirector of the Berkeley Center of Law and Technology, warns, "[A]ny data in digital form—not just sound recording and motion pictures—can be protected by technical measures [. . .]. Those who disseminate digital data may want to restrict what researchers can do with that data" (2029).

In addition to giving copyright holders dramatic new powers over copying through access, the DMCA emboldens owners to censor users out of court. It should be noted that the DMCA was not intended as a tool of censorship, but some well-publicized cases suggest that content owners have learned to use the DMCA to not only dictate fair use of their copyrighted digital productions but also censor academic discussions and online criticism. A famous example of the DMCA censoring academic speech is the case of Princeton University professor Edward Felten. In April 2001, the Recording Industry Association of America (RIAA), invoking the DMCA, threatened to sue Professor Felten if he delivered a presentation at a scientific conference on cracking digital watermarks protecting sound and image files (Knight). Consequently, he was forced to withdraw his presentation. The Felten case suggests how freedom of expression, particularly academic discussion, can be impaired by the mere threat of a lawsuit or DMCA violation. This is because, as Felten himself notes, "litigation is costly, time-consuming, and uncertain, regardless of the merits of the other side's case" (Brown). Speaking at a lecture at Stanford University, Felten warned his audience that copyright owners like those in the music industry can seek "control over what we could write in our papers." He added, "If it happened to [computer scientists], it could happen to other disciplines as well" (quoted in Bowman). Currently, Professor Felten is challenging the DMCA in federal court on the grounds of free speech.

Due to mounting criticisms of the DMCA by scientists like Felten and law professors like Peter Jaszi, who argue for the academic value of fair use, the Library of Congress issued on November 27, 2006, six classes of work that are exempted from the DMCA's prohibition against circumventing technology. One of the six includes "audiovisual works included in the educational library of a college or university's film or media studies department, when circumvention is accomplished for the purpose of making compilations of portions of those works for educational use in the classroom by media studies or film professors" (U.S. Copyright Office, "Statement"). However, there are many problems with this narrowly phrased exemption criterion. First, this exemption only covers the "compilation" of audiovisual works that are already "included in the education library of a college or university film and media studies department." This means that more current audiovisual material released in the public (such as on the Internet) cannot be used unless it is officially part of the library's collection. Second, this exemption explicitly applies to "media studies or film professors": if read strictly, it does not apply to other professors outside of the disciplines who might also make media commentary such as composition teachers and scholars; if read loosely to include all professors who teach media, this exemption still excludes the use of audiovisual work by students for educational purposes. Finally, the exemption has an expiration date of three years. According to the Librarian of Congress, "These exemptions expire after three years, unless proponents prove their case once again" (U.S. Copyright Office, "Statement"). Not only are these exemptions for fair use provisional and vulnerable to termination, but these particular fair use circumstances require proponents to continually advocate and justify their existence.

As I've noted earlier in this chapter, the DMCA—with its current exemptions—still prevents students from the opportunities to learn through one of the oldest forms of education: modeling and design. This is particularly critical for those of us who study and teach visual strategies in digital writing and rely on providing examples of multimedia writing. Mary E. Hocks observes, "Interactive digital texts can blend words and visuals, talk and text, and authors and audiences in ways that are recognizably postmodern" (629–30). While Hocks points to the need for teachers to recognize and teach a new hybrid form of visual communication that is "at once verbal, spatial, and visual" (631), her observation also highlights the potential problems that might beset a teacher who asks students to create the examples and models of hybrid visual communication on the web, or through other multimedia, to illustrate their knowledge and understanding of digital writing. Students, for instance, might use a PowerPoint presentation to analyze the strategic use of music in recent commercials to target audiences. Even under the exemption rules of the DMCA, these students could not use circumventing technology to 1. use audiovisual material that is not in the library, or 2. create an audio clip from the original source that would help contextualize the use of music because they are not teachers. While studies have shown that students acquire a deeper understanding of rhetoric and communication skills when they themselves become creators and communicators, the DMCA would prohibit students from adequately learning strategies of digital communication in an age where understanding and applying digital information and communication is central to proficient media literacy.

Furthermore, since Richard Lanham published *The Electronic Word*, rhetoricians who study new media communication have moved from merely analyzing the visual rhetoric of the digital environment to employing criticism and constructing scholarship that relies on "interactive digital texts." These e-rhetoricians, like media scholars and documentary filmmakers, rely on verbal-visual forms of argumentation—the kind of hybridity that depends on extensive use of media content in order to comment on or critically analyze current digital communication practices. As incorporations of audio and visual clips from popular culture are vital to the work of documentary filmmakers, so too are music or film clips integrated in e-rhetoricians' new media criticism. The DMCA slows—if not precludes—the growth of this critical practice. The recent exemptions to the DMCA do not necessarily ease the difficulty as they limit the source (only library-held material), the creators (professors only), and the duration applied (three years). If anything, the exemptions expose the severe limitations of the DMCA, which does not explicitly take into account fair use or the range of public users who engage in noninfringing uses of copyrighted work through the circumvention of access controls.

In addition to a trend toward favoring copyright holders in courts and legislation, Jaszi identifies a parallel development in copyright law that narrows the practice of fair use in the "dramatic development in secondary liability for copyright infringement, and dramatic increases in civil and criminal penalties" (United States 20). As another legal scholar has noted:

> In the past, Congress has instituted criminal copyright penalties only in situations in which substantial levels of piracy existed.[. . .] In 1997 and 1998, however, the United States Congress expanded the scope of criminal copyright infringement law far beyond any previous attempts to curtail piracy. Specifically, Congress lowered the threshold for criminal copyright infringement through the passage of the No Electronic Theft (NET) Act, and expanded the scope of criminal penalties for infringement through the Digital Millennium Copyright Act (DMCA). ("Criminalization" 1706)

The DMCA makes it a criminal offense to violate copyright through copyright-infringing technology by setting up "a 500,000 fine or up to five years imprisonment for the first offense, and up to a $1,000,000 fine or up to 10 years imprisonment for subsequent offenses" (U.S. Copyright Office, "Digital Millennium Copyright Act" 7). The severe monetary and criminal penalties create more than a cautious atmosphere; they deter productive and reasonable application of fair use. The DMCA rules out potential fair use of copyright materials because "[t]he possibility of criminal penalties for using copyrighted works [. . .] chill[s] the dissemination of information and may deter other productive uses of copyrighted works because of the uncertainty regarding the legality of use" ("Criminalization" 1718–19).

Censorship by Internet Service Providers

While the DMCA's monetary and criminal penalties for copyright violation "chill" fair use by scholars, they also encourage a second type of censorship we may encounter through Internet Service Providers (ISPs), who are charged to act on copyright owners' claims of infringement. Although the DMCA does limit the liability of online service providers for copyright infringement, the harsh penalties encourage Internet Service Providers to censor the infringing material and capitulate to the copyright owner's claim of unauthorized use, or find themselves in violation of the law. So, in addition to blocking users' ability to apply the technology for fair use purposes, the DMCA, Lawrence Lessig points out, creates "strong incentives for ISPs to remove from their sites any material claimed to be a violation of copyright" (64).

In addition to fines, the language of the DMCA itself gives ISPs no room to question the copyright owner's claim or investigate the fair use of an infringing work. Section 512(b) of the DMCA demands that "[a]ny material that was posted *without the copyright owner's authorization* must be removed or blocked promptly once the service provider has been notified [. . .]" (U.S. Copyright Office, "Digital Millennium Copyright Act" 11, my italics). This command runs contrary to some of the central tenets of fair use. According to legal scholars, the fair use doctrine maintains that the condition of fair use does not require the copyright owner's authorization; furthermore, it permits fair use of copyrighted material, even if owners decline consent. Concerned over the rising practice of censorship under the DMCA, Deirdre K. Mulligan, director of the Samuelson Law, Technology and Public Policy Clinic at the UC Berkeley School of Law, notes: "When the DMCA passed, many were concerned that the takedown provisions were heavily tilted against speakers—by merely claiming copyright, any individual or business can silence speech.[. . .] [T]here are certainly [. . .] instances of speakers being wrongfully silenced under the DMCA" ("FatWallet Victorious"). An example of how copyright owners have used the DMCA to force an ISP to censor text on the Web is the oft-cited case of Google and its capitulation to the Church of Scientology in 2002. According to *Wired Magazine*, the Church of Scientology cited the DMCA as a basis for demanding that Google remove anti-Scientology websites from its search engine. Google removed the URLs and, in a letter to the anti-Scientology websites, noted: "Had we not removed these URLs, we would be subject to a claim for copyright infringement, regardless of its merits" (quoted in McCullagh). Accordingly, ISPs are not only asked to defer to copyright owner's claims of infringement, but also forced to become collaborators in regulating copyright infringement: the DMCA, in other words, "makes the owner of every Internet service provider, content host, and search engine an untrained copyright cop. The default action is censorship" (Vaidhyanathan).

The censorship practiced by copyright holders and ISPs points to a trend in which viable fair use cases are invalidated even before they could be defended in court. More recently in 2005, Wal-Mart invoked the DMCA to shut down a small parody website: WalMart-Foundation.org. The infringing web site was created by a Carnegie Mellon University student for an art class that, focusing on visual rhetoric, taught students about the "tactical use of satire in mainstream media" (Papsian). After Wal-Mart sent the DMCA violation notice to Papsian's ISP, he was forced to remove the graphics, which were taken and altered from the original Wal-Mart website. Although under fair use provisions Papsian's work appears defensible in court by factors of transformation and criticism or parody, Papsian's case was never defended. While fair use scuffles here and there by little-known individuals like Papsian may not seem serious, continual exercise of censorship weakens fair use overall. The preemptive censorship activities of copyright owners and ISPs normalize the action and, in due course, alter fair use practice on the Internet.

CONVERSATION WITH THE PUBLIC: STATEMENT OF BEST PRACTICES IN FAIR USE

In the previous sections of this chapter, I've identified two factors that contribute to the vulnerability of scholarship and criticism in digital media—the chilling effect of censorship from copyright holders who use the DMCA to grant or deny permission and censorship from ISPs who are obliged by the DMCA to act under copyright holders' interest. These forms of censorship generated by the DMCA lead to a changing understanding and practice of the existing fair use doctrine for digital scholars. While one might criticize Congress for the passage of the DMCA, some fair use proponents like Siva Vaidhyanathan place equal amount of blame on "teachers, writers, and researchers" who failed to heed and significantly act on the early warnings. "When the DMCA was being considered, the Digital Future Coalition put up an admirable defense of the principles of access and fair use for teaching, research, and criticism," Vaidhyanathan writes in *The Chronicle Review*, an online magazine of *The Chronicle of Higher Education*. "But the commercial forces allied against it were too formidable. In the absence of widespread public outcry, Congress could only rely on what the most powerful interested parties told it: that if some copyright protection is good, then more must be better. Had there been some grassroots activism by teachers, writers, and researchers, Congress might have realized that it was considering reckless legislation" (Vaidhyanathan). Regardless of whether grassroots activism by "teachers, writers, and researchers" might have made a difference in preventing the passage of the DMCA, we can still change how fair use on the Internet is applied to our work and our teaching. More specific and explicit guidelines of fair use for composition scholars and teachers need to be created, not only for the sake of clarifying how we apply fair use but also in helping organizations like ISPs, publishers, and universities understand what is at stake in our claims of fair use.

Like the CCCC-IP's statement of fair use, which works to primarily enlighten composition scholars about fair use misinformation and their rights, the Documentary Filmmaker's Statement of Best Practices in Fair Use, released on November 18, 2005, calibrates the definition of fair use and corrects misinformation regarding fair use of digital media, so that filmmakers can be emboldened to use copyrighted material and defend their fair use claims. However, it also presents an explicit description of documentarians' fair use practice and limitations, and elicits sympathy for creative need of documentary filmmakers while clarifying the legal perimeters in which documentary filmmakers agree to work.

The Statement of Best Practices provides three key strategies, which may be useful for composition studies if we aim not only to *apply* "fair use" practice but to *maintain* this practice through the solicitation of allies in professional communities and sympathetic appeals to a larger public.

1. First, the Documentary Filmmaker's Statement of Best Practices involves media and legal experts to establish credibility. The Statement of Best Practices involves important allies of documentary filmmakers who help legitimate their cause and highlight their observation of copyright law. The opening sentence of the statement identifies the various institutions at American University that the film associations consulted, including the Center for Social Media in the School of Communication and the Program on Intellectual Property and the Public Interest in the Washington College of Law directed by Peter Jaszi. In addition, the statement includes endorsements by media groups such as Arts Engine and the Independent Television Service. By identifying endorsements and consultants, the documentary filmmakers' Statement demonstrates that its arguments have been examined and approved by media and copyright experts.

Moreover, the critical involvement of these professional organizations is meant to suggest that the fair use concerns in the Statement of Best Practices resonate not only with documentary filmmakers but also with a greater public. Indeed, a few months after the statement's release, one blogger on Lawrence Lessig's FreeCulture.org website noted the following:

> This is a powerful tool: not just for filmmakers who want to use the work of another, but on the supply side as well. *Not only does this document inform filmmakers of their rights, it informs them of their obligations as well.* Not only will this embolden filmmakers when they receive a cease & desist letter or are told they have to get permission to quote in their film—hopefully this will reduce the number of cease & desist letters sent in the first place. (Baker)

The support of professional communities thus provides a dual function: to establish the cultural currency and legal authority of the stance provided and to indicate that the fair use issues applied by filmmakers (and scholars alike) are part of a broad cultural experience. Likewise, composition scholars have already found allies in law professors such as Lawrence Lessig of Stanford University, who spoke on fair use at the CCCC in 2004, or Peter Jaszi of American University, who coauthored "The Law of Texts: Copyright in the Academy" with Martha Woodmansee. Drawing on an advisory board of copyright experts like Lessig and Jaszi and bringing in media scholars whose understanding of the value of fair use is similar to our own, we can strengthen our argument.

2. Second, the Statement of Best Practices elicits sympathy through explanation of noninfringing copyright use. While the statement is undoubtedly a guideline for helping documentary filmmakers understand fair use in the making of their film projects based on current legislation and court decisions, it also aims to remind an outside audience of the legitimacy of their noninfringing use of copyright material as well as their critical role in informing and educating the public through documentary films. The statement begins by relating that "over the last decade, [documentarians are] increasingly constrained by demands to clear rights for copyrighted material" (Documentary Filmmakers'). What this approach makes clear to its audiences is the transformation of "fair use" laws—that documentarians are not dealing with the status quo but with far more restrictive legal demands. This point is then followed by an explanation of why these restrictions damage the production of fine documentary film. The statement is careful to clarify that the understanding of fair use of copyright material does not mean piracy or "exploitative or abusive application of fair use": in fact, the language in the statement puts documentarians on the side of copyright holders. It states that "documentarians are themselves copyright holders" who are interested in "honor[ing] [. . .] claims as copyright owners" (Documentary Filmmakers'). However, the statement issues the case that documentarians' "ability to communicate effectively is being restricted by an overly rigid approach to copyright compliance," which "compromises" both "knowledge and perspectives that documentarians can provide" their audiences—ultimately, "the public suffers as a result" (Documentary Filmmakers').

The lesson that composition scholars might take from this approach is how the statement provides emotional appeal to an outside audience that may include lawmakers or copyright holders in the film industry. It identifies the copyright problems that documentarians face with restrictive "fair use" demands in terms of its ultimate impact on the public; additionally, it frames its noninfringing use of copyright material in terms of respect for the rights of copyright owners.

3. Finally, the Statement of Best Practices describes "actual practices" and recommendations of "what would be appropriate if [documentarians] were free to follow their own understanding of good practices." In addition to explaining how copyright material is vital for professional practice, the statement provides recommendations for documentary filmmakers in "four classes of situations" involving the fair use of copyright materials. These four classes of fair use "reflect the most common kinds of situations" encountered by filmmakers. They are: (class one) "employing copyrighted material as the object of social, political, or cultural critique"; (class two) "quoting copyrighted works of popular culture to illustrate an argument or point"; (class three) "capturing copyrighted media content in the process of filming something else"; and (class four) "using copyright material in historical sequence" (Documentary Filmmakers'). In each case, the Statement provides the description of situation, principle of fair use applied, and limitations of such use for documentary filmmakers. The "description" category explains why a particular fair use situation is critical to documentarians. For instance, for "capturing copyrighted media content in the process of filming something else," the description argues the capture of copyrighted media content is only "incidental" and that it is necessary to represent a "real-life setting." The "principle" category either cites existing fair use principles such as media citation for criticism or analysis (class one) or argues how fair use applies to the documentary medium when it contributes to social and educational history (class four). Finally, the "limitation" category provides documentarians with guidelines for fair use but also reassures copyright holders that their application of fair use observes the law. For example, for class two (quoting copyrighted works of popular culture), the statement includes the limitation that clearly appeals to the concerns of holders: "the quoted material is not employed merely in order to avoid the cost or inconvenience of shooting equivalent footage" (Documentary Filmmakers').

Ultimately, this Statement of Best Practices was written not only to clarify fair use principles to documentary filmmakers or to identify situations of fair use but also to inform and educate outside communities about what documentary filmmakers do, why they do it, and how fair use enables their creative process. It is not enough that filmmakers are informed of their rights to fair use of copyright material so that they may take advantage of them with a greater degree of confidence; there is a sense that they must continue to employ their fair use rights or face losing them. The Statement of Best Practices describes this situation best: "Fair use is shaped, in part, by the practice of the professional communities that employ it" (Documentary Filmmakers'). This is a critical communiqué for scholars as more and more third parties begin to interpret, shape, and control the fair use practice in which we participate. Only when we involve the broader community within our discussions of fair use can we defend our fair use practice and protect it from the "chilling" repercussions of aggressive copyright legislation.

THE PUBLIC CASE FOR FAIR USE

Our academic community encourages the teaching and scholarly study of "nonprintcentric" media such as digital texts that are found on the Internet; however, these professional goals and practices run against the DMCA and a Congress that is hostile or at least ambivalent to fair use. Three years ago, the National Council of Teachers of English (NCTE) formally endorsed the position that compositionists should embrace multimedia composition, arguing that we should help students become literate in multimedia forms of communication (NCTE, "Nonprint Media"). But as our own profession moves toward online publishing and digital criticism, we encounter the same censorships and limitations faced by documentary filmmakers, computer scientists, and others who wish to exercise fair use on the Internet. The copyright rules articulated in the DMCA will determine the media content of arguments we circulate in the digital public sphere and limit the means by which we distribute our arguments. Because of these limits, we can only half answer Patricia Sullivan and James Porter's call for innovative scholarship that takes into account new types of composition shaped by computer-writing technology (Sullivan and Porter xiv).

Ultimately, the means for us to defend fair use might be in discovering who defines fair use. In the first half of this chapter, I have tried to argue that our evolving fair use culture is shaped by many factors and two major participants: the copyright holders and ISPs. The Constitution supplies the copyright clause and language supporting limited rights to holders. Court rulings offer common law precedent for fair use claims and practice. The legislation of the Copyright Act codifies fair use, and other more recent legislative acts like the DMCA limit fair use for users of copyright materials in various ways, directly and indirectly, through prohibitions, penalties, restrictions, and censorship. The current tendency toward a more restrictive interpretation of fair use by publishers, ISPs, and holders contributes to defining our existing and emergent practices of fair use in digital scholarship and teaching. I stress "emergent" because, as many legal scholars have noted, current fair use practice, as it is misunderstood by the public and furthered unwittingly by users, may eventually be normalized and codified if it is not challenged. For this reason, our ability to defend our fair use rights under the U.S. Code must not only be practiced to be maintained, but also be understood by those outside our field as good and legal practice; thus, is it crucial that we, like documentary filmmakers, make a strong and consistent rhetorical case to the public, develop coalitions with sympathizing professional organizations, and delineate our intentions for fair use. The most important of our efforts involve appealing to a broader public, buttressing the documentarians' common practice of fair use, and establishing the credibility of their position.

As composition scholars, we also need to correct the public's understanding of fair use in our work, particularly as our scholarship—in synch with technological changes in media culture—begin to further involve digital technologies. We need to make clear that scholars, like artists, filmmakers, and members of news media, also require the use of popular images for purposes of argumentation and critique and, further, that our students learn effectively by quoting copyrighted media from popular culture or transforming its content as a function of expression, criticism, or analysis. In short, we need to produce a Statement of Best Practices that makes our stakes in protecting fair use the stakes of many communities and, ultimately, the public's self-interest. While it is not certain how profoundly the DMCA will change the future of multimedia scholarship, one thing is clear: in order to argue, research, and teach digital media, e-rhetoricians need to have available all the possible means of critical argumentation at their disposal; otherwise, our ability to persuade is hampered and our ideas incomplete.

WORKS CITED

Baker, Gordon. "Fair Use Best Practices: Film Making and Beyond." FreeCulture. org. 11 Dec. 2005. 23 Feb. 2006 <http://freeculture.org/blog/2005/12/11/fair-use-best-practices-filmmaking-and-beyond/>.

Bowman, Lisa M. "Professor Warns of Threat to Free Speech." C/Net News.com. 3 Mar. 2001. 3 Mar. 2007.

Brown, Janelle. "Is the RIAA running scared?" Salon.com. 26 Apr. 2001. 3 Mar. 2007 <http://archive.salon.com/tech/log/2001/04/26/felten/>.

CCCC Caucus on Intellectual Property. "Use Your Fair Use: Strategies toward Action." *College Composition and Communication* 51.3 (2000): 485–88.

Committee on House Education and the Workforce Subcommittee on 21st Century Competitiveness. United States Congress. "Combating Internet Piracy on College Campuses." *Congressional Quarterly.* 26 Sept. 2006. Lexis Nexis. Stanford University

Conference on Fair Use. "Multimedia Fair Use Guidelines." Office of General Counsel, University of Texas. 25 Nov. 2006 <http://www.utsystem.edu/OGC/IntellectualProperty/ccmcguid.htm>.

Crews, Kenneth D. "The Law of Fair Use and the Illusion of Fair-Use Guidelines." *Ohio State Law Journal* 62 (2001): 602–700.

"The Criminalization of Copyright Infringement in the Digital Era." *Harvard Law Review* 112.7 (1999): 1705–22. JSTOR. Stanford University Lib. 15 Oct. 2006.

"Documentary Filmmakers' Statement of Fair Use." Nov. 2005. Center for Social Media, School of Communication, American University. 1 June 2007 <http://www.centerforsocialmedia.org/files/pdf/fair_use_final.pdf>.

"FatWallet Victorious in Challenge to Wal-Mart's Frivolous Digital Millennium Copyright Act Subpoena." *Ascribe* 5 Dec. 2002. 4 Mar. 2006 <http://www.nyfairuse.org/dmca/walmart.fw.xhtml>.

Folsom v. Marsh. 9F. Cas. 342 (1841). Legal Research. Lexis Nexis Academic. Stanford Lib., Stanford, CA. 24 Nov. 2006.

Gimbel, Mark. "Some Thoughts on the Implications of Trusted Systems for Intellectual Property Law." *Stanford Law Review* 50.5 (1998): 1671–87.

Ginsburg, Jane E. "Copyright and Control over New Technologies of Dissemination." *Columbia Law Review* 101.7 (2007): 1613–47.

Hocks, Mary E. "Understanding Visual Rhetoric in Digital Writing Environments." *College Composition and Communication* 54.4 (2003): 629–56.

Knight, Will. "Censored Music Protection Research Revealed." *New Scientist* online. 14 Aug. 2001. 3 Mar. 2006 <http://www.newscientist.com/article.ns?id=dn1154>.

Lanham, Richard. The Electronic Word: Democracy, Technology, and the Arts. Chicago: U of Chicago P, 1993.

McCullagh, Declan. "Google Yanks Anti-Church Sites." *Wired Magazine.* 21 Mar. 2002. Online. 25 Nov. 2006 <http://www.wired.com/news/politics/0,1283, 51233,00.html>.

Lessig, Lawrence. "Internet Under Siege." *Foreign Policy* 127 (Nov.–Dec. 2001): 56–65.

Lunsford, Andrea, and Susan West. "Intellectual Property and Composition Studies." *College Composition and Communication* 47.3 (Oct. 1996): 383–411.

Mennecke, Thomas. "Wal-Mart Uses DMCA Against Parody Site." *Slyck News* 28 Apr. 2005 <http://www.slyck.com/story765.html>.

NCTE Board of Directors. "On Composing with Nonprint Media." *NCTE Online.* 8 Mar. 2007 <http://www.ncte.org/about/over/positions/category/comp/1149 19.htm>.

NCTE Standing Committee Against Censorship. "Guidelines for Dealing with Censorship of Nonprint Materials" NCTE Anti-Censorship Center. Online. Oct. 2004. 7 Mar. 2007 <http://www.ncte.org/about/over/positions/category/ cens/107611.htm>.

Papsian, Daniel. "Press Release." 28 Apr. 2005. 24 May 2007 <www.walmart-foundation.org/walmart-pr.pdf>.

Phan, Dan Thu Thi. "Will Fair Use Function on the Internet?" *Columbia Law Review* 98.1 (1998): 169–216.

Reyman, Jessica. "Copyright, Distance Education, and the TEACH Act: Implications for Teaching Writing." *College Composition and Communication* 58.1 (2006): 30–45.

Samuelson, Pamela. "Anticircumvention Rules: Threat to Science." *Science* www.science.mag.org. 14 Sept. 2001. 2028–30. <http://www.law.upenn.edu/law619/ f2001/week09/samuelson_dmca.pdf>.

Sullivan, Patricia, and James E. Porter. *Opening Spaces: Writing Technologies and Critical Research Practices.* Westport, CT, and London: Ablex Publishing, 1997.

United States. Cong. House. Committee on Energy and Commerce. Subcommittee on Commerce, Trade, and Consumer Protection. *Fair Use: Its Effects on Consumers and Industry.* 109th Cong. 1st Sess. H. R. Washington: GPO, 2005.

United States Copyright Office. The Digital Millennium Copyright Act of 1998. U.S. Copyright Office Summary. December 1998.

————. "Statement of the Librarian of Congress Relating to Section 1201 Rulemaking." 22 Nov. 2006. 1 Dec. 2006 <http://www.copyright.gov/1201/docs/2006_statement.html>.

Vaidhyanathan, Siva. "Copyright as Cudgel." *The Chronicle Review* 2 Aug. 2002 <http://chronicle.com/temp/email2.php?id=qjhv6fhDdkkdtF9jkkGfPVPZ4XrtrSKg>.

Woodmansee, Martha, and Peter Jaszi. "The Law of Texts: Copyright in the Academy." *College English* 57.7 (1995): 769–87.

CHAPTER 3

"Some Rights Reserved"

Weblogs with Creative Commons Licenses

CLANCY RATLIFF

The weblog, by design, is a collaborative genre of writing that challenges traditional notions of authorship and intellectual property. Since the late 1990s, bloggers are becoming increasingly aware of this fact, and they are seeking out and implementing alternatives to the current, and some would argue problematic, model of heavy copyright protection of ideas. One of these alternatives is getting a Creative Commons license for content, which enables an author to retain some protections afforded by copyright law but give up others; for example, a blogger can specify a license that allows readers to copy and distribute his or her writing, as long as the blogger is given credit for the writing and the use is not for commercial gain. Thousands of bloggers have now acquired Creative Commons licenses for the content on their weblogs, which includes creative writing, essays, photographs, graphics, and even video. In this chapter, I will give a brief review of copyright law as it has developed in the United States, explain what Creative Commons and its mission are, and examine the trend of Creative Commons licenses on weblogs, using bloggers' own statements about why they are in favor of Creative Commons licenses. I will argue that blogging emerged pari passu with several other important technological and cultural occurrences: the *United*

States v. Microsoft case and the rise of GPL (General Public License) and open source software, the tightening of copyright restrictions that came with the Digital Millennium Copyright Act, and the popularity of peer-to-peer networks combined with the music industry's attempts to eliminate them. Such a confluence of factors—and bloggers' acquiring Creative Commons licenses in reaction to them—make weblogs particularly important in the fight for an intellectual commons.

A NOTE ON METHOD

In early 2003, I became interested in bloggers' enthusiastic adoption of Creative Commons licenses, as this phenomenon was a connection of my interests in copyright law and weblogs. In order to learn more about bloggers' motivations for acquiring Creative Commons licenses, I decided to solicit some commentary from them about their decisions to use these licenses, which, at the time, were still very new. I formulated the following questions:

> How did you find out about Creative Commons licenses?
>
> Why did you get a Creative Commons license?
>
> What do you think the value of a Creative Commons–licensed blog site
> is over a traditional "All Rights Reserved" site?

I then posted the questions at Kairosnews.org, a weblog maintained by a large community of rhetoric and composition scholars, so that readers could leave their answers to the questions in the comments section of the post. Three readers responded. I then visited a site called Blogdex, which tracked posts on weblogs and served as an early weblog search tool, and I used this tool to see which weblogs linked to Creative Commons' website. I visited these weblogs and contacted the bloggers who had listed their email addresses. Of these, I received responses from six bloggers. I contacted them again in May of 2007, including in my email each blogger's responses to my questions, to find out if they had changed their minds about what they had written. No one had: all the bloggers wrote that the stances they expressed in 2003 had not changed. I cite these bloggers' replies to my questions here not to make any statistical conclusions about bloggers' adoption of Creative Commons licenses, but rather to contextualize and inform my observations about the rise of Creative Commons licenses as one response to a significant moment in the history and rhetorical context of copyright law.

THE HISTORY AND AIMS OF CREATIVE COMMONS

With the aid of founding member Lawrence Lessig, Creative Commons began in 2001 as a collaborative effort between Harvard Law School and Stanford Law School. The goal of the project was "to develop a rich repository of high-quality works in a variety of media, and to promote an ethos of sharing, public education, and creative interactivity" (Creative). In December 2002, inspired by the General Public Licenses for software, they released their Creative Commons licenses. The licensing options include Public Domain Dedication, Attribution, Noncommercial Use, No Derivative Works, and ShareAlike. Another Creative Commons project is the "Founder's Copyright." If an author licenses a book or an artist licenses a piece of art under a Founder's Copyright, the creator will hold the copyright for fourteen years with an option to renew for an additional fourteen. In support of the Founder's Copyright, some bloggers have a button on their weblogs that reads, "Create like it's 1790!" For weblogs, the most popular combination of selection items in the range of licenses offered is Attribution, Noncommercial Use, and ShareAlike. That is, people may use that particular blogger's work as long as they attribute it to the author of the weblog, do not use it for commercial gain, and, if they create derivative works based on the weblog, license them in a similar "Some Rights Reserved" way. This combination, although popular among bloggers, is not the only combination of licensing terms that bloggers use. Lessig, for example, has Attribution as the only term in his license; blogger Doc Searls uses a Public Domain Dedication license, meaning that he has relinquished all rights to his weblog writing.

A BRIEF HISTORY OF COPYRIGHT

Copyright law was originally meant to encourage creativity and innovation. It began with the public's interests in mind: first, it was conceived as a quid pro quo, meaning that the public gave the exclusive right of distribution and creative control to the creator for a limited time, with the understanding that the work would enter the public domain at the end of the time allotted. Then it became a sort of bargain, in which the public "bribed" creators to produce more work by granting exclusive copyright (Litman 78). The original Copyright Act of 1790 gave the creator these rights for fourteen years, with an option to renew for an additional fourteen years. In 1831, Congress made it possible to renew the copyright for another fourteen years. Congress extended the copyright term again in 1909, 1976, and then again in 1998.

Under current copyright law, as soon as any creative expression enters a fixed medium—for example, as soon as any file is saved on any hard drive, or as soon as an exposure is made onto a piece of film, or any words are written with pencil on paper—the work is automatically copyrighted for the life of the author plus seventy years.

Recently, organizations such as the Electronic Frontier Foundation and the Berkman Center for Internet and Society have critiqued copyright law on the grounds that it is no longer congruent with its original intent: to balance the interests of creators of intellectual and creative works with the interests of the public, who benefit from having a public domain of content, which they can draw from to create new work: an intellectual and cultural commons, or as Benkler puts it, a collection of work that "is not intended to supplant all other forms of creating and disseminating information. Rather, it is intended to offer a background resource available to all as *users*" (577, emphasis in original). In *Digital Copyright*, Jessica Litman critiques the process by which copyright laws are made, claiming it is skewed in favor of the private industries and their copyright lawyers. In other words, the content industries—record companies, motion picture companies, television networks, cable television companies, satellite television companies, and publishers—want longer terms of copyright because longer terms are in their economic interest. Their lobbyists present this agenda to congressional representatives, who, in turn, pass legislation without much consideration of its implications for the public interest. Critics also argue that recent extensions of copyright terms move toward making copyright perpetual and leaving the public not only without representatives of their interest in the intellectual property debate, but without ideas to use for new innovations and creations.

It should be noted that critics of copyright law do not want to abolish copyright or prevent artists, scholars, and inventors from being compensated for their work. The argument is not that people should be free to download music without paying for it or to copy movies onto discs and sell them on the street corner. Critics of copyright law argue that creativity and innovation are fostered when artists, inventors, and scholars are free to take existing ideas and works and make something new out of them. Examples from literature include the novels *Wide Sargasso Sea*, by Jean Rhys; *I, Tituba, Black Witch of Salem*, by Maryse Condé; and *Ahab's Wife: Or, the Star-Gazer*, by Sena Jeter Naslund. Each work is a subversive, feminist take on a canonical work of literature, told from the point of view of a minor character. Rhys's novel is the story of Bertha Mason, Rochester's first wife in Charlotte Brontë's *Jane Eyre*, Condé's novel is the story of Tituba, a slave in Arthur Miller's *The Crucible*, and Naslund's novel is the story of Captain Ahab's unnamed wife from Herman Melville's *Moby-Dick*. Each of these novels uses the stories of the works on which they are based, but each author creates a new story. Because *Jane Eyre* and *Moby-Dick* are in the public domain, meaning that their copyright terms have expired, authors are free to create spin-offs or variant narratives of these works.

Since the emergence of the Internet in the early 1990s, authors have continued to write narratives based on canonical and noncanonical popular fiction, including movies and television shows. Online communities, many of which include bloggers, have formed, where users write and post fan fiction, or "fanfic," stories with characters from television and movie franchises such as *Star Trek* and *Buffy the Vampire Slayer*. The ease with which digital video and audio compositions can be created has resulted in a proliferation of multimedia compositions called mashups. One such mashup was a whimsical, quirky trailer for the Stanley Kubrick film *The Shining*, which repurposed footage from the film and edited it in such a way that the audience, had they not seen it, would think it was a feel-good romantic comedy. The voiceover says:

> Meet Jack Torrance. He's a writer looking for inspiration.
>
> Meet Danny. He's a kid looking for a dad.
>
> Jack just can't finish his book.
>
> But now, sometimes, what we need the most is just around the corner.

The trailer then cuts to Jack Torrance driving his car on a picturesque, expansive country road, and Peter Gabriel's heartwarming and upbeat tune "Solsbury Hill" swells. These kinds of creative works are what critics of copyright law believe culture is built upon; it is what culture needs in order to renew itself. Web authors want to create these compositions: essays, stories, digital videos, songs, images. Most of the time, as with the alternative trailer of *The Shining*, they only want to amuse friends and strangers; they are not intent on making mashups for commercial gain. Critics of copyright law want these creators to be able to compose these works without fear of litigation.

Given their involvement with creative online communities, bloggers in particular have been critical of copyright law's reach. When asked why he chose to use a Creative Commons license for his weblog, Timothy Jarrett replied:

> Because I've been arguing the cause of the intellectual commons long enough that I felt I should take action once an alternative was

available. Also, I think that explicitly enabling reuse of content through RSS (technological means) and the license (legal means) ensures that I do my part to make sure the "virtuous cycle" of blogging (author-subscriber-reader-author) continues.

Jarrett expresses a view of composition that acknowledges the collaborative nature of all writing, and he refers to web technology's facilitation of that process. To illustrate the "virtuous cycle," let us suppose that Jarrett writes a weblog post. I subscribe to his weblog (for no cost) through RSS, or "Really Simple Syndication," a technology that allows me to have an inbox of new content from specific websites I choose to add to my subscriptions. I read his posts once I see his new content in my RSS reader, and then I use his ideas to help me write posts on my own weblog. Because he has a Creative Commons license, I know that I can quote from his post liberally without having to worry about whether or not I am quoting too much, for my use of his post falls under fair use guidelines.

Andrew Ó Baoill expresses the view of authorship and art that many critics of copyright law espouse:

> I am not a believer in strong copyright protections. I believe that all creative work builds on that which has gone before (we stand on the shoulders of giants)—perhaps nowhere is this more obvious than in weblogs, which are so overt about the links (online or off-line) on which they rely. Having said that, I understand, and sympathise with, the rationale for copyrights, as expressed in the U.S. Constitution— to encourage creativity for the benefit of society, using temporary monopolies as a reward.

Ó Baoill's comment also illustrates the way that blogging especially embodies the bricoleur approach to authorship. Whereas a great poet such as T. S. Eliot may use Greek mythological, biblical, and Hindu symbols in his poetry, bloggers also use allusions in their writing. However, they can make the allusion text link explicitly, or, as Ó Baoill says, overtly, to its source, so that the "shoulders of giants" quality of the writing is actually networked and visible. The rhetorical situation of blogging lends itself to the recognition of all writing and art as inherently collaborative. Being able to use others' content without an arduous and expensive rights clearance process is in bloggers' and the public's best interest, but as Ó Baoill mentions, a *temporary* monopoly for the author, artist, or inventor is also in the public's interest, as it functions as an incentive for the creation of more works. The key is to achieve a balance that fairly compensates creators but also ensures that new works enter the public domain regularly; however, with such lengthy copyright terms and regular extensions of those terms, copyright law's critics may be right to fear that copyright could become perpetual. Ó Baoill observes the way that blogging's networked architecture reveals the collaborative qualities of writing, but I argue that this architecture is only one of several reasons that bloggers are seeking alternatives to traditional copyright. The cultural context of weblog technology's emergence is also worth exploring.

THE CONTEXT: WEBLOGS, OPEN SOURCE SOFTWARE, AND PEER-TO-PEER NETWORKS

Weblogs emerged in the early 1990s, but they did not become mainstream until 1999. The cultural context with regard to copyright and piracy is particularly important to establish here because I intend to show how blogging emerged alongside three other phenomena that have greatly influenced the way members of the public, especially those with access to and knowledge of digital technology, view the copyright system. The first phenomenon is Microsoft's attempt to create a monopoly with its Windows interface and MS-DOS (Microsoft Disk Operating System) while, at the same time, refusing to share the source code from any versions of its products. In *The Future of Ideas*, Lessig states:

> While Microsoft had built an important platform upon which developers across the world had constructed code, Microsoft had adopted a practice that chilled certain kinds of innovation. When an innovator had a technology that threatened Microsoft's platform, Microsoft, the government claimed, adopted a strategy to kill that innovation. The platform, in other words, turned against some kinds of innovation, while no doubt protecting others. (62)

In response to this threat of monopoly, open source software and operating systems, as well as software and operating systems licensed under a General Public License (GPL), have become a public commons alternative to Microsoft and other proprietary software. A GPL states that if a user adds to or modifies the code of a software tool or operating system, he or she must release that new version under a GPL as well. While open source software can be bought and sold, the source code must still be made public.

The early adopters of weblogs were early adopters of technology in general, such as web and software developers, and some of these early bloggers were involved in open source software development communities and forums. Responses from bloggers to my question of how they found out about Creative Commons suggest such an association with open source software. Charlie Lowe and Dave Munger cited Slashdot as their original source of information about Creative Commons. Andrew Ó Baoill and Kara Kane could not remember exactly where they first heard about Creative Commons, but they cited Slashdot, Lawrence Lessig's weblog, Declan McCullough's email list, Politech, and Kuro5hin, another technology weblog. Ryan Eby cited general "press around the open source community," and Timothy Jarrett credited Doc Searls's weblog. Doc Searls is an editor of *Linux Journal*, and he writes about open source software on his weblog regularly. In 2003, when blogging and Creative Commons were still fairly new, the bloggers who adopted Creative Commons were already persuaded that corporations were using copyright law against the public interest. Many followed open source conversations and news developments about copyright law, especially during and after the year 1998, which presented a dramatic change for copyright in both the Sonny Bono Copyright Term Extension Act and the Digital Millennium Copyright Act (DMCA), which was also a galvanizing force for copyright critics.

The 1998 passing of the DMCA is, in fact, the second significant cultural factor to consider with the emergence of blogging. Lessig argues that the "particularly troubling" aspect of the law was its endorsement of Digital Rights Management (DRM), which refers to architectural controls in software and hardware that prevent users from copying files and playing audio, video, or text files on unauthorized devices, in the form of its anticircumvention provision, which "regulates code that cracks code that is intended to protect copyrighted material" (*Future* 187). As Lessig recounts, companies that produce DVDs and CDs began putting CSS (Content Scramble System) technology on their products so that only machines licensed to play CSS-encrypted discs—machines with Macintosh OS and Windows MS-DOS—could play them (*Future* 188–89). I would argue that this move on the part of the content industries, which was considered totalitarian by many, served as a direct challenge to the anarchist ethos of computer aficionados, including early adopters of weblog technology. When a program called DeCSS was released to enable CSS-encrypted discs to play on computers using Linux OS and other operating systems, "the industry went nuts" (*Future* 189).

The third phenomenon to emerge along with blogging is the popularity of file sharing applications and peer-to-peer networks such as KaZaa,

Gnutella, and Napster and the recording industry's subsequent attempts to quash file sharing and copying of digital copies of compact discs. The aggressive lobbying of content industry leaders such as Hilary Rosen, spokesperson for the Recording Industry Association of America (RIAA) from 1996 to 2003, and Jack Valenti, president of the Motion Picture Association of America (MPAA) from 1966 to 2004, have facilitated perhaps the biggest backlash of all against the current copyright system. Users who enjoy music want to be able to download songs to their hard drives for free, and cite the high price of CDs and DVDs as the reason they would rather download than purchase them. While the free downloading of content is problematic if it means that artists, writers, and inventors are undercompensated for their work (as copyright law's critics would generally agree) regulation of the technology used to open and copy files is equally as problematic, and some critics argue that copyright is moving in the direction of a pay-per-single-use model. The popularity and subsequent criminalization of peer-to-peer file sharing have coincided with the rise of blogging. I maintain that blogging has developed in tandem with these intellectual property debates because bloggers are the *same people* who follow conversations about copyright law, open source software, and peer-to-peer networks.

The rhetorical context in which Creative Commons and blogging emerged constitutes part of the motivation for bloggers' adoption of Creative Commons licenses, but each blogger has his or her individual motivations, which can vary widely. Charlie Lowe, for example, acknowledges his background as a teacher and scholar as an influence on his opinions about intellectual property:

> I believe in the principles of copyleft, from an ideological standpoint. I am convinced that our society would be better off with copyleft as the default mode of publishing/software publication and creation. After all, copyleft and open source are a more collaborative model for knowledge creation than the current intellectual property paradigm. And as a teacher, I think it's important for us to designate the use we would normally grant someone of our texts if they asked. So, for example, I suggested the Creative Commons license with Kairosnews because I feel at minimum, we as teachers should be willing to assign some usage beyond fair use.

The term *copyleft* refers to a type of license that lets users appropriate an author, artist, or inventor's content in a variety of ways: users can copy and distribute the content, they can create derivative works based on that content, and they can use the work for commercial purposes. The only stipulations are that the author, artist, or inventor is given credit, or attribution, for the work, and that the copy or derivative work is licensed under the same copyleft license, which in Creative Commons parlance is the Attribution-ShareAlike license. The GPL, which is commonly used for software, is also a copyleft license.

Lowe thinks of copyright issues in terms of knowledge creation, and he views them through his role as a teacher. Lowe, as a teacher, not only wishes to share his own knowledge freely with students, but wishes to help them produce knowledge as well. Dave Munger concurs: "The Web site I run (commontext.org) is on a cc license because I'm committed to the idea of public licensing, particularly for teaching texts." Commontext is no longer online, but for a brief time it was Munger's writing textbook. He hoped to create a space in which a writing textbook could be collaboratively authored by any teacher who wanted to participate in its creation by contributing teaching resources. Then the resulting textbook could be used by students free of charge. Because Commontext was available under a Creative Commons license, other teachers were free to make paper copies of chapters of the textbook, or the whole book, and distribute them to students. Individuals could also make derivative works based on the textbook, such as audio recordings of the book for students or teachers with impaired vision.

Matthew Haughey, a graphic artist and web developer who maintains Creative Commons' organizational weblog, only became familiar with Creative Commons when the organization approached him to design and develop their website, but his experience as a designer made him favorable to Creative Commons and their aims:

> I licensed my weblog posts, my photographs, and my essays [under Creative Commons] because I believe having a large, rich pool of content to build on is important. When I was first starting out in web design, I remember not having much in the way of free images or public domain photos that could be used online. I couldn't afford to buy stock photos so I usually ended up taking my own photographs to use in page designs. Ideally, in the future I would hope there would be plenty of music, images, movies, and text to use in various ways to build new works.

Haughey's comment here serves to illustrate how the process of creating new visual art—or new music, or new writing—is enhanced and facilitated by having a public domain, or commons, of intellectual and creative work. Admittedly, taking one's own photographs is not such an unreasonable expectation, but the freedom to use others' works without having to endure an often arduous rights clearance process, pay steep royalties, face cease-and-desist orders, or worse, fight infringement lawsuits is invaluable in a remix culture.

BLOGGERS' CONTRIBUTIONS TO AN INTELLECTUAL COMMONS

When Creative Commons licenses first became available for websites in February 2003, the bloggers who adopted them began immediately to speculate about their value for the Web as a whole, and also for particular users such as writers, artists, and educators. Ryan Eby describes how the process works and how he envisions his contribution via his role as a blogger:

> I think [a Creative Commons licensed site] promotes sharing of information and in turn promotes the creation of more information. If I come across an online journal of someone doing some scientific research, I might be prone to want to use it in my science class for some reason. I will be much more likely to use it if I know off the bat what rights there are for the content.

The potential pedagogical uses of Creative Commons content are quite promising. Eby points out that if he reads "an online journal" dealing with science, he may want to use it in class. Here "online journal" could refer to a weblog, but it could also refer to one of the online scholarly journals that are using Creative Commons licenses. In composition studies, several journals currently license articles under Creative Commons licenses: *The Writing Instructor, Enculturation, Kairos, Lore*, and *Computers and Composition Online*. Parlor Press, a scholarly press that publishes books in rhetoric and composition studies, allows authors to use Creative Commons licenses or Founder's Copyright policies for their books.

With a Founder's Copyright, which has also been embraced by bloggers (though not generally used for weblogs themselves), a work is copyrighted for fourteen years with an option to renew for an additional fourteen years, but after a maximum of twenty-eight years, the work enters the public domain. For most critics of copyright, the goal is for the work to enter the public domain after the author has a brief, limited opportunity to profit from the work, an opportunity intended as an incentive to create more work. The result is that the public has a continually replenished public domain. Dave Munger expresses this view about the public domain:

The value of a [Creative Commons license] is that others don't have
to ask permission before they use the material. It also sends a powerful
signal to an audience that "this is for sharing." I'm also personally very
interested in the public domain. Even a public license can be limiting,
and the public domain makes the process of building new works much
simpler, because any notion of "property" is completely stripped from
the work. But I think there's room in the world for both public licenses
and the public domain.

The notion of intellectual and creative work as property has been critiqued
by scholars in composition studies, including Lunsford and West, who question the author as the proprietor of the work he or she creates. In "Intellectual
Property and Composition Studies," they describe the problem with property
in the context of the teaching of writing:

> Teachers can generally move up in prestige, power, and even financial
> gain by laying claim to pieces of intellectual property, evidence that
> authorizes in direct proportion to number (and origin) of degrees and
> published documents—material traces of intellectual labor commodi-
> fied. Within the classroom, teachers extend the practice of claiming
> knowledge as marketable property, selling knowledge goods to student
> consumers. Now, surely, teachers (of all people) deserve to be compen-
> sated for work; but should teachers operate under a tacit assumption that
> we somehow own the knowledge on which we build CVs and which we
> "give" to students or "rent" to others, who must cite us as the autono-
> mous authors who have created and thus necessarily control what we
> claim to know? The academy's nearly compulsive scholarly and teach-
> erly attention to hypercitation and endless listing of sources are driven,
> for the most part, by the need to own intellectual property and to turn it
> into commodities that can be traded like tangible property, a process of
> alienation that is at the heart of copyright doctrine based on the abstract
> concept of "work." (397)

Lunsford and West see the creative process as being always already collaborative. We make new knowledge based on connections we make among existing
research, arguments, and observation of practices. Once that new knowledge
is made, it is not necessarily the property of the person who expresssed it;
rather, it is a contribution to a resource, which is beneficial to all: or, a commons. For Lunsford and West, ideas are meant to be shared, and they should

be placed in a rhetorical situation in such a way that will facilitate the sharing of those ideas.

Les Jenkins agrees, and he explains how Creative Commons, as an alternative model of copyright, helps bring about more sharing:

> One of the concepts that seems to be a big part of blogging for a lot of people is the sharing of ideas. [. . .]A blog with a Creative Commons license has laid down exactly what rights the author is defining for the work on his blog and removes any confusion or guesswork for anyone who wants to use part of that authors work on their own site. If one sees "all rights reserved" they should assume the author doesn't want their material being used elsewhere. With a CC license you can easily find out exactly what you can and can't do with the work in question which should help to encourage the spread of ideas and the sharing of efforts.

Here it is apparent that Jenkins sees himself and bloggers, in general, as contributors to the Web as a commons for ideas. These ideas can take the form of texts, images, music, software code, and more. The fact that the concept of commons is working at the levels of content and software code is especially important. Benkler sets forth the idea of thinking of the Web in layers: the content layer (the texts, images, and sound compositions we upload and download daily), the logical layer (the software that enables us to access the content), and the physical layer (phone lines, cable lines, and wireless spectrum). Commons advocates are working to open up free spaces on each of those layers, and Creative Commons developers, as well as some software developers for blogging tools, have been working to integrate the content layer and logical layer.

THE LOGICAL LAYER: CREATIVE COMMONS IN WEBLOG SOFTWARE CODE

Creative Commons license options are built into the content management software tools of three blogging applications: Movable Type, WordPress, and Drupal. In Movable Type, the Creative Commons options are built into the core code of the software, while Drupal and WordPress have modules of code that users can install separately. In all cases, users are able to select the terms of their Creative Commons licenses within the administrative settings of the software, without having to paste the license code into the template of the blog site. A blogger who gets a Creative Commons license usually pastes the following code into his or her site:

```
<a rel="license" href="http://creativecommons.org/licenses/by-sa/3.0/">
<img alt="Creative Commons License" style="border-width:0src="http:
//i.creativecommons.org/l/by-sa/3.0/88x31.png" /></a><br />This
work is licensed under a <a rel="license" href= "http://creativecommons.
org/licenses/by-sa/3.0/">Creative Commons Attribution-ShareAlike
3.0 License</a>
```

The integration of Creative Commons and weblog software not only makes for a more seamless way for bloggers to display the license on their site, but it also helps bloggers to know when Creative Commons releases new versions of their licenses and gives them opportunities to update the licenses. Arguably, having Creative Commons' licensing code in the weblog software also enables Creative Commons to reach a new audience: people who have not followed the news about copyright and open source software. Two bloggers I corresponded with in 2003, Timothy Jarrett and Les Jenkins, added Creative Commons licenses to their blog sites through Movable Type. Jenkins wrote:

> The first contact I had with [Creative Commons] came about because of the software that I use to maintain my blog. The folks at Six Apart who write MovableType added in the ability to quickly and easily construct a Creative Commons license and have the metadata for it created automatically in version 2.6 of the script released back in February. I didn't look into it right away, but saw that a lot of other blogs were putting up CC licenses so I decided to check it out and see what it was. I liked the idea and decided to make use of it.

Jenkins extols the ease with which such a license can now be added to a site, but more important than that is the insertion of the Creative Commons code into software as a rhetorical and technological countermeasure to Digital Rights Management, which locks down content. Before Creative Commons was founded, Benkler called for such countermeasures:

> It is of central importance to reverse the attempts to use the DMCA to close up the software layer of the information environment and diminish the possibility that a robust public domain will in fact lead to widespread accessibility to the basic building blocks of participation in our public conversation. (577)

Creative Commons' inclusion in software is a reversal of certain aspects of the DMCA, which, according to Benkler, "permits the owners of copyright to design the logical layer of the distribution media of their work to assure that their works are perfectly protected by technology," even if "the uses that users are seeking to make of these works are privileged by law," as in the case of fair use (571). By virtue of the technology's architectural controls, then, the user receives the message that he or she has no rights, not even the rights that the law guarantees: fair use. Instead, the Creative Commons metadata's presence in third-party software applications tells the users what *extra* rights they have in addition to fair use. Whereas the Digital Millennium Copyright Act "builds the mass media model into the very logic of the information environment and undermines the capacity of each user in this environment to partake of our common cultural conversation" (572), Creative Commons' presence in the software helps users participate in the conversation more freely.

CONCLUSION: CREATIVE COMMONS FOUR YEARS LATER

Since 2003, the implementation of Creative Commons licenses has become akin to a meme in the blogging community. Because blogging is a community activity—in other words, people who keep weblogs read and link to others' weblogs as well—the Creative Commons license phenomenon has spread quickly. The communal nature of the activity of blogging plays a role in weblogs' contribution to the Web as an intellectual commons. Prominent group weblogs such as Slashdot and Kuro5hin have been powerhouses in the spread of Creative Commons licenses as resistance to ownership of culture.

The vast majority of bloggers do not get paid for keeping their weblogs at all; they do it in order to freely publish their ideas and receive other ideas in return. The notion that composers need a financial incentive in order to create and distribute content is not the reality of the blogging community. Bloggers keep their weblogs for pleasure, to write and be read by others, and to engage in a collaborative meaning-making process. Timothy Jarrett said, "The philosophy of subverting the continued elimination of the intellectual commons through explicitly declaring a share-alike license struck me as brilliant." Other bloggers I corresponded with echoed similar sentiments, preferring a shared-knowledge, anti-ownership model of producing content. They advocate the sort of freedom Lessig refers to in *The Future of Ideas*:

> Because our bias is to ignore the choice between the free and the controlled, we ignore the costs of a system of control over a system that remains free. We fail to see the benefits from freedom because we

assume that freedom is not possible. We assume that creativity and innovation and growth will occur only where property and markets function most strongly.

Against this ideology, I offer the Internet. Against this bias, I submit a tradition that has understood balance better. The past decade has demonstrated the value of the free; that freedom came from the Net's architecture. (238)

Since its inception, Creative Commons has experienced a great deal of growth. Weblogs, according to Matthew Haughey, "have turned thousands of former web readers into web writers, and they're creating hundreds of thousands of pages of web content." Developers for Creative Commons have worked with the metadata of CC-licensed content, data which show the terms under which the content is released. In 2003, Ó Baoill speculated that "[a]s XML reading tools improve it may allow better syndication—automated harvesters can check whether reprinting is allowed (and under what conditions) and use this to create aggregator-style sites." Four years later, we are much closer to seeing a site such as the one he describes. Search engines can now read the metadata that specifies what content is licensed through Creative Commons. Users are now able to filter out anything that does not have a Creative Commons license, which means that if an individual wants to search for potential material to use in teaching, or public domain clip art to use in graphic design, he or she can filter out any "All Rights Reserved" material. Creative Commons has their own search engine on their site, and in their advanced search options, Yahoo! has Creative Commons options. Users are able to check a box that says, "Find content I can use for commercial purposes" and a box which says, "Find content I can modify, adapt, or build upon." In an advanced search on Google, a user can scroll down to "Usage Rights" and select an option from a pull-down menu: "free to use or share," "free to use or share, even commercially," "free to use, share, or modify," or "free to use, share, or modify, even commercially." Flickr, a photograph displaying and sharing service owned by Yahoo!, also has Creative Commons searching built in. A search for "cupcake" on Flickr with the "Find content I can modify, adapt, or build upon" box checked yields 6,542 images, any of which a Web designer or graphic artist could use in a collage or site template. Soundclick and Jamendo are services which let users upload their musical compositions and license them under Creative Commons licenses. Revver, a video sharing service, lets users select Creative Commons licenses. In all of these tools, Creative Commons licensing is built into the software, the logical layer of the Internet.

In 2003, Haughey mused, "the value is that the content of licensed blogs can be reused in ways we can't imagine [. . .] I suspect soon we'll see someone do something creative with all the blog content being licensed right now." Blogging has helped Creative Commons' proliferation, and, in turn, bloggers have helped raise the profile of this alternative copyright model. I hope to see composition teachers and scholars use these services to create teaching materials and to incorporate these more collaborative authoring practices in their writing pedagogy.

WORKS CITED

Bausch, Paul, Matthew Haughey, and Meg Hourihan. *We Blog: Publishing Online with Weblogs*. Indianapolis, IN: Wiley Publishing, 2002.

Benkler, Yochai. "From Consumers to Users: Shifting the Deeper Structures of Regulation Toward Sustainable Commons and User Access." *Federal Communications Law Journal* 52.3 (2000): 561–79.

Creative Commons. 26 Apr. 2003 <http://new.creativecommons.org/learn/aboutus/>.

Ebyryan. "Re: Creative Commons Licenses on Weblogs." *Kairosnews: A Weblog for Discussing Rhetoric, Technology, and Pedagogy*. 26 Apr. 2003 <http://www.kairos news.org/modules.php?op=modload&name=News&file=article&sid=1824& mode=flat&order=0&thold=0>.

Haughey, Matthew. "Harvard Blogs and Creative Commons." *Creative Commons Weblog*. 26 Apr. 2003 <http://creativecommons.org/weblog/entry/3648>.

———. "Notable Recent CC Licensors." *Creative Commons Weblog*. 2003. 26 Apr. 2003 <http://creativecommons.org/weblog/entry/3615>.

Kerwin, Kara. Personal Communication. 2003.

Lessig, Lawrence. *The Future of Ideas: The Fate of the Commons in a Connected World*. New York: Vintage, 2001. .

———. "Great CC News." *Lessig Blog*. 26 Apr. 2003 <http://cyberlaw.stanford.edu/ lessig/blog/archives/2003_04.shtml#001065>

———. "Ticketstubs." *Lessig Blog*. 26 Apr. 2003 <http://cyberlaw.stanford.edu/lessig/ blog/archives/2003_01.shtml#000823>.

———. "Ways Say 'Some Rights Reserved.'" *Lessig Blog*. 26 Apr. 2003 <http:// cyberlaw.stanford.edu/lessig/blog/archives/2003_03.shtml#001032>.

———. "Weblogs and the Public Domain. *Lessig Blog*. 26 Apr. 2003 <http://cyber law.stanford.edu/lessig/blog/archives/2003_04.shtml#001066>.

Litman, Jessica. *Digital Copyright*. Amherst, NY: Prometheus Books, 2001.

Lowe, Charles. "Re: Creative Commons Licenses on Weblogs." *Kairosnews: A Weblog for Discussing Rhetoric, Technology, and Pedagogy*. 26 Apr. 2003 <http://www.kairos news.org/modules.php?op=modload&name=News&file=article&sid=1824& mode=flat&order=0&thold=0>.

Lunsford, Andrea, and Susan West. "Intellectual Property and Composition Studies." *College Composition and Communication* 47.3 (Oct. 1996): 383–411.

Moore, A. D. Intellectual Property and Information Control: Philosophic Foundations and Contemporary Issues. New Brunswick, NJ: Transaction, 2001.

Mortensen, Torill, and Jill Walker. "Blogging Thoughts: Personal Publication as an Online Research Tool." *Intermedia*. 2002. 26 Apr. 2003<http://www.intermedia.uio.no/konferanser/skikt-02/docs/Researching_ICTs_in_context-Ch11Mortensen-Walker.pdf>.

Munger, David. "Re: Creative Commons Licenses on Weblogs." *Kairosnews: A Weblog for Discussing Rhetoric, Technology, and Pedagogy*. 26 Apr. 2003 <http://www.kairosnews.org/modules.php?op=modload&name=News&file=article&sid=1824&mode=flat&order=0&thold=0>.

Rodzilla, John, ed. *We've Got Blog: How Weblogs Are Changing Our Culture*. Cambridge, MA: Perseus Publishing, 2002

Searls, Doc. "The Whatever License." *The Doc Searls Weblog*. 28 Apr. 2003 <http://doc.weblogs.com/2003/04/13#theWhateverLicense>.

Trott, Mena. "Version 2.6." Moveable Type News Blog. 12 Aug. 2008 <http://www.moveabletype.com/blog/2003/01/version-26.html>.

Winer, Dave. "Creative Commons, RSS and Manila." 26 Apr. 2003 <http://manila.userland.com/creativeCommonsRssManila>.

CHAPTER 4

In Defense of Obfuscation

Questioning Open Source and a New Perspective on Teaching Digital Literacy in the Writing Classroom

———

BRIAN D. BALLENTINE

This opening anecdote comes from my years spent working as a software engineer for a major medical company. We were developing and testing new Web-based software applications that enabled doctors to view patient scans from medical imaging devices such as magnetic resonance imaging (MRI) and computed tomography (CT) machines through a Web browser. Our competition was, of course, doing the same, and we were all working with hospitals to beta test our products for different uses in their facilities. A hospital in New York was using similar software for preoperative reviews. Doctors examined patient data and scans on the computer as a supplement to their notes. In this instance, a software engineer working for the hospital had modified, or hacked, the application's code in order to provide an additional feature for the software. All of the software in use came with strict warnings about not tampering with an application's code. In addition, companies went out of their way to deliberately obfuscate their code. That is, we wrote code to try and protect our code. The unfortunate side-effect of the hospital engineer's alterations was that it caused some of the images under review to be in a mirrored or reversed format. Consequently, in a procedure to remove a brain tumor, a surgeon actually started an operation on the wrong side of a patient's head.

This is, of course, an isolated incident, but I believe the flagrant disregard and disrespect for the obfuscation techniques employed in the hospital software point to a larger cultural, legal, and ethical disconnect regarding copyrighted works in digital form. This article will attempt to interpret how we have arrived at this more liberal treatment of digital copyrighted material and then enter the debate about how best to contribute to the establishment of a balance between copyright and the ease in which digital technology enables copying, editing, and redistribution. Scholars like Yochai Benkler, Jessica Litman, Lawrence Lessig, and Siva Vaidhyanathan have already been working toward the goal of balance, but there does not appear to be a stop in the slide toward leveraging copyright law (law developed to function in the analog world of print) for more, not less, regulation. In turn, copyright law in the digital domain fosters a reputation of disrespect or, as Lessig has plainly stated, the law is often perceived as an "ass" ("Remix"). If the law cannot divest itself of such a reputation, or rather, be reinterpreted as meaningful, then there is little surprise that medical software is hacked. More problematic, if we begin with the assumption that a hacker may have the best intentions, how would we as educators teach the critical thinking skills necessary for this individual to recognize that what he or she is about to do is wrong? Wrong, not just in the petty sense of "this is mine; I want to keep it from you," but in the much more severe sense of "if you alter this there could be unforeseen and dire consequences." In other words, if the only protection available for the digital underpinnings of our medical, legal, financial, and educational data is a law otherwise known as an "ass," then we must take an active and immediate role in advancing a digital or technical literacy to aid in establishing a balance for copyright law as it applies to digital environments.

In this chapter, I will begin by examining some of the key works by Lessig including his address at the 2005 Conference on College Composition and Communication. This process will illuminate the precarious state of writing and writing instruction due to the discordant relationship of copyright law and new digital technologies. Lessig offers suggestions for striking a balance that may or may not ensure the practice of writing or what will be discussed as digital remix, for the future. I will argue that part of Lessig's plan is founded on the free software movement's obligation for code to remain open, editable, and redistributable, which, as I will demonstrate, is untenable as the de facto model for rhetoric and composition studies to work within our remix culture. Following will be my own suggested modifications for finding a balance, including a discussion of a new digital literacy that includes an intellectual property component for the writing classroom

ENABLING AND RESTRICTING THE FREEDOM TO WRITE

At the 2005 Conference on College Composition and Communication Lessig appeared as a featured speaker and offered attendees the challenging and provocative prompt of whether or not writing will be "allowed" for our future students. Before answering the question, Lessig wanted to be very clear that he believes existing copyright law established for regulating printed works, such as a traditional book, is in fact "good." The law as it regulates the technology of the book allows for the practice of remixing. Remixing is how we evaluate, criticize, reexpress, or simply put our own spin on the texts we read, the films we see, or the music we hear. According to Lessig, all that we know of "culture and knowledge" is a remix of information ("Remix"). The relevance of the message for the writing instructors in the room became clear with the reminder that we all teach the practice of remixing texts. In other words, the essence of writing is remix. The freedom to remix, that is, whether or not writing will be allowed, is now in question.

The freedom to "write" is in jeopardy because the technology used to remix has changed. In the past, a critic could write and publish a scathing book review discussing the details of a text without asking and obtaining permission from the author. Copyright law allows for the fair use of materials in order to facilitate criticism, teaching, reporting, and scholarship. In turn, copyright law prohibits the reviewer from republishing the book, or large portions of it, as part of the review. That is, the reviewer cannot make a copy of the text and redistribute that material without permission as that practice *could* decrease profits to the author. And this brings us to our current dilemma: in this digital age, our technologies facilitate the copying of copyrighted works with an ease never before possible. In fact, every use and viewing of a digital text effectively creates a copy of that text in a computer's memory. Combine the ability to copy with the growing speed and distributive reach of the Internet, and the result is copyright owners (often large corporations or associations) calling for increased regulation. The copy produced when working with digital texts means these uses of digital remix technology become illegal automatically and, as instructors, we are left to teach (or not) what has been labeled "piracy."

In his presentation, Lessig offered three suggestions for striking a balance between copyright law and new digital technologies. First and most important to my argument, those interested in defending remix must make an effort to "connect with the other side." Those individuals wishing to stop the trend of increasing copyright control have a responsibility to publicly acknowledge and condemn illegal practices such as mass music file sharing. To ignore that copyright violations occur online only "inspires insanity" in organizations such as the Motion Picture Association of America (MPAA) or the Recording Industry Association of America (RIAA). Second, there must be reforms in copyright law itself. Left with the choice of reforming the law or reforming the technology, Lessig advocates the former. Scholarly publications, for example, need and could benefit from different *models* of protection than, say, a Disney film. The real challenge, however, will be to "restore the practice of our culture to distinguish between these models" ("Remix"). Lessig's final offering is itself a new method for licensing creative work and promotes reform through individual action. This third suggestion introduces the Creative Commons organization and its CC- licensing options: "Creative Commons provides free tools that let authors, scientists, artists, and educators easily mark their creative work with the freedoms they want it to carry" (Creative Commons). For those interested in supporting and participating legally in remix culture, the capabilities and functionality of the Creative Commons website enable a truly remarkable project. The site stresses simplicity and clear language along with easy-to-follow licensing steps, so the services of a lawyer are not required. Lessig has gone on to promote a "Just Ask" campaign encouraging academic scholars to approach publishers with a request to use this new model of copyright.[1]

My critique does not find fault with the Creative Commons itself. On the contrary, I would be remiss if I did not pause and elaborate on this initiative that works so successfully with copyright law to promote knowledge sharing. As Lessig explains, so much depends upon the active participation of authors, artists, and other innovators:

> A Creative Commons license constitutes a grant of freedom to anyone who accesses the license, and more importantly, an expression of the ideal that the person associated with the license believes in something different that the "All" or "No" extremes. Content is marked with the CC mark, which does not mean that copyright is waived, but that certain freedoms are given. (*Free* 283)

The licensing options afforded to authors, including Public Domain, Developing Nations, Sampling, Founder's Copyright, and Music Sharing, demonstrate an achievable alternative by exercising new models of copyright (Creative, "Choose"). However, while the Creative Commons is an excellent initiative for moving forward, it does little for works using traditional copyright law or corporations and individuals who wish to continue to enforce strict control of their work. As was the case with the hospital software, the "expression of the ideal" happened to be, and needed to be, no access. In essence, Lessig's second and third recommendations, recognizing new models for copyright and the Creative Commons initiative itself, offer little to the vital first requirement of making peace with the other side. There is no gesture of respect on the part of the hacker/remixer/author to hold up the law as anything more than that which should be worked around. And yet, Lessig worries that the "rule of law depends upon people obeying the law. The more often, and more repeatedly, we as citizens experience violating the law, the less we respect the law . . . And I do care if the rules of law sow increasing disrespect because of the extreme of regulation they impose" (*Free* 202).

Confusion sets in when we consider why a hacker or a remixer views the obfuscation of proprietary code as an "extreme regulation" of freedom. Where would the perceived implicit right to remix, for example, hospital software come from? I argue that our understanding and treatment of digital work is inherited from a culture of presumed openness dating to the early days of computing and software development. The influence of this culture provides an unsustainable foundation for arriving at a balance with the "other side."

THE FREEDOM TO HACK: A CULTURE AND HISTORY OF OPENNESS

Along with the rise in personal and business computing came a massive expansion in the world of software development. Initially, the code controlling many software applications was largely nonregulated, not protected, and left open. Computer platforms were not yet cross-platform, which meant that an IBM user, for example, had no motive to copy code from an application running on another platform because that code simply would not run. The public Internet was not yet in existence and there was no means to easily distribute copied works over a network. With no need to lock-up that which would not get away, programmers grew accustomed to a culture of openness when it came to viewing and remixing code.

Accounts of the arrival of protected code are well documented by the writings (and the subsequent reactions) of free software pioneer and advocate Richard Stallman. In 1971, Stallman began working for MIT's Artificial Intelligence Lab and joined in the sharing of software among an expanding community of developers that included other universities and major corporations. However, by the early 1980s, new computer technology and systems such as Digital's PDP-10 and VAX, along with Motorola's 68020, contained proprietary information and code. Access to the code was available only to those willing to sign nondisclosure agreements that forbade sharing alterations and improvements (Stallman 53–54). Stallman was outraged. For him, "ordinary common-sense morality" should be enough to inform any programmer that they instead "should be free to modify programs to fit their needs, and free to share software, because helping other people is the basis of society" (Stallman 55). Instead, corporations began to treat code as property in a traditional sense and believed in the economic potential of restricting access to that property

Perhaps the most significant case of a code base switching from open to closed is that of AT&T's UNIX operating system. Prior to 1984, AT&T's government contracts and agreements barred the company from competing in the computing industry. Since there was no money to be made, AT&T's programmers convinced corporate officials to keep UNIX open. The operating system quickly grew to have one of the most popular and improved upon code bases in large part due to the involvement of many universities. After AT&T split apart in 1984, the company declared ownership of UNIX and, along with it, all of the code contributions of every programmer ever having worked on the operating system. This was Stallman's cue. Not wanting to jeopardize any of his future work falling under similar control, Stallman quit the MIT lab in 1984 to work on his own free operating system, dubbed GNU.[2] In order to support and protect his project, Stallman founded the Free Software Foundation, which, among its many initiatives, promotes the use of its own General Public License (GPL) for software developers. Software using the GNU GPL cannot be altered and shared unless the source code for the application continues to remain open.[3] In essence, Stallman located a productive and legal method of using existing copyright law to bring back the freedom his community of programmers once knew.

DEFINING FREEDOM

Stallman remains president of the Free Software Foundation, and there is no question that his efforts (and those of other major contributors to the free code movement) have had a profound effect on promoting a culture of openness and the "freedom" associated with free software. Freedom for Stallman's foundation means always enabling and retaining the right to *run*, *modify,* and *redistribute* source code. The GNU GPL, which has come to be known as a "copyleft" license, requires derivative work to be released under the same licensing terms. This requirement prevents code from either falling unprotected into the public domain or being obfuscated within a proprietary project. While there is not enough time to explore the nuances of the ongoing dispute, it should be noted that projects within the *open* source camp (including some of the versions of Linux) are not all licensed the same or as strictly as Stallman's *free* software camp and do not make use of the GNU GPL.[4] Other popular licenses include the Mozilla Public License (MPL), the Apache License, and the Modified BSD License. However, most licensing methods do not prohibit turning a profit. Perhaps Stallman's most famous remark to clarify what he means by "free" is his request to "think of free as in free speech, not as in free beer" (GNU). What may come as a surprise is that the Free Software Foundation allows for the freedom to *sell* free software as long as access to the code travels with the software. There is *never not* access to code; anything else would be a moral offense.[5]

Freedom, then, is the freedom to hack. Hack, not as in the pejorative sense of how the term is now commonly understood, but to program with the intention of enabling functionality not previously available. For Stallman, a hacker is "[s]omeone who loves to program and enjoys being clever about it" (Stallman 53). However, absent from this definition is any sense of critical or ethical reflection prompting programmers to consider whether or not they *should* hack just because they *can.* A key and thus far missing component of striking a balance with those in favor of greater control of intellectual property is demonstrating the ability and the desire for critical and ethical reflection on hacker activity in digital environments. While the term *ethics* is prevalent in free software literature, the concern for an ethical approach to free software is framed typically in developers' responsibility to continue to share their knowledge with the community. Less formal codes have coalesced with monikers such as "white hat hackers," but these so-called codes are far from standardized.

For example, those within the hacker community who identify themselves as white hat hackers break into software, networks, or systems to search for security flaws or other ways code could be exploited. By most definitions, however, "white hat hackers crack their own systems or the systems of a client who has specifically employed them for the purposes of security auditing" (Red Hat Linux 9). For some, this practice has grown to include proprietary and deliberately obfuscated software. The actions are said to be justified in that after finding a problem with the code or network, these individuals are supposed to contact the software provider and alert them of the issue. White hat hacking (here "white" is associated with purity or good) practices may also deem that individuals do not broadcast the code flaw to the detriment of the company that produces the software. Conversely, those that hack for nefarious purposes (crashing networks or stealing information) are labeled "black hat hackers." In practice, most hacking is much more grey than either of these terms and in fact the term grey hat hacker has grown out of the ambiguous black/white labels. Red Hat, one of the most popular and success-ful commercial Linux offerings, attempts to clarify white/black/grey distinc-tions in an online security guide:

> The *grey hat hacker*, on the other hand, has the skills and intent of a white hat hacker in most situations but uses his knowledge for less than noble purposes on occasion. A grey hat hacker can be thought of as a white hat hacker who wears a black hat at times to accomplish his own agenda. Grey hat hackers typically subscribe to another form of the hacker ethic, which says it is acceptable to break into systems as long as the hacker does not commit theft or breach confidentiality. Some would argue, however that the act of breaking into a system is in itself unethical. (Red Hat Linux 9)

Indeed, not only is it unethical but often illegal. Regardless, ethics and a hacker's accountability for the safety, privacy, or general well-being of others is an undeveloped issue.[6]

While there are those who seek to distance themselves from Stallman's rhetoric on free software and hacking, his philosophy continues to influence both the free and open source communities. In "Free Software Philosophy and Open Source," authors Niklas Vainio and Tere Vadén claim:

> Arguments presented by Stallman in the early 1980s still form some of the most lucid and coherent positions on the social and political impli-cations of software development. Most importantly, the polarization of the FOSS [free open source software] community into the FS and OS camps has been only partial. All of these facts point out how FS has acted as a necessary background for OS. (9)

There are other powerful voices but Stallman is far from marginalized. In fact, his Free Software Foundation just released the third version of the GPL in June of 2007 and the use and influence of that license continues. What is more worrisome is that "as OS software becomes more commonplace and even omnipresent, the ideological underpinnings are often overlooked with or without purpose" (Vainio and Vadén 9).

However, there is no need to drift into an ad hominem attack on out-spoken proponents of free software and their moral ideals. That, for better or worse, has been done.[7] Instead, the concern is that the current drive to strike a balance in intellectual property law, especially among those who favor less control, has inherited much from the free software ideology of keeping everything open and free but with insufficient regard for the responsibility of having that access. Siva Vaidhyanathan framed the issue best when he wrote: "One of the chief challenges of the twenty-first century will be to formulate ethics, guidelines, habits, or rules to shape an information environment that provides the freedoms liberal democracy needs as well as the stability that commerce and community demand" (xiv). This challenge has not been met.

BUILDING ON FREE SOFTWARE: AN INHERITED IDEOLOGY

The influence of the Free Software Foundation evinces itself in the work of many contemporary legal scholars, including Lessig, who is among the seven board members leading the foundation. The preface to his last book, *Free Culture: The Nature and Future of Creativity*, acknowledges a debt to Stallman and even suggests being derived from Stallman's initiatives. Lessig writes:

> The work of a lawyer is always derivative, and I mean to do nothing more in this book than to remind a culture about a tradition that has always been its own. Like Stallman, I defend that tradition on the basis of values. And like Stallman, I believe those values are the part of our past that will need to be defended in our future . . . Like Stallman's arguments for free software, an argument for free culture stumbles on a confusion that is hard to avoid, and even harder to understand. A free culture is not a culture without property; it is not a culture in which art-ists don't get paid. A culture without property, or in which creators can't get paid, is anarchy, not freedom. Anarchy is not what I advance here. Instead, the free culture that I defend in this book is a balance between anarchy and control. (xv–xvi)

There is no doubt we are stumbling on that confusion now, but our current proposition or offer of balance between anarchy and control is doomed to "inspire insanity" on the "other side" if we hold too tightly to a tradition of unconditional open code and the right to redistribute code for free. Under-standing code as material property whose owner or developer retains the right to the protections afforded by intellectual property law, if that protection is desired, is impossible to grasp if we begin with Stallman's premise of pro-prietary code as moral offense. That is, locating a balance between anar-chy and control becomes an unachievable goal without accepting code and commercial software as a type of writing or remix that may benefit (indeed, benefit everyone) with protection. Many early attempts to clarify this digital dilemma for intellectual property law were based on loose or faulty compari-sons between "brick and mortar" businesses and software.

For example, Lessig complains in his second book, *The Future of Ideas*, that the "reigning view about software speaks as if a rational company would never write code unless it had complete control over what it produces. But perfect control is rarely assured in any free market, not with code or anything else" (70). Lessig continues by making analogies to coffee shops and other businesses that would enjoy keeping their ideas untouchable as they entered the marketplace. While his depictions of Starbucks having to compete with upstart coffeehouses (Peet's Coffee, for example) are convenient, they over-simplify and, I believe, misrepresent the role that code plays in a real business and development process.

If I want to compete with Starbucks, I am certainly free to open my own chain of coffeehouses. More importantly, there is nothing stopping me from visiting Starbucks to study their products, pricing, store design, and so forth. I can research their store locations, try to understand their target markets, and view their earnings. There are a host of things that I *should* do before endeav-oring to compete. And, as Lessig reminds us, "Starbucks didn't get a govern-ment monopoly before it risked a great deal of capital to open coffee shops around the world. All it was assured was that people would have to pay for the coffee they sold; the idea of a high-quality coffee shop was free for others to take" (*Future* 70). Fair enough.

However, I cannot go to the headquarters of Starbucks and demand information on all of their suppliers. There are no laws stating that I should have access to all of the contracts the company has with their vendors. I can-not demand Starbucks divulge any of their business plan or philosophy simply because I want to be a better competitor. I cannot get the recipe for an Iced Caramel Macchiato to make comparable drink specials, and there is no moral imperative to "hack" that drink. All of these elements are the underpinnings that contribute to the success of Starbucks. None of these elements must be "free," and here I am entitled to nothing.

The code for proprietary software represents, more or less, property in the form of drink recipes for a successful coffee start-up. If I were considering developing a new application to compete with Adobe's Photoshop, for example, it would be foolish not to buy, use, and study a copy of the program. I should read reviews of the product, learn all of its features, and research who uses it, how, and why. There are, of course, numerous other considerations as I develop my business plan in an effort to launch a company that competes with Adobe's product. Just like the start-up costs associated with opening a new coffeehouse, my new software company will need money for computers, software, connectivity, and of course the salaries of developers who will write the application's code from the ground up. In the case of the coffeehouse, I do not get Starbucks's drink recipes. In the case of the competing software company, I do not get Adobe's source code. These are items in which both companies researched and invested their own resources and which, if they so desire, should be protected. True, Starbucks did not get a government monopoly to protect the concept of a high-end coffee shop but neither did Adobe before risking resources on a high-end graphics program. Lessig is only partially right when he states, "innovators in the ordinary market can't keep good ideas to themselves" (*Future* 71). Actually, Starbucks has the right to keep some of their business to themselves but not included in those rights is the protection of the idea for a high-end coffee shop. Likewise, Adobe has introduced groundbreaking functionality that has been appropriated, improved upon, and even *mirrored* by their competitors. But mirroring functionality does not mean copying source code. The competitors, my new software company included, need to gamble on their own development. Most importantly, the ideas of a high-end coffee shop and graphics program remain free and part of culture. The recipes or codes that make the implementation of those ideas a success are entitled protection if desired by their owners. In other words, intellectual property law does not protect ideas—only instantiations of ideas.

Instead of wrestling with analogies, why not abandon the loose-fitting brick and mortar stories for anecdotes and the growing history depicting what free software and proprietary code *enable* or *disable* in digital spaces? To begin, there should be a representation of both the dangers (my opening anecdote about the hospital) and the powerful benefits of free code.

So, in contrast to the hospital story, this Linux versus Microsoft anecdote was retold in an article in *The Economist* in 2003. When the government representatives of the city of Munich decided to switch to Linux from Windows, the "modest" $35 million deal (modest in terms of Microsoft accounts) prompted

Microsoft CEO Steve Ballmer to fly in for a meeting with the mayor. Ballmer reportedly lowered Microsoft's asking price but could not sway the mayor, who claimed the decision was a matter of "principle." According to *The Economist*, "the municipality wanted to control its technological destiny. It did not wish to place the functioning of government in the hands of a commercial vendor with proprietary standards which is accountable to shareholders rather than to citizens" ("Microsoft"). Munich's mayor wanted the city free of the proprietary standards and the limitations of Microsoft's closed code, which is deliberately obfuscated. Open source projects such as Linux-based operating systems do not contain obfuscated code so it may be remixed to adjust to the needs of the city and its constituents. If programmers working for the city of Munich wanted to remix Microsoft's latest operating system, they would either not be able to or would be doing so illegally. Proponents of free code fear actively controlling or disabling code *stagnates* information sharing and, with it, culture.

LITERACY IN A READ/WRITE WORLD

Stagnation, according Lessig, will manifest in the form of a "read only" culture. The United States Constitution states copyright law should "promote the progress of science and useful arts" and that, at some point, means permission for write access. Without this permission, Lessig bemoans what will soon be our collective condition:

> Passive recipients of culture produced elsewhere. Couch potatoes. Consumers. This is the world of media from the twentieth century. The twenty-first century could be different. This is the crucial point: It could be both read and write. Or at least reading and better understanding the craft of writing. Or best, reading and understanding the tools that enable the writing to lead or mislead. The aim of any literacy, and this literacy in particular, is to "empower people to choose the appropriate language for what they need to create or express." (*Free* 37–38)

Here, considerations for the term *literacy* exist based only on the needs or wants of the users (ensuring openness) and not on the needs of someone who may wish to protect proprietary work. Again, to reach out to the other side requires tweaking perspectives on proprietary information. Literacy *is* the key, and expanding on the criteria and qualifications for a new literacy will be the marker of success for gesturing toward those in favor of control. More specifically we will need to learn to teach a digital or technical literacy that includes intellectual property as well as demonstrate the ability to show a proficiency in that literacy.

The word *literacy* is a difficult term on which to hang a definition, and which, when paired with *digital* or *technology*, becomes more problematic. In the most general sense, a literate person possesses the skills to read and write. Coupled with technology, literacy is often meant to convey an ability to operate or handle computers or other digital devices. In many respects this is because technology is studied, understood, and taught primarily with a focus on its functional characteristics. The rhetorical tradition, however, suggests a more complicated but useful interpretation. As rhetoricians have long discussed, technology is a concatenation of *techné* and *logos*, where the former "refers to art, as the result of productive reason, and *logos* is generally translated as word or explanation" (Colvino and Jolliffe 760). As such, technology may be studied by way of the arguments and explanations for productive arts rather than with an eye on the functional attributes of an artifact. For the moment, however, the "metamorphosis of the meaning of technology from an explicitly discursive process to a product that stands on its utility and efficiency" continues to drive a wedge between writing and the mere functionality of our digital tools (Colvino and Jolliffe 760). As an antidote, if composition instructors can approach hacking or remixing with digital technologies as a discursive process similar to traditional writing practices, those instructors will be able to introduce remix as a writing practice in need of critical reflection, including formation of argument, audience and situational analysis, comprehension of goals, issues of ethics and plagiarism, and research practices. The technology of writing/remix has indeed changed; a writing instructor's mission to teach critical reflection along with writing/remix has not. The job is just more challenging.

DIGITAL LITERACY, ETHICS, AND IP IN THE CLASSROOM

Several years ago, Laura Gurak called for a "critical technological literacy" that, along with knowledge of the operation of technology, "also relies heavily on people's ability to understand, criticize, and make judgments about a technology's interactions with, and effects on, culture" (13). Her discussion regarding a future free culture of remix aligns with Lessig's message but with no sense of the importance of reaching out to the other side. Her concern is that while "it's the ethos of the Internet to share" (122) corporate forces coupled with existing copyright law will stomp out a culture of remix:

> Cyberliteracy means more than just surfing the Internet and knowing
> how to click a few buttons. It means understanding your legal rights and
> paying attention to how the forces behind the technology of cyberspace
> are changing our social spaces. In terms of privacy and copyright, these
> changes are being driven by laissez-faire, market-dominated model, and
> unless we participate in the decision making, the Internet of the future
> will be driven solely by corporate interests, not those of citizens. (126)

Gurak's point is well taken; however, my argument is not to sit back and hope
that the market will create space for collaboration that enables and nurtures
a remix culture. Nor is it my position to protect antiquated business models
that may or may not survive in online spaces. Instead, to promote the desired
balance between the two sides, the instruction and the understanding of intellectual property and ownership in digital environments must include and go
beyond the rule of the law to incorporate the "effects on culture" and our
system of values. Discussions of ethics and technology have thus far engaged
important issues such as privacy, anonymity, flaming, gender (in)equality, and
the digital divide. However, other work, such as scholarship by James Porter,
has made the important connection between ethics, digital environments, and
discourse or rhetoric. The composition classroom, where digital remix must
now be taught, can become a space for "keeping ethics, rhetoric, and writing
together as an intertwined set" (23). Ethics takes us beyond the letter of the
law, enabling explorations of our own subjectivities and rhetorical situations.
When the situation requires a critical judgment call regarding digital remix
practices, Porter offers cautionary advice: "we are in an ethically sensitive and
important time right now because what we as users (and as teachers of users)
do on the networks will help constitute the norms for such discourse as they
become stabilized and legally sanctioned (or not) in the future" (8). While
Porter's warning came almost ten years ago, our normative practices on the
network often do not translate well into a reach across to the other side.

    In a much more recent work, Stuart Selber artfully outlines a three-part
structure comprised of functional, critical, and rhetorical literacy, which
coalesce to define what he calls "multiliteracies for a digital age." Along the
way, Selber manages to make a convincing case for the humanities' involvement in shaping and instructing this new literacy. While Selber finds fault with
programs for often taking a strictly functional approach to teaching multiliteracies, he still views functional know-how as an essential part of the equation.
In addition to the *uses* of technology, students must also become "question-
ers of technology" (critical) and "producers of technology" (rhetorical) (25).

At the close of his first chapter Selber asks, "What does it really mean for a student to become critically literate in a digital age?" (27–28). His answer is that "There is no one right answer to this question, nor should there be, but the profession must provide responses that are concrete, comprehensive, and capable of being implemented" (28). Selber's book does not focus specifically on issues of intellectual property and copyright (neither term makes it into the index), but I want to add to what Selber calls "the special responsibilities of humanities teachers in a digital age" (23) the deliberate instruction of the current intellectual property debate.

In the present struggle for balance, it is rare that the observations of Gurak, Porter, or Selber are heeded. As such, ethics paired with technology has little to do with our conduct regarding respect or understanding of intellectual property in digital spaces. When the subject is broached, ethics receives brief treatment. For example, Lessig's understanding of what it means to hack derives from Stallman's definition, but Lessig does add, "there's a well-deserved respect that goes with the talent to hack ethically" (*Free* 154). However, guidelines or parameters for ethical hacking (even those of the white/black/grey variety) are not offered. Instead, Lessig reminds us that regulations such as those on our automobiles and our tax system result in environments where many of us "violate the law everyday." He expands on the dilemma and what the relationship between the law and ethics means to his teaching:

> It is a particularly salient issue for teachers like me, whose job it is to teach law students about the importance of "ethics." As my colleague Charlie Nesson told a class at Stanford, each year law schools admit thousands of students who have illegally downloaded music, illegally consumed alcohol and sometimes drugs, illegally worked without paying taxes, illegally driven cars. These are kids for whom behaving illegally is increasingly the norm. And then we, as law professors, are supposed to teach them how to behave ethically—how to say no to bribes, or keep client funds separate, or honor a demand to disclose a document that will mean your case is over. Generations of Americans [. . .] can't live their lives both normally and legally, since "normally" entails a certain degree of illegality. (*Free* 201)

Living with illegal activity brings Lessig back to his concern of perpetuating a culture of disrespect for the law. The solution, of course, is not to repeal every law that poses a challenge but, instead, to actively introduce ethics into the discussion. I do not doubt that Lessig endeavors to instill all of the ethical lessons he mentions in his own students but, the subject of ethics here receives little attention other than its presentation as a daunting task. In the fight over a balance in intellectual property law, both sides would benefit from an overt and frank discussion of ethical concerns.

My own attempts to bring ethics into a classroom dealing with digital remix began with the insights of Gurak, Porter, and Selber but continue with a more practical tact. I located a formalized code of ethics that acknowledged the role of and our relationship to technology. The logical choice was the Institute of Electrical and Electronics Engineers (IEEE), a global, nonprofit institution and the leading professional organization in support of the advancement of technology. On ethics, IEEE first accepts the role technology has in "affecting the quality of life throughout the world" and then asks its members to adhere to the "highest ethical and professional conduct" by agreeing to the ten points in their code ("IEEE Code"). Below are four excerpted points from IEEE's code that may be introduced easily into a writing classroom as matters of debate regarding student responsibility or "membership" to digital environments such as the Internet:

1. [T]o accept responsibility in making decisions consistent with the safety, health and welfare of the public, and to disclose promptly factors that might endanger the public or the environment; [. . .]

5. to improve the understanding of technology, its appropriate application, and potential consequences;

6. to maintain and improve our technical competence and to undertake technological tasks for others only if qualified by training or experience, or after full disclosure of pertinent limitations; [. . .]

9. to avoid injuring others, their property, reputation, or employment by false or malicious action. ("IEEE Code")

The goal is not to foist ideologies on students but, instead, to bring them into the debate. Strictly speaking, IEEE does not actively police its code, nor does it possess a means to do so. A professional may still find herself a member of the organization after an ethical violation. As ethicist Michael Davis remarks, "Apart from pangs of conscience, the only repercussion she is likely to suffer is the poor opinion of those who know her well enough to know what she did. Her primary concern should be one of justifying her conduct to those concerned, including herself" (48). However, without a code to assist in the evaluation of our use or misuse of technology, many hackers rely (consciously or not) on the inherited ideology of the free software movement.

At the very least, beginning with IEEE's ethical points creates a different perspective for a hacker about to approach, for example, obfuscated hospital software. Rather than beginning with the premise that everything must be left open or that it is a moral offense to be closed, the would-be remixer may instead consider the resulting injury or harm if the code is altered. While the IEEE promotes the advancement of technology, the organization wisely fore-grounds the responsibility inherent in possessing new technology. As instruc-tors of remix technology, we should do the same.

WRITING ABOUT REMIX: BRINGING THE DEBATE
INTO THE COMPOSITION CLASSROOM

Advocates of bringing the "anarchy" versus "control" debate surrounding intellectual property into the writing classroom often emphasize case stud-ies from our rich legal history. Indeed, foundational cases such as the *Sony Corporation of America v. Universal City Studios*[8] (otherwise known as the *Beta-max* case) and *Diamond v. Chakrabarty*[9] are excellent introductions to issues of copyright and patent law respectively. More recent cases such as *A&M Records v. Napster*,[10] *MGM v. Grokster*,[11] and *Eldred v. Ashcroft*[12] provide backdrops for writing assignments, short presentations, and in-class debate. While cases such as *Napster* and *Grokster* resonate with students they both represent examples of corporate concerns (the "other side") defeating file sharing. There are tri-umphs (along with *Betamax*) for the side favoring less control and cases such as *Lexmark v. Static Control*[13] and *Kelly vs. Arriba Soft Corporation*[14] should be part of the curriculum. In order to create a balance between anarchy and control, the composition classroom requires a balance of cases so as not to vilify or glorify one side automatically.

In the tug-of-war between more versus less control over information, factions representing both sides produce a significant amount of marketing and promotional materials. These websites, commercials, videos, posters, and even stickers, are fodder for rhetorical analyses. For example, labeled by some as the nemesis of information sharing, the Recording Industry Association of America (RIAA) produces and distributes antipiracy videos complete with interviews of college students pulled out of class by the FBI. In addition to introducing the frightful possibilities of a felony record or overwhelming legal bills, the video attempts to shock the viewer with the fear-inspiring question,

"So you think it can't happen to you?" ("Campus"). From the side favoring less control, the popular technology review blog Gizmodo.com publicly called for a March 2007 boycott of all RIAA affiliated materials complete with an anti-RIAA manifesto ("Gizmodo's"). Likewise the Electronic Frontier Foundation (EFF), an advocacy group whose agenda includes fighting the expansion of copyright law, now sells stickers that read "Come Back with a Warrant," "Coding Is Not a Crime," and "P2P Is Not a Crime" (Electronic). Such maxims, devoid of any context or rationale, quickly devolve into mere platitudes for openness and at best appear as ironic counterbalances to the fear mongering of the other side.

While there are numerous possibilities for the composition classroom, imagine, for example, asking students to apply the four tenets of stasis theory to the EFF's last claim regarding "P2P." What is it, how did it come to be, is it good or bad, and what should we do with it? Are there logical fallacies in play? There are equal opportunities for the RIAA video and the tactics supporting its claims. Do the claims use or misuse a position of authority to advance their argument? Are there emotional or pathetic appeals? In short, in the process of investigating the claims and reasoning for the arguments made by both sides, students gain a more informed understanding of the struggle itself.

CONCLUSIONS

The concept of writing as remix did not necessarily arrive at the doorstep of literary or rhetoric and composition studies as a unique premise. We need only return to the poststructural theorists (the same theorists that digital and hypertext studies rely on so heavily) for claims that an author's "only power is to mix writing" (Barthes 146). For some scholars, it has become a cliché to announce that "we live in remix culture" (Manovich). Indeed, this is true. The work of Lessig and others has brought that point home to composition studies. It is time to move beyond this statement of fact and bring the debate surrounding a balance of control over digital works and networked environments into the composition classroom. If we do not include our students or teach only from a position mirroring that of Stallman's "freedom," we miss not just an opportunity to reach out to the other side but an opportunity to provide our students with a more robust perspective of the debate. Currently, we have not prepared for circumstances that arise where the public good is best served by the continued protection or even the deliberate obfuscation of copyrighted material, nor have we taken an active role in providing students the new digital literacy called for years ago by Gurak and Porter and, more recently, by Selber. We can change this. A deliberate introduction of a code of ethics, such as the code offered by the IEEE, can facilitate a classroom discussion on the ethics of digital remix that is informative without being prescriptive. In conjunction, legal case studies representing both sides of the intellectual property debate serve as an introduction to what is at stake regarding the advancement of knowledge sharing and the potential effects on the market. In the struggle to influence the debate, both sides aggressively publish propaganda ripe for analysis in the writing classroom. Creating fresh assignments with these materials as the central focus will only deepen student awareness of digital remix.

We are in an era of digital remix. Grabbing electronic images and text from the culture around us is a new type of writing and calls for a new type of writing instruction. For the younger generation, it is intuitive to interact with digital texts in this fashion and, according to Lessig, the network "begs" for this use. These methods shape how our students understand, how they make meaning, and how they think. Now that writing tools have changed from printed text to digital, do freedoms change? With effort, the answer could be no.

NOTES

1. Without entering a debate regarding how CC licensing may or may not complicate what is often referred to as the "crisis" in scholarly publishing, some academics other than Lessig are succeeding in obtaining CC licenses for their materials. For example, see: John Logie, *Peers, Pirates, and Persuasion: Rhetoric in the Peer-to-Peer Debates* (West Lafayette, IN: Parlor Press, 2006).

2. GNU is a recursive acronym for "GNU is Not Unix." While Stallman completed major components for his GNU project, including an editor and compiler, he did not finish the core operating system. It was not until Linus Torvalds released the code for the first version of Linux that hackers began to combine and grow the work of the two men. Those that wish to continue to acknowledge Stallman's contribution refer to Linux as "GNU/Linux."

3. The Free Software Foundation also encourages developers to license and include any supporting documentation for the free software. Documentation is licensed with the GNU Free Documentation License or FDL. See: http://www.gnu.org/licenses/.

4. For example, applications such as the popular Web server software Apache are developed "open" but may be legally appropriated and then closed off because the Apache Software Foundation uses its own license that does not block the code from being incorporated into a proprietary project. Stallman is on record as speaking

against such practices. See Lessig, "Open Source Baselines: Compared to What?" *Government Policy Toward Open Source Software*, ed. Robert W. Hah (Washington, DC.: American Enterprise Institute Press, 2003).

5. Microsoft, often represented with the symbol "M$," is regarded by many in the free software community as the egregious offender. The Free Software Foundation is currently sponsoring a website titled "Bad Vista" with a mission of deterring the adoption of Microsoft's new operating system. See: http://badvista.fsf.org/

6. For example, Stallman views ethics as the obligation to advance "human knowledge" and the responsibility to make that knowledge available to all. See "The Hacker Community and Ethics: An Interview with Richard M. Stallman, 2002" 18 Apr. 2007 <http://www.gnu.org/philospohy/rms-hack.html>.

7. See Bertrand Meyer's "The Ethics of Free Software" in the March 2000 issue of *Software Development Magazine* at: http://www.ddj.com/dept/architect/184414581. Meyer reacts to the "morally unjustifiable" and "extremist" views of Stallman and the Free Software Foundation stating, "The character assassination performed on commercial software developers by the extremists of free software, and their failure to accept people with different views of the world, can be honest and even idealistic in their own ways, has no moral basis." Even harsher, Bob Metcalfe found himself apologizing to Stallman for calling him a "communist." See: http://www.infoworld.com/articles/op/xml/99/10/25/991025opmetcalfe.html

8. *Sony Corporation of America v. Universal City Studios*, 464 U.S. 417 (1984). This cornerstone case ruled that Sony's VCR possessed significant "non-infringing capabilities" that superseded the technology's ability to record copyrighted material. The *Betamax* case is often cited when attempting to protect new technology from lawsuits seeking damages due to the copyright infringing capabilities of that technology. Often called the "Sony safe harbor" principle, this defense does not guarantee success in court.

9. *Diamond, Commissioner of Patents and Trademark v. Chakrabarty*, 447 U.S. 303 (1980). While this is a patent rather than a copyright case, it is excellent for starting classroom conversation. Chakrabarty, a genetic engineer, developed and sought a patent for newly engineered bacteria capable of breaking down crude oil. His application was initially rejected, but the Supreme Court ruled in his favor, stating that since the bacteria is man-made and not naturally occurring it could be patented.

10. *A & M Records, Inc. v. Napster, Inc.*, 239 F.3d 1004 (Ninth Circuit 2001) was the first case to handle peer-to-peer file sharing and copyright infringement. The court ruled against Napster, citing the software's contribution to infringing activity. Napster enabled both the reproduction and distribution of copyrighted material.

11. *MGM Studios, Inc. v. Grokster, Ltd.*, 545 U.S. 913 (2005). Grokster, another maker of peer-to-peer file sharing software, was sued out of existence for promoting the copyright infringing capabilities of its technology. This promotion is otherwise known as inducement.

12. *Eldred v. Ashcroft*, 537 U.S. 186 (2003). This case challenged the constitutionality of the 1998 Sonny Bono Copyright Term Extension Act (CTEA). Eric Eldred had published noncommercial, digital versions of works by authors that had fallen into the public domain. The CTEA added twenty years of protection and pulled some of the work out of the public domain. Lessig served as lead council for Eldred before the Supreme Court. The court found the CTEA constitutional by a decision of 7–2.

13. *Lexmark International, Inc. v. Static Control Components, Inc.*, 387 F.3d 522 (Sixth Circuit. 2004). Lexmark, a computer printer company, attempted to prevent other companies from refilling and profiting from Lexmark toner cartridges. The company offered discounted prices for those willing to agree to return and recharge cartridges only with Lexmark. To enforce the agreement, Lexmark included a computer chip and program on each cartridge that authenticated the cartridge. Without authentication the printer would cease to function. Static Control created a rechargeable printer cartridge complete with a computer chip to circumvent Lexmark's controls. In an appeal, the court found that Static Controls did not violate copyright or the Digital Millennium Copyright Act.

14. *Kelly v. Arriba Soft Corporation*, 280 F.3d 934 (CA9 2002). A commercial photographer, Leslie Kelly, sued Arriba and its search engine for reproducing thumbnail images of her photographs on its search results page. Since the search engine did not store the full-sized versions of Kelly's photographs on its servers, the court ruled in favor of Arriba Soft on the basis of fair use where public benefit outweighed any damage to the commercial value of the photographs.

WORKS CITED

Barthes, Roland. *Image Music Text*. Trans. S. Heath. New York: Hill & Wang, 1977.
"Campus Downloading." 28 Mar. 2007 <http://www.campusdownloading.com/dvd.htm>.
Colvino, William, and David Jolliffe, eds. *Rhetoric: Concepts, Definitions, Boundaries*. Boston: Allyn and Bacon, 1995.
Creative Commons. "Choose a License." 27 Mar. 2007 <http://creativecommons.org/license>
———. "Share, Reuse, Remix—Legally." 27 Mar. 2007 <http://creativecommons.org>.
Davis, Michael. *Thinking Like an Engineer: Studies in the Ethics of a Profession*. New York: Oxford UP, 1998.
Electronic Frontier Foundation. 28 Mar. 2007 <https://secure.eff.org/site/Ecommerce/1391638416?JServSessionIdr001=vjirkxtrk1.app13b&VIEW_PRODUCT=true&product_id=1005&CAMPAIGN_ID=1102>.
"Gizmodo's Anti-RIAA Manifesto." 28 Mar. 2007 <http://gizmodo.com/gadgets/home-entertainment/gizmodos-antiriaa-manifesto-239512.php>.

GNU. "Selling Free Software." 27 Mar. 2007 <http://www.gnu.org/philosophy/selling.html>.

Gurak, Laura J. *Cyberliteracy: Navigating the Internet with Awareness.* New Haven, CT: Yale UP, 2001.

Institute of Electrical and Electronics Engineers. "IEEE Code of Ethics." 28 Mar., 2007 <http://www.ieee.org/portal/pages/about/whatis/code.html>.

Lessig, Lawrence. "Remix Culture." Featured Session. CCCC. San Francisco, CA: 17 Mar. 2005.

———. *Free Culture: The Nature and Future of Creativity.* New York: Penguin Books, 2004.

———. *The Future of Ideas: The Fate of the Commons in the Connected World.* New York: Vintage Books, 2001.

Manovich, Lev. "Generation Flash." 27 Mar. 2007 <http://www.manovich.net/DOCS/generation_flash.doc>.

"Microsoft at the Power Point." *The Economist.* 11 Sept. 2003. 28 Mar. 2007 <http://www.economist.com/business/displayStory.cfm?story_id=2054746>.

Porter, James. *Rhetorical Ethics and Internetworked Writing.* Greenwich, CT: Ablex, 1998.

Red Hat Linux 9: Red Hat Linux Security Guide. "Attackers and Vulnerabilities." 4 Nov. 2007 <http://www.redhat.com/docs/manuals/linux/RHL-9-Manual/security-guide/ch-risk.html>.

Selber, Stuart A. *Multiliteracies for a Digital Age.* Carbondale, IL: Southern Illinois UP, 2004.

Stallman, Richard. "The GNU Operating System and the Free Software Movement." *Open Sources: Voices from the Open Source Revolution.* Ed. Chris DiBona, Sam Ockman, and Mark Stone. Sebastopol, CA: O'Reilly, 1999.

Vaidhyanathan, Siva. *The Anarchist in the Library: How the Clash Between Freedom and Control Is Hacking the Real World and Crashing the System.* New York: Basic Books, 2004.

Vainio, Niklas, and Tere Vadén. "Free Software Philosophy and Open Source." *Handbook of Research on Open Source Software: Technological, Economic, and Social Perspectives.* Ed. Kirk St. Amant and Brian Still. Hershey, PA: IGI Global, 2007.

PART II

Teaching the Conflicts

*Copyright Law in Pedagogical
Theory and Practice*

CHAPTER 5

A Refrain of Costly Fires

Visual Rhetoric, Writing Pedagogy, and Copyright Law

STEVE WESTBROOK

In this chapter I treat public and educational contexts as sites of comparison, analyzing the ways in which copyright law is conceptualized, discussed, and applied in both arenas. First, I examine how copyright owners' rights to derivative works affect writers, musicians, artists, and publishers in the public sphere. Then, I examine how the enterprise of composition understands derivative rights and, more importantly, presents the problem of copyright to students of visual rhetoric, whose image-based texts are particularly susceptible to claims of infringement. Calling attention to both the restrictive capacities of the law and the absence of significant discussion of copyright within the pedagogical materials designed to introduce students to visual rhetoric, I suggest that those of us who teach composition need to make a renewed effort to more thoroughly discuss how students' appropriations of images may affect their ability to lawfully circulate their texts outside of the classroom. Further, I argue that in order to treat students of visual rhetoric professionally we should introduce them to fair use analysis through conversations that better link their academic composing practices to a variety of public contexts.

HOW MUCH FOR YOUR METAPHOR?
PERMISSIONS IN THE PUBLIC SPHERE

Expressing frustration with the practical ramifications of copyright law, Susan Bielstein compares the task of tracking down permissions to "having to jump through endless tiny hoops of fire" (32). Anyone who has faced the task of acquiring permission to reproduce textual, auditory, or visual material within the publishing or entertainment industry can relate immediately to this comparison. The process can take months, require exorbitant fees, consist of intense negotiations, and cause many headaches, often leading permission-seekers to feel, as Miller's metaphor suggests, like a cross between a Sisyphean bureaucrat and a charred circus flea. At the very least, the process requires acquiescence with no guarantee of success; copyright holders may simply refuse to grant permission and thus effectively veto the production or circulation of a new work that relies on the appropriation of their material—in some cases, even if this appropriation is small in scope and transformative in nature. Take, for instance, a rather publicized request for permissions from a few years ago: in 2004, Sula Miller, a television producer affiliated with Big Grin Productions, sought to use lyrics from the hit song "Ring of Fire" (popularized by Johnny Cash in 1963) in a commercial for a hemorrhoid-relief product. She succeeded in gaining permission to use the lyrics from Merle Kilgore, who originally cowrote the song with June Carter Cash; however, Miller's efforts were blocked by the heir of Johnny and June Carter Cash's estate, Roseanne Cash, who could legally claim her deceased mother's copyright to the song. Asserting that she did not want her mother's work to be demeaned, Roseanne Cash said in a statement released to the press, "the song is about the transformative power of love [. . .] and that's what it will always mean" ("Cash"). Although Cash had licensed the rights to a number of bands like Social Distortion, whose cover versions did not radically reinvent the lyrics' meaning, she drew the proverbial and proprietary line at Miller's commercial. The lyrics were not permitted to be contextually transformed from expressing love to expressing the flaring pain of hemorrhoids, and the commercial never aired.

While this anecdote has, of course, a certain humor, it also reveals important implications for understanding copyright law. Namely, it demonstrates the radical power of control that the law affords copyright holders—whether or not these holders are actual producers of a given text—under the provision of rights to derivative works. Let me explain: in our present example, Miller did not seek to use Johnny or June Carter Cash's version of "Ring of Fire";

in fact, she did not seek to use even a portion of the song as performed by any members of the Cash family. Rather, Miller wanted to use an audio sample of Kilgore's own recording of the song. She was prevented from incorporating a small portion of Kilgore's performance into her larger multimedia production largely because of the law's treatment of derivative works. Title 17 provides copyright owners with "the exclusive rights [. . .] to prepare derivative works based upon the copyrighted work" (17 U.S.C. Sec. 106), and it defines a "derivative work" as:

> a work based upon one or more preexisting works, such as a translation, musical arrangement, dramatization, fictionalization, motion picture version, sound recording, art reproduction, abridgment, condensation, or any other form in which a work may be recast, transformed, or adapted. (17 U.S.C. Sec. 101)

As Lawrence Lessig explains in *Free Culture*, this provision "protects works that are based in any significant way on the initial creative work" (136). Kilgore's recorded version of "Ring of Fire" is thus considered a derivative version of the song that he and June Carter Cash originally cowrote. In this particular (and peculiar) incident, *either* original coauthor retained the power to veto a public performance that relied on appropriative sampling of the lyrics by another party. This distribution of power allowed Roseanne Cash to prevent Kilgore from performing his own song for Miller's commercial and thereby enabled Cash to authorize her preferred version of the song, controlling, in her words, "what it will always mean" or, at least, what it will mean in its authorized legal articulation until the limit of the copyright expires in 2073.

As this example demonstrates, in contemporary U.S. culture, the use of text and the control of its meaning is afforded to the copyright owner and in many cases determined less by contextual rhetorical practices than by economic and judiciary policies (both formal and informal). To be clear, this predicament is not necessarily the result of the actual codified law itself but, rather, of cultural perceptions of and reactions to the very threat of litigation. As Rosemary Coombe reminds us in *The Cultural Life of Intellectual Properties*, "hegemonic power is operative when threats of legal action are made as well as when they are actually acted upon" (9). Further, these threats carry with them a hefty price tag, especially for individuals who are not already enfranchised within the content industries, moneyed institutions, or estates. As Martine Courant Rife reveals while summarizing the findings of Fisher and McGeveran, "the average cost of defending a copyright infringement lawsuit is just under one million dollars" (3). In the end, the conflict involving Miller, Kilgore, and Cash never went to trial, largely because Kilgore rescinded his permissions agreement with Miller for fear of disrupting relations with the Cash estate; as a result, Miller decided not to pursue the project further. Regardless, copyright law's cultural power to radically affect text-making and alter rhetorical practices comes across clearly.

Understanding this power and its ramifications, a number of legal experts and composition scholars, including David Bollier, Jessica Litman, Lawrence Lessig, Siva Vaidhyanathan, John Logie, and Andrea Lunsford, have recognized how copyright owners' assertion of their rights to derivative works may represent a potential threat to creativity, democratic exchange, and the freedom of speech guaranteed by the First Amendment of the U.S. Constitution. Discussing copyright within the larger context of intellectual property in *Silent Theft: The Private Plunder of Our Common Wealth*, Bollier suggests that many rights holders do not want their works to be "*freely usable* by the culture. They want to sanction only a controlled, consuming relationship [. . .] not an open, interactive one we associate with a democratic culture" (121, italics in original). In its current articulation of derivative rights, copyright law privileges exactly this kind of sanctioning, as revealed by the example of Roseanne Cash's assertion of control.

Clearly, the logic of derivative rights—while complicated by commercial profit motives within a capitalist system—flies in the face of much artistic tradition. A countless number of text-makers, ranging from playwright William Shakespeare to photomontage artist John Heartfield, who "recast, transformed, or adapted" others' texts may not have been able to produce (or afford to produce) their most famous works if subject to the constraints of derivative rights under contemporary U.S. copyright law. Discussing his attempt to integrate a song lyric into his own fiction, contemporary writer Jonathan Lethem complains of the economic problem of acquiring permissions: "I've expressed irritation when I've tried to quote a Brian Wilson lyric in a novel and it turned out that I couldn't afford to do it." This predicament ranges from mildly frustrating to virtually career-ending; Public Enemy stopped recording music largely because the cost of acquiring permissions for their sampling practices became economically unfeasible. As Lethem and others suggest, permissions have become a kind of commodity market controlled by copyright owners and, at the very least, a trying reality for those who must seek consent for perfectly ordinary appropriations that might, nonetheless, be considered infringing. In fact, copyright industries comprise approximately 6 percent of the U.S. gross domestic product (Logie, *Peers* 109).

As I have begun to suggest, in contemporary practice, the problem of derivative rights and the metaphor of jumping through "endless tiny hoops of fire" extend well beyond music to other forms of performance and publication; they contain particularly troublesome effects for individuals seeking to reproduce or transform visual texts. In *Permissions, A Survival Guide*, Bielstein points to an irony that defines contemporary book publishing: "as we turn more and more to the object of vision for information and learning, it is becoming harder and harder and impossibly expensive to include illustrations in books" because of the cost of acquiring permissions (9). In fact, Bielstein, a veteran in the field of art history publishing, advises contemporary writers to use as few images as possible in their book manuscripts. Addressing them directly, she states, "chasing [permissions for] images is time consuming and expensive. So if you can live without images, do it" (101). One of the major problems with including images of artwork is the recent trend among individuals and institutions to claim multiple layers of copyright. As Bielstein explains, even if the copyright of a historical piece of artwork has expired, the reproduction of this artwork may have been newly copyrighted. In more tangible terms, this means that the photograph of, say, an eighteenth-century illustration may be copyrighted by an individual photographer or, more often, an institution like an art center or museum, which may lay claim to exclusive rights to the photograph through the work-for-hire doctrine. At the risk of being reductive, I offer my simplest explanation of a complicated, systemic problem: recognizing the profitability of, in effect, "selling" permissions, museums often disallow public photography of their major holdings; instead, they hire their own photographers who transfer their copyright to the museum (under the work-for-hire doctrine), which can then maintain control over the photographic reproductions and thereby maintain its market for permissions fees. That is, anytime writers want to make use of an image of a particular art object, they must seek the consent of the museum, which effectively owns the right to reproduction, and pay accordingly. The College Art Association's Committee on Intellectual Property expands on this problem in their newsletter:

> Even if a depicted work is in the public domain, a photographic reproduction of that work may carry additional layers of copyright protection claimed by photographers, publishers, or museums. As many scholars can attest, the procedure of separating these layers and seeking requisite permissions for the sake of publication can be complex, painstaking, and financially onerous. (4)

Pushed to its logical extreme, this bias threatens to encourage art historians to author books that contain purely alphabetic descriptions of artwork instead of actual images. In fact, this is exactly the case with Jonathan Katz's forthcoming book, *Jasper Johns, Robert Rauschenberg, and the Collective Closet: How Queer Artists Came to Dominate Cold War American Art*. Because Rauschenberg and representatives of Johns's estate disagreed with Katz's argument and disliked its representation of the artists under examination, they collectively refused Katz's request for permission to reproduce their copyrighted images. Faced with this problem, Katz and his publisher, the University of Chicago Press, are obliged to offer readers a specialized study on the artwork of Rauschenberg and Johns without reproducing any images of this artwork, however crucial the images may be to the content of the study (Zervigon). Although seemingly absurd, this example reveals both the logic and effect of dominant interpretations of standard U.S. copyright law and applies not only to reproductions of whole artworks in the field of art history, but to a broad range of visual compositions and appropriative practices.

In an interview with Salon.com, Lethem comments on the discrepancy the law appears to make between prose writing and visual genres. Using the popular cartoon character of Homer Simpson as an example, he states the following:

> the truth is, I could write a whole book [. . .] describing Homer's yellow skin and protuberant eyes, and no one would ever be able to block my choice as an artist there, or make it too expensive for me to do it. But if a visual artist or a filmmaker or a digital montage maker tried to capture that image, which is just part of a visual language that is floating around, they wouldn't have my freedom.

Thus when considering visual paradigms, we come somewhat full circle, as it were, and return to the frustration of facing our "endless tiny hoops of fire"—this time reflected in a prose description of Mr. Simpson's glinting eyes.

CAN I USE THAT METAPHOR FOR FREE?
CONFUSION IN THE CLASSROOM

The metaphor of jumping through these "tiny hoops of fire" is not only applicable to the commercial settings of the music, art, and publishing industries, but also to a different context as well—one more immediate to our circumstances as composition teachers working in the twenty-first century. It might represent the frustration we experience when attempting to understand the very implications of copyright law for the writers we teach, especially when they are engaging in the production of visual texts. After all, those of us working in the field of composition are presently "turning more and more toward the object of vision" as we and our students embrace visual rhetoric and new media. How, then, should our treatment and understanding of copyright law differ from those of professional writers, musicians, and publishers?

Recent developments in law and technology have made it increasingly difficult to determine the legality of students' new media composing behaviors, particularly when students appropriate and transform digital images. Even seemingly mundane activities of digital composition give rise to a number of complicated procedural questions. Imagine, for instance, a relatively simple scenario: a student finds a picture of a hoop of fire on a popular Internet search engine and wants to incorporate this picture into her essay. What steps should she take to integrate this image ethically and/or legally? Does she need to locate its owner and seek permission to reproduce or transform the image within the context of her paper, or is she exempt from this process because she is writing for "educational purposes," which are often cited in fair use defenses? How exactly do we understand what constitutes a fair, educational use of copyrighted materials, especially if this student creates her visual text for class but then decides to share it with a public audience by "publishing" it on her own personal website? How much should our determination depend on the publication context, or on the amount, portion, or percentage of the image being appropriated? What exactly should we encourage our students to do, or restrict our students from doing, when they produce not only relatively simple genres like essays containing pictures but more complex, hybridized forms of visual rhetoric that rely on fluid appropriative and combinatory practices and target multiple public and private audiences?

This short list of questions could quickly become a litany of koans for legal experts and laypeople alike, especially since, according to one scholar, the relationship between the law and recent developments in digital technologies is full of "contradictory rulings, failed legislation, and muddled policies" (Logie, "Champing" 201). I offer the questions not to function as precursors for ready solutions or definitive answers but, rather, to echo Andrea Lunsford and Susan West's early call in "Intellectual Property and Composition Studies" for composition instructors to investigate the relevance of intellectual property debates to the practices of teaching and text-making. Since the publication of Lunsford and West's article in 1996, significant progress has been made in this direction by individual scholars and the collective body of the Conference on College Composition and Communication's Intellectual Property Caucus (CCCC-IP). Of course, much more progress still needs to be made. In light of the law's apparent discrepancy between alphabetic and imagistic texts, and our discipline's recent trend toward the visual, we need to more thoroughly investigate and understand the particular intersections of copyright law and visual rhetoric—not necessarily to come to a procedural consensus but to come to an intellectual, ethical, and theoretical understanding of the larger consequences at stake, particularly for our students.

My purpose in the remainder of this chapter is to begin this investigation by focusing on three interconnected concerns. First, I examine how relevant issues of permissions, derivative rights, and copyright law are being presented to students through the pedagogical materials of visual rhetoric textbooks. Second, based on my findings, I reflect on how our discipline's ideas about what students do and do not need to know about copyright law reveal troubling assumptions about the identities of students and the functions of their new media texts. Third, I offer suggestions for reform that address issues relevant to both public and educational contexts and, moreover, complicate the construction of any easy distinction between these interconnected spheres, which students and their new media compositions pass between on a daily basis.

WHAT HOOPS OF FIRE? VISUAL RHETORIC TEXTBOOKS AND THE PEDAGOGY OF DENIAL

Given the complications associated with the process of securing rights to reproduce images in the publishing world, how exactly do our pedagogical materials address the problems of permissions, derivative works, and larger issues of copyright? After conducting research into this matter, I'm afraid the answer I have to report is rather short and cynical: they don't. Of the eight visual rhetoric textbooks I recently surveyed—*Beyond Words* (Ruszkiewicz, Anderson, and Friend); *Compose, Design, Advocate* (Wysocki and Lynch); *Frames of Mind* (DiYanni and Hoy); *Picturing Texts* (Faigley et al.); *Rhetorical Visions* (Hesford and Brueggemann); *Seeing and Writing 3* (McQuade and McQuade); *The Writer's Eye* (Costanzo); *Writing in a Visual Age* (Odell and Katz)—none deploys the terms *derivative works* or *fair use* or alludes to the four-factor analysis used to determine whether a use of intellectual property is fair or infringing under current copyright law; only *Picturing Texts* mentions the issue of acquiring permissions. Here, the authors offer one sentence of advice to students within the context of discussing documentation: "If you use someone else's images, including those you find on the Web, you need to obtain permission from the owner and to credit the image just as you would a quotation" (455). This might be sound advice, but I have reproduced in full the beginning and end of the discussion. The authors present seeking permissions as a rather arbitrary requirement for producers of visual rhetoric but do not include any sort of larger cultural or intellectual framework that would reveal what exactly seeking permission entails, what it might cost, or why it needs—or, perhaps, does not need—to be sought (ethically, legally, creatively, economically). In other words, there appears to be no significant discussion of what copyright law means for composers of new media and no compelling effort to let students into contemporary debates about intellectual property or an understanding of how and why these debates might already affect their own visual composing practices.

The remaining textbooks reveal two dominant tendencies: to over-look the issue of copyright altogether, or to assume that students need only document their appropriation of images through practices of conventional academic citation. In *Writing in a Visual Age*, Odell and Katz offer students guidelines characteristic of the latter tendency; instead of discussing per-missions as something distinct from documentation, they claim that "all visuals copied from another source should be cited, either in the caption or in the text, according to the documentation style you are using" (623). By ignoring the preliminary step of obtaining permissions, the authors do not acknowledge that copyright holders may claim the authority to disallow someone from using an image altogether and thereby make the very issue of documentation irrelevant. Textbooks subscribing to the former tendency, such as *Beyond Words*, *Rhetorical Visions*, and *The Writer's Eye*, require stu-dents to compose photo essays or advertisement parodies explicitly by appro-priating images from websites; they simply do not mention relevant issues of copyright. In the case of *Design, Compose, Advocate*, the authors, in fact, exaggerate students' liberties, suggesting that they have free rein to make use of others' intellectual property without acknowledging the real restric-tive capacities of copyright law: "Use whatever materials and technologies you have available to produce your own visual argument—for any purpose, context, and audience" (313). While these guidelines may offer radically democratic conditions (or, rather, a utopian *lack* of conditions), they deny proprietary economic realities to offer students a delusional perspective of writers' freedoms. Under U.S. law, we are simply not free to use any materi-als we like in any contexts, especially those defined as commercial and pub-lic. In fact, according to the Digital Millennium Copyright Act (DMCA),

certain infringing uses of materials may be considered a felony, the penalty
for which may include "up to a $1,000,000 fine or up to 10 years imprison-
ment" (U.S. Copyright Office 7).

I bring this issue up not to suggest we should scare our students into
complying with copyright law—this is certainly not my intention, as I hope
to demonstrate shortly—but rather to reveal how glaring the absence of a significant conversation on copyright is from these teaching materials. It would
seem that those textbooks that encourage new media composition particularly
through the appropriation and transformation of digital images would need
to at least acknowledge this conversation, if not actively participate in it. After
all, these texts are implicated in a cultural information industry and evolving
system of law that powerfully affect writers' production, reproduction, and
dissemination of visual material. Although it has been over a decade since
Lunsford and West claimed, "The time has passed when teachers of composition and communication could ignore debates about intellectual property, if
indeed we ever should have" (383), the textbook evidence would suggest that
in the field of visual rhetoric—where the connections are most apparent—we
are indeed ignoring these debates, at least as they pertain to students.

A number of rationales might be used to explain this glaring absence.
First, some may suppose that significant discussions of copyright law within
the context of visual rhetoric function mainly as distractions to the real work
of learning how to compose. That is, teachers of composition (whether defined
from the bias of print or digital cultures) should stick to teaching composition
and leave legal concerns to lawyers. The problem with this perspective is that
in our historical present, a time in which intellectual property law is strug-
gling to catch up to innovations in technology—particularly the technology
of text-making—a clean separation of these spheres simply is not possible,
especially in classes concerned with new media. As John Logie has suggested,
"Whenever composition instructors use computer technology in their classrooms, they raise exponentially the likelihood that the work completed within
their classes will run afoul of current intellectual property laws" ("Champing" 201). A second rationale assumes that to acknowledge the problem of
copyright is to acquiesce to the tenets of the law and, in this sense, verify or
bolster its power through acknowledgment, a prospect that many academics
are justifiably hesitant to encourage. Adopting silence as a resistance strategy,
this sort of conscientious denial further asserts that education is, or should be,
relatively immune to the more insidious abuses of copyright law. Although I
sympathize with this perspective, I'm not sure that the strategy of resistance
through silence or denial is the most effective for us or the most ethical for our

students. In short, I remain unconvinced by these justifications, and I don't think they represent the real reason for visual rhetoric textbooks' failure to integrate discussions of copyright.

I suspect that underlying these and other rationales is an ideological tendency to assume that students do not need to be informed about infringement and fair use because their compositions are only "academic," in the most pejorative sense of this term: that is, they don't matter. At worst, the compositions are not taken seriously; at best, they are assumed to be merely school exercises irrelevant to public audiences. In short, the absence we are confronted with would not exist if textbook authors and the larger enterprise of composition believed that students' visual rhetoric should circulate meaningfully in the public sphere, where copyright law—however undemocratic some of its restrictions may seem—undoubtedly applies and where permissions fees abound (it would appear for both commercial and nonprofit representations). In other words, the absence of discussions of copyright in visual rhetoric textbooks is evidence of our continuing to treat students' visual compositions as more or less disposable after the issuance of our evaluation.

The tendency to treat students' visual texts as merely "academic" is made possible by both composition's history of treating students' writing as a relatively inconsequential imitation of "real" writing and by the law's very definition of an educational context. Let me begin with the law: while copyright law, itself, does not create a safe haven for academic activity, it supports a distinction between educational and noneducational practices, and tends to offer increased restrictions for the latter. Interpretations of the fair use doctrine of U.S. Code encourage a radical distinction between educational and public spheres. The first of the four factors that define the fair use provision claims the following as a chief consideration for determining infringement: "The purpose and character of the use [of copyrighted materials], including whether such use is of a commercial nature or is for nonprofit educational purposes" (17 U.S.C. sec. 107). To be clear, this provision is what has allowed us, to a certain degree, to avoid "having to jump through endless tiny hoops of fire" when we appropriate images for the multimedia presentations we offer in class, show students films or television clips without paying enormous fees, photocopy and distribute teaching materials relatively freely, and engage in any number of what we consider ordinary teaching activities. In short, it is an important protection, which we depend upon daily. However, the clause ensures that at least part of the defense of fair use be predicated on drawing a firm line between educational and noneducational purposes, and the very definition of "purposes" is highly problematic.

Let me explain what I mean by calling attention to the disparity between the text of Section 107 and the normative interpretation of this text. Although the legal language defines the determining factor as "educational purposes," in application, this term is understood to mean something more akin to "educational contexts." For instance, authors of scholarly articles or books that are written for the purpose of educating readers are usually not protected by this section of the fair use doctrine; even if their work may be aptly described as criticism, comment, scholarship, or research, they must usually pursue permissions. As John Logie suggests in *Peers, Pirates, and Persuasion*, "academic texts, by and large, are subject to the same copyright regime that was developed to protect works like Sheryl Crow's most recent hit single" (146). And, as my brief illustration of the "Ring of Fire" case demonstrates, proprietary rights for hit singles are heavily coveted and radically protected. This copyright regime is, of course, also applied to the reproduction of visual images in scholarly works. As Bielstein asserts, "allowances for education and research do not normally translate into publishing images, for *publishing, even the nonprofit variety, is not considered an educational enterprise*" (91, my italics). Rather, it is considered part of a commercial industry, and even though education is certainly also a commercial industry, the interpretation of the law makes a firm distinction here. It would seem that in order to qualify as having an educational purpose, the practice under consideration must occur within the walls of an educational institution or a protected online equivalent, and, further, the circulation of texts must remain limited to this closed environment. In fact, since the passage of the TEACH Act, the criteria for qualifying a use of new media as "educational" within the context of distance education has been radically restricted, so much so that certain image-based texts may not be made downloadable or even available to students outside the time constraints of online class sessions.

As the law encourages the isolation of students' texts from larger commercial and cultural arenas, so too does the enterprise of composition. The treatment of students' writing as disposable might be considered "traditional" in our field, for here it has a long and contentious history. In *Composition in the University*, Sharon Crowley reveals how this tradition developed in relation to the norms of the first-year required writing course and came to define composition through most of the twentieth century. She claims that these norms led to students' writing being treated as "an imitation, or better, a simulacrum, of the motivated writing that gets done elsewhere [. . .] in the culture at large" while divorcing this writing from the actual rhetorical contexts in which it would ordinarily be produced (8). She argues convincingly that as a result of this history writing becomes a purely "academic" task of generating text for purposes of evaluation: "The primary motivation for composing is to supply teachers with opportunities to measure student performance" (8). Often in our assignments we ask students to imagine they are writing for specifically defined audiences outside of the academy, and when we approach the task of assessment we assume the persona of boss, peer, or public policy maker as appropriate. Through such performances, we may offer the kind of situational simulacrum to which Crowley alludes on a relatively frequent basis, but we rarely move beyond such imaginary performances to actually provide students' writing a post-evaluative public life or afterlife, as it were.

That said, as much as a history of disposable writing defines the present condition of our field, so too does a more recent countertradition of attempts to reconnect students' writing to actual rhetorical contexts within the public sphere. Various articulations of service-learning and internship programs represent perhaps the most tangible attempts to bridge the gap between so-called academic and so-called real-world writing. But even when not working with these distinct models, a diverse range of compositionists have been arguing for providing students external audiences (i.e., bringing writing instruction outside of the classroom) or, alternatively, for better recognizing the ways in which academic settings indeed already represent "real-world" contexts and consequences. Those advocating the former position include, among many others, Kay Halasek and Susan Miller. In *A Pedagogy of Possibility*, Halasek suggests that audiences for student writing should be expanded beyond "the person of a writing instructor or a panel of placement evaluators" (102), and in *Textual Carnivals* Susan Miller suggests that students need to be provided more educational opportunities to experience public writing's "social and economic consequences" (197). Pointing out academic writing's inevitable "real-worldliness," Joseph Harris and Johndan Johnson-Eilola have each offered, in their very different ways, the latter perspective. In *A Teaching Subject*, Harris claims that "A college is a place where people work [. . .]. It is thus not something separate from the world of actions and events but an integral part of it" (18). Given developments in new media, suggests Johnson-Eilola in "The Database and the Essay: Understanding Composition as Articulation," no matter if we try, "we can't separate writing from the economic sphere" (212). In other words, recent developments in technology reveal that attempts to divorce academic writing from larger civic contexts are misguided or fictional endeavors at best. As the efforts briefly represented here suggest, in the last twenty years composition has been deconstructing the false binary that would separate education from the "real world" in an attempt to teach writers to navigate a variety of rhetorical contexts within and beyond the college or university. Regardless of the particularities of our theoretical orientations, most of us can probably agree that this is a good idea. Nevertheless, the most technologically innovative of our visual rhetoric textbooks remain, in this particular regard, entrenched in composition's older tradition of academic isolationism.

The practical problem with sustaining a false binary of educational and noneducational contexts should be readily apparent: it radically disserves students who wish to display their "academic" experiments with visual rhetoric in larger public arenas, however immediately or eventually. And, if education is working effectively to connect theory and practice, learning and life, this sort of display should be the exact goal of student-writers. Let me return to art history to offer an example of this problem made immediate. Bielstein asks her audience to consider the case of writing a dissertation that relies on the reproduction of images. She claims, "Fair use applies to Ph.D. dissertations that include illustrations because [. . .] the dissertation is educational" (91), in the sense that it is produced within the context of an educational program and usually not disseminated to a terribly broad reading public. However, she argues that because professional publication—whether through a popular, university, or nonprofit press—tends to fall outside of fair use's educational provision, student-writers may face challenges when trying to convert their dissertations into monographs. Addressing her readers directly, she states, "if you have obtained a slide for 'research purposes only' and then decide you want to publish it, you may find yourself contractually obligated to go back to the provider for permission to do so, even if you are writing a highly specialized monograph" (91). Of course, a provider can always refuse permission, as demonstrated by Katz's failed appeal to Rauschenberg and Johns's estates. Depending on how heavily an author has relied on images, the sudden intrusion of copyright law from outside of the educational sphere can lead to radical revision, the removal of images, or, in extreme cases, a blocked, cancelled, or recalled publication.

I think those of us who teach visual rhetoric might learn a lesson from art history in this regard: we would serve our students well by understanding that because they will likely seek to share their visual rhetoric with different publics, they should be informed about copyright law during their course of study. In other words, if we aim to treat the writers in our classrooms at all professionally—whether they are college freshmen or doctoral candidates— we should assume that their new media texts might, in fact, be designed to reach publication venues outside of the academy; if we take this prospect at all seriously, we need to initiate conversations about permissions, copyright law, and intellectual property. Of course, we might begin this conversation by making students aware of databases that contain freely appropriable images, so that from the early stages of their experimenting with visual rhetoric they may use others' material legally in a variety of contexts defined as both educational and public. Lawrence Lessig's Creative Commons project, which offers a "Some Rights Reserved" alternative to standard copyright law, houses archives of materials that may be reproduced perfectly legally and free of charge. Works commissioned under the Library of Congress's public works project present another free and unquestionably legal alternative. But beyond the immediacy of providing these practical resources, how exactly do we engender more substantial conversations about copyright in ways that do not reinforce the false bifurcation of academic and public/commercial spheres, and in ways that afford students significant agency to negotiate the rather hegemonic system of standard U.S. copyright law?

DOUSING THE FLAMES AND INTERLOCKING THE CIRCLES: TOWARD AN EDUCATIONAL PUBLIC?

Despite the paucity of materials that adequately address issues of copyright, we have several pedagogical models to work from. I know of two books designed for students that, although not marketed as visual rhetoric textbooks, contain at least some exercises in visual production and include discussions of fair use and copyright law. In *Everything's an Argument*, Lunsford and Ruszkiewicz ask students to experiment with visual texts within the broader context of a rhetorical/cultural studies paradigm, and in the short handbook *Designing Writing*, Mike Palmquist offers students practical advice on document design. A comparison of these texts' treatment of fair use offers insight into how we might frame our conversations about copyright with our students, especially with regard to the issues of context and agency.

Lunsford and Ruszkiewicz devote an entire chapter to issues of intellectual property. Addressing students directly, the authors offer the following advice regarding copyright law:

> Although they are currently in danger, "fair use" laws still allow writers to quote brief passages from published works [. . .]. For graphics, photos, or other images you wish to reproduce in your text, you should [. . .] request permission from the creator or owner (except when you are using them in work only turned in to an instructor, which is "fair use"). And if you are going to disseminate your work beyond your

classroom—especially by publishing it online—you must ask permission for any material you borrow from an Internet source. (408)

Unlike the vast majority of visual rhetoric textbook authors, Lunsford and
Ruszkiewicz discuss the problem of permissions, make key distinctions
between the applicability of fair use to alphabetic and imagistic texts, and
warn students about the discrepancy between academic and larger public contexts. At the same time that the authors present this vital information, however, they also reinforce the division of educational and public spheres that,
as I have suggested, risks disserving students by encouraging them to write
for an audience of one, or as Janice Walker states somewhat sarcastically in
"Copyrights and Conversations: Intellectual Property in the Classroom" to
choose "between *real* writing and writing only for the teacher" (245, italics
in original). Further, the authors simplify the criteria for determining fair
use according to these contexts, assuming that students "must" imperatively
seek permissions for material in the online public sphere and that educational
uses are automatically considered "fair" when neither of these assumptions
holds definitively true. Such concrete polarization reinvents contested norms
as established rules and denies students the opportunity to participate in what
is really a larger, complex process of negotiation, to which they should be
exposed as both producers of visual text and citizens of a democracy.

    In contrast, Palmquist's discussion of fair use, albeit exceedingly brief,
leads students directly to the law itself. In a section of *Designing Writing* entitled "Avoiding Plagiarism: Considering Copyright and Fair Use" he includes
the following advice: "As you design your document, it's particularly important to consider [. . .] copyright and fair use regarding the use of digital
illustrations, such as photographs and other images, audio clips, video clips,
and animations" (28). Including a URL, Palmquist then points students to
"The fair use provision, which is defined in Section 107 of the Copyright Act
of 1976 (available at http://www.copyright.gov/title17/92chap1.html #107)"
(28). He concludes this section of his handbook with less absolutism than
Lunsford and Ruszkiewicz: "If you intend to publish your document, you
might need to request permission to use an image" (28, my italics). Though
perhaps seemingly inconsequential, the distinction reveals a significant discrepancy in the treatment of students. In Palmquist's text, the conversation
about fair use attributes students more agency by granting them exposure
to the language of the law and enabling them to make their own decisions
about whether permissions need to be sought rather than suggesting these
be ultimately determined by any definitive schism between academic arenas

and public performances. It is this sort of exposure, I argue, we should grant to students, for if we are truly going to treat them professionally, we need to afford them the right and responsibility to understand the doctrine of fair use in its rhetorical complexity. And the only way to achieve this understanding is to enable them to access the text itself and encourage them to practice their own fair use analyses.

The official fair use provision is based upon four factors, only the first of which is concerned with education:

> In determining whether the use made of a work in any particular case is a fair use the factors to be considered shall include—
>
> (1) the purpose and character of the use, including whether such use is of a commercial nature or is for nonprofit educational purposes;
>
> (2) the nature of the copyrighted work;
>
> (3) the amount and substantiality of the portion used in relation to the copyrighted work as a whole; and
>
> (4) the effect of the use upon the potential market for or value of the copyrighted work. (17 U.S.C. Sec. 107)

Amendments and additions aside, this constitutes the criteria for determining whether a use of materials is infringing or lawful; it is exactly what judges use to determine their verdicts. Clearly, the doctrine offers no transcendent or absolute proclamations; rather, its only mandate is that interpretation based on all four factors occur on a case-by-case basis. Although some educational institutions offer concrete guidelines for fair use based largely on percentages of appropriable material (e.g., one may use 10 percent of a visual image), these guidelines have no legitimate legal authority. As Kenneth Crews points out in "The Laws of Fair Use and the Illusion of Fair-Use Guidelines," all percentage- or portion-based rules, many of which emerged from the Conference on Fair Use (CONFU), may have been adopted by educators but were never enacted into law. He writes, "All of the guidelines fail any valid claim that they might have binding, legal authority . . . From a source-based analysis, one can unequivocally conclude that the guidelines are not themselves binding on the public as a rule of law" (664). In short, the aforementioned four factors are *the* legal criteria, and they are continually subject to interpretation and reinterpretation.

It is important that we provide students of visual rhetoric access to four-factor analysis not only so that they receive accurate information with which to make their own informed decisions, but also for two other, interrelated reasons. First, gaining familiarity with four-factor analysis may offer them a relative position of power from which to argue the legality of their appropriations, should the need arise. In other words, they might not necessarily be beholden to the control of copyright holders in the public sphere if they can demonstrate how and why their use of materials should be considered fair according to the four factors. That is, they may be able to at least douse the flames of the "endless tiny hoops of fire" that permission-seekers so often face; more significantly, they may be able to understand and assert their rights if confronted with abusive applications of copyright law by powerful corporations or media conglomerates within the content industries. For those readers who may suspect I am exaggerating the importance of this kind of empowerment (regardless of how cliché the goal of "empowerment" may have become in the discourse of education), I offer the publicized example of Swarthmore students Nelson Pavlosky and Luke Smith from several years ago. Pavlosky and Smith successfully resisted Diebold's cease and desist letters and continuous legal threats when the company attempted to assert the provisions from the Digital Millennium Copyright Act to prevent them from circulating leaked emails that revealed Diebold's admission of flaws in their electronic voting machines. In short, these two students became publicly recognized, and Diebold's acknowledgment of problems with its machinery in the presidential election became public information because, rather anomalously, two students resisted the hegemonic threat of litigation. As their example reveals, the stakes in our democracy are high, as is the value of an individual's ability to understand (and form a successful defense based upon) four-factor analysis.

Second, relying on and actively teaching all of the four factors (rather than assuming a decisive split between educational contexts and public performances) establishes a preferable basis for legal reform. Given the increasing interrelation of academic and public spheres and the importance of this relation to our students, we should be arguing less for preserving special exceptions within an isolated academic environment and more for extending the reach of education to include a wide range of public spaces. To do so, we need to return to the language of the law itself and recover the term *educational purposes* so that it applies in practice to a diverse variety of contexts—including publication—that may not be cripplingly limited to the classroom or its online virtual equivalent. To revert to a separate educational sphere would quite simply be to work against the pedagogical and technological progress of the last twenty years. I find this point particularly important because, as Martine Courant Rife suggests, we are currently working within a crucial time frame, in which "we still have a space to shape law by practice" (14).

For this reason, we should be highly conscious of our strategies for addressing copyright law and of our responsibilities as educators.

Personally, I'd like to make one point very clear as I conclude this essay. Although I have focused on the restrictive capacities of copyright law, I don't mean to suggest by any means that intellectual property is not worth protecting; as Brian Ballentine reveals in his chapter in this collection, certain exclusive proprietary rights should undoubtedly remain in place. In other words, I am not advocating any sort of black-and-white approach to the matter or arguing for any absolute or anarchic dissolution of copyright. As I hope to have made clear, however, I do believe, along with an incredible range of scholars, that interpretations of copyright law—particularly rights to derivative works—have grown increasingly and unnecessarily restrictive in reaction to developments in the digital technology of text-making and text-sharing, or as Andrew Ross states, "the result of the technology-driven IP property grab [. . .] has resulted in an aggressive expansion of copyright" (745). Further, this expansion has come to privilege institutions already enfranchised within the content industries. As I have suggested here and elsewhere, it is affecting our students in negative ways, and I believe that we should join with each other and with students in lobbying to alter its course. Several compositionists are already doing so through acts of resistance in their own writing, which extend the applicability of "educational purpose" outside of the classroom. At the end of his recent book, *Peers, Pirates, and Persuasion*, which relies on the reproduction of several crucial images, John Logie states the following: "While I have done my best to identify and acknowledge the copyright holders for these images, *I have determined not to seek permissions* for these obviously fair uses" (149, my italics). In our roles as teachers we may feel justifiably hesitant to indoctrinate students to such bold positions of resistance; it may not be our job to do so. However, we can certainly agree that it is our job, if not to advocate, to at least inform and educate. That is, we share a responsibility to provide students the resources that will enable them *to make their own determinations* about whether, when, and how to go about seeking permissions. If we want to uphold this responsibility within the field of visual rhetoric, we need to start by making the language of fair use visible.

WORKS CITED

Bielstein, Susan M. Permissions, A Survival Guide: Blunt Talk about Art as Intellectual Property. Chicago: U of Chicago P, 2006.

Bollier, David. Silent Theft: The Private Plunder of Our Common Wealth. New York: Routledge, 2002.

"Cash Family Blocks Haemorrhoid Ad." *BBC News.* 18 Feb. 2004. 25 May 2007 <http://news.bbc.co.uk/1/hi/entertainment/music/3498749.stm>.

College Art Association Committee on Intellectual Property. "Q & A." *CAA News: Newsletter of the College Art Association* 29.1 (January 2004). 20 May 2007 <http://www.collegeart.org/pdf/caa-news-01-04.pdf>.

Coombe, Rosemary. *The Cultural Life of Intellectual Properties: Authorship, Appropriation, and the Law.* Durham: Duke UP, 1998.

Costanzo, William V. *The Writer's Eye: Composition in the Multimedia Age.* Boston: McGraw-Hill, 2008.

Crews, Kenneth. "The Law of Fair Use and the Illusion of Fair-Use Guidelines." *Ohio State Law Journal* 62 (2001): 599–702.

Crowley, Sharon. *Composition in the University: Historical and Polemical Essays.* Pittsburgh: U of Pittsburgh P, 1998.

DiYanni, Robert, and Pat C. Hoy II. *Frames of Mind: A Rhetorical Reader with Occasions for Writing.* Boston: Thomson Wadsworth, 2005.

Faigley, Lester, Diana George, Anna Palchik, and Cynthia Selfe. *Picturing Texts.* New York: W.W. Norton & Company, 2004.

Halasek, Kay. *A Pedagogy of Possibility: Bakhtinian Perspectives on Composition Studies.* Carbondale and Edwardsville: Southern Illinois UP, 1999.

Harris, Joseph. *A Teaching Subject: Composition Since 1966.* Upper Saddle River: Prentice Hall, 1997.

Hesford, Wendy S., and Brenda Brueggemann. *Rhetorical Visions: Reading and Writing in a Visual Culture.* Upper Saddle River: Prentice Hall, 2007.

Johnson-Eilola, Johndan. "The Database and the Essay: Understanding Composition as Articulation." *Writing New Media: Theory and Applications for Expanding the Teaching of Composition.* Logan, UT: Utah State UP, 2004. 199–236.

Lessig, Lawrence. *Free Culture: How Big Media Uses Technology and the Law to Lock Down Culture and Control Creativity.* New York: Penguin Press, 2004.

Lethem, Jonathan. Interview. *Salon.com.* By Amy Benfer. 25 Mar. 2007. 20 May 2007 <www.salon.com/books/feature/2007/03/25/lethem_interview/print.html>.

Logie, John. "Champing at the Bits: Computers, Copyright, and the Composition Classroom." *Computers and Composition* 15.2 (1998): 201–14.

———. *Peers, Pirates, and Persuasion: Rhetoric in the Peer-to-Peer Debates.* West Lafayette: Parlor Press, 2006.

Lunsford, Andrea A., and John J. Ruszkiewicz. *Everything's an Argument.* 3rd ed. Boston: Bedford/St. Martin's, 2004.

Lunsford, Andrea, and Susan West. "Intellectual Property and Composition Studies." *College Composition and Communication* 47.3 (October 1996): 383–411.

McQuade, Donald, and Christine McQuade. *Seeing and Writing 3.* Boston: Bedford/St. Martin's, 2006.

Miller, Susan. *Textual Carnivals: The Politics of Composition.* Carbondale and Edwardsville: Southern Illinois UP, 1991.

Odell, Lee, and Susan M. Katz. *Writing in a Visual Age*. Boston: Bedford/St. Martin's, 2006.

Palmquist, Mike. *Designing Writing: A Practical Guide*. Boston: Bedford/St. Martin's, 2005.

Rife, Martine Courant. "Ideas Toward a Fair Use Heuristic: Visual Rhetoric and Composition" *Composition and Copyright: Perspectives on Teaching, Text-making, and Fair Use*. Ed. Steve Westbrook. (Chapter 7 in this volume).

Ross, Andrew. "Technology and Below-the-Line Labor in the Copyfight over Intellectual Property" *American Quarterly* 58.3 (2006): 743–66.

Ruszkiewicz, John, Daniel Anderson, and Christy Friend. *Beyond Words: Reading and Writing in a Visual Age*. New York: Pearson Longman, 2006.

U.S. Copyright Office. Digital Millennium Copyright Act of 1998. U.S. Copyright Office Summary. December 1998.

Walker, Janice R. "Copyrights and Conversations: Intellectual Property in the Classroom." *Computers and Composition* 15.2 (1998): 243–51.

Westbrook, Steve. "Visual Rhetoric in a Culture of Fear: Impediments to Multimedia Production." *College English* 68.5 (2006): 457–80.

Wysocki, Anne Frances, and Dennis A. Lynch. *Compose, Design, Advocate*. New York: Pearson Longman, 2007.

Zervigon, Andres. Personal Interview. 1 June 2007.

CHAPTER 6

Beyond the Wake-up Call

Learning What Students Know about Copyright

LISA DUSH

The field of English studies is today in the midst of what might be called the "third wave" of its attention to copyright. The first wave, ushered in by the important work of Lunsford and West[1] and Woodmansee and Jaszi[2] in the mid-1990s, came as a response to drastic intellectual property policies proposed in the Clinton administration's green and white papers. These proposed policies, drawn up by a computer- and music-industry-friendly group and touted as the blueprint for intellectual property norms on the new World Wide Web, envisioned the Web as a commercial space, available only to those who could pay for access. First-wave copyright scholarship from English studies argued against the romantic notion of solitary authorship that informed such policies. Then, at the end of that same decade, another dramatic public policy issue, the Sonny Bono Copyright Term Extension Act, was debated and then signed into law, adding twenty years to copyright holders' sole control over their copyrighted texts. In response, a second wave of copyright and IP scholarship surfaced in English studies, including a special issue on intellectual property in *Computers and Composition*[3] and book-length explorations of theories of the public domain, fair use, and the rhetorical systems surrounding text ownership.[4] The recent third wave of attention to copyright has coalesced around several developments. First, as instructors in English departments and writing programs teach more multimedia and multimodal composition courses, we must deal much more concretely with copyright. Second, the broader movement to oppose proprietary copyright, largely led by Lawrence Lessig and his nonprofit licensing and advocacy group, Creative Commons, has grown into an organized and visible force. Lessig sees compositionists as important allies in the fight to reclaim the intellectual commons, and has made a number of appearances at our major conferences. Finally, a host of composing and consumption behaviors that involve computers and the Web—from fan fiction, to file sharing, to composing videos with inexpensive and widely available technologies—have made copyright an issue that our students will likely have thought about and experienced, if not inside the classroom, then outside of it.

In the mid-1990s, the late-1990s, and even today, however, the prevailing tenor of scholarship on copyright and intellectual property has been that of the wake-up call. We have been repeatedly told the history of copyright, reminded that the Founding Fathers' intention with the copyright clause of the Constitution was to create a balance, now destroyed, between individual and public rights. We have been asked to keep informed on the laws, to prepare ourselves to be public advocates, and to continue to make clear the constructed and intertextual nature of texts in our classrooms. The existing research, whether historical or theoretical, however, leaves unanswered the question of *how* we talk with students about copyright and IP issues. And as any teacher of multimodal composition will attest, the *how* of dealing with copyright is more problematic than the why. Time is always a constraint in writing classrooms, but the logistics of digital writing seem to leave even less of it for discussions about complicated issues like copyright. And while all academic institutions have some sort of official plagiarism policy, which teachers of print composition can adopt or build upon, dealing with copyright is generally a matter of inventing policy. In the face of these constraints, it is not uncommon for even the most thoughtful of teachers to simply issue their students a blanket prohibition, perhaps highly qualified, on using copyrighted texts.

This chapter addresses a key unknown when it comes to talking about copyright in the classroom: what students might already know and think about the subject. The chapter begins to lay out for examination some student attitudes about copyright, intellectual property, and authorship, by reporting on comments from one class of multimodal composers. The students I discuss were asked to reflect on copyright in both in-class writings and interviews

(see appendixes A, B, and C for a discussion of the study's methods) in a
research project that began with three questions: 1. Do students have any pre-
existing knowledge of and experience with copyright law, and if so, of what
sort? 2. Are copyrighted texts important to students' multimodal composition
processes and if so, how? and, 3. What discourse and metaphors do students
use when they speak about their composing behaviors with copyrighted texts?
The research was gathered in an elective multimodal writing course, called
Digital Storytelling, which a colleague and I co-taught in the English department of a large public university. The course centered on the question of
whether different media encourage different sorts of narratives, and the bulk
of the class was devoted to three major projects, each focusing on a different
medium—first images, then audio, then video. Prior to the course, my colleague and I decided that we would explicitly address the ethics and legality
of using others' texts in our class. We knew that students would likely want
to use images and music tracks that were copyright protected, and we wanted
them to use others' texts in a responsible way. What we meant exactly by
"responsible way," was unclear: some of the most compelling articles on multimedia classroom work, such as Daniel Anderson's "Prosumer Approaches
to New Media: Consumption and Production in Continuum" and Geoffrey
Sirc's "Box-Logic," display student texts with very heavy use of proprietary
texts, yet make no mention of how copyright issues were addressed, or not
addressed, in the class.

    As the comments in this chapter show, students are not blank slates; they
have already had experiences with, appropriated discourses about, and adopted
stances toward copyright. Hearing these voices should help us to imagine how
we might frame classroom discussions on copyright, and also provide a few
new reasons for why it is important to have these discussions.

FILE SHARING AND FAN FICTION:
STUDENTS' EXPERIENCE WITH COPYRIGHT

The word *copyright* has a whiff of dry legality about it—it's difficult to imagine
an exciting classroom conversation centered on copyright law. But the day we
discussed copyright was one of the classes when we learned the most about
our students' lives outside of the classroom, particularly about their lives as
producers and consumers of texts. Our copyright discussion came roughly
halfway through the semester, as our students were just in the planning stage
of their video projects, which we had assumed would invite heavy use of
copyrighted texts. To stimulate the discussion, we first watched two short

films on the Creative Commons website. Both films are animated and about six minutes long; one tells the history of the Creative Commons, the other details some successful projects by and between Creative Commons licensees.[5] We then posted several addresses of websites related to copyright, and asked students to post a response discussing their attitudes about and behaviors regarding copyright (see appendix B). These questions were designed to gather some initial information about my first research question: what, if any, experience did students have with copyright.

We planned this discussion anticipating that the students' interest would be minimal; however, we were impressed to see them watch the Creative Commons videos with rapt attention, and then to bang away at their keyboards, enthusiastically discussing the issue in the online forum. When the verbal discussion began, the enthusiasm continued. The most obvious thing to note was that although the discussion was framed (by the Creative Commons movies and us) around using copyrighted texts in your own creative compositions, the class immediately began to talk about peer-to-peer file sharing. In fact, the students seemed desperate to talk about illegal downloading. As our student Candice said in her WebCT post, "I steal music and movies from online, I'm not sure I'm supposed to tell anyone about that, it seems to be a thing that everyone does but no one talks about too much."

While it may seem that file sharing—downloading free MP3s—is a red herring, a hot topic that a teacher needs to cool down before moving on to the "real" discussion of how copyright law affects composition, it has important links to students' understanding of and attitude toward copyright and composition. In "Why Napster Matters to Writing: Filesharing as a New Ethic of Digital Delivery," DeVoss and Porter write convincingly on the fundamental connections between file sharing behavior and composition. Our students are file sharers, DeVoss and Porter claim, and the "attitudes and expectations" they learn in virtual spaces like Napster—such as giving credit to authors, sharing alike, and acting not just the role of consumer, but also of distributor on the Internet—are not left outside of the classroom door (179, 187–91). DeVoss and Porter suggest that students, by participating in peer-to-peer file sharing networks, are learning a "new ethic of digital delivery," and that a shift in the ethic of delivery has profound effects on the perceived "economies of writing" in which students participate, and thus on their notions of

> value, exchange, and capital; [. . .] production and consumption of goods; [. . .] giving, receiving and sharing; [. . .] purpose, desire, and motivation; [. . .] the distribution of resources, products and services;

and [. . .] the systems of understanding that people rely on when they engage in such activities. (194)

Our students' comments suggest that young people feel quite a lot of cognitive dissonance around file sharing: everyone does it, even though it's wrong . . . but is it really wrong? "What's different," said one student, Allison, "about me just putting a tape in the radio and recording songs? I used to do that in junior high, and no one prevented me from doing that." Most of the students began their discussion of file sharing with strong condemnations of the record industry, but then got tangled in the concern that their favorite musicians might lose money if everyone downloaded their music for free. In our classroom discussion, there was an interesting dialogue about the various compensations students had developed to send monetary reward to their favorite artists, even as they downloaded their albums for free, such as buying concert tickets and T-shirts. In these discussions of file sharing, then, arose questions and ethical dilemmas that drill down to key issues around copyright policy: How can the rights of artists and the public be balanced? How is profit to be made through creative works? How much protection and profit do artists need in order to be motivated to create their art? What role do publishers and distributors play in the creative industries? Is the "tragedy of the commons," wherein individual desires run wild, depleting the unregulated commons, a real tragedy, or, as David Bollier argues in "Reclaiming the Commons," a myth?

While DeVoss and Porter focus on the positive values associated with file sharing—giving credit, an ethic of sharing—our students framed file sharing as an antagonistic, largely individual act against an unresponsive, irrational and fat-cat recording industry. As Kathy said, "I don't have much sympathy for the vast machinations of advertising and other nonsense that stand between the public and the texts in question, and that's probably what's at the heart of the matter for a lot of this. That's what I tell myself when I take stuff, anyway." Comments like Kathy's complicate, then, some of the existing scholarship on copyright and intellectual property. It's not that DeVoss and Porter have it wrong about file sharing, but rather that students may not be framing their own extracurricular activity in the same productive ways that we do.

Besides file sharing, a second activity that exposed students in our classroom to copyright law was fan fiction. In fact, the two students that had the most sophisticated understanding of copyright were Ellen and Sandy, the most avid fan fiction writers and readers in the class. Both reported having many conversations with other members of fandom—virtual spaces where fans of books, TV shows, or movies use the worlds and characters of published texts to create their own stories and art—as Sandy said, about "copyright, parody law, and not getting caught." Ellen and Sandy both knew much about the attitudes of various writers toward their own copyrights: J. K. Rowling, of Harry Potter fame, encourages fan fiction, while Anne Rice, author of *The Vampire Chronicles*, "FREAKED over the idea of fan fiction," reported Ellen. Not surprisingly, both Ellen and Sandy had a very collaborative and social understanding of writing, and their comments suggest an appealing way of understanding reading and writing. Ellen said:

> To a lot of fans, fanfic is one of the ultimate compliments—it means that the work was so interesting, so engaging, so good, that they couldn't stop thinking of it. To some fans, saying "You may absolutely not write fan fiction about my work" is kinda like saying "Please give me your money, but leave your brain at the door."

Ultimately, the students' comments suggest that copyright is not new to them, and that to discuss it is far from boring. Teachers need not presume that students have no experience with copyright law; in any given classroom students can be found with strong opinions and valuable expertise. In our group of ten students, three had friends who had received cease and desist (C and D) letters from copyright lawyers, one student was involved in a video production company with a group of friends and had contacted record companies about song permissions, four were fanficcers, and all had participated in peer-to-peer file sharing networks. These experiences frame students' attitudes about copyright and give them language for discussing both copyright law and the conceptions of authorship and cultural ownership that stem from the law.

CREATIVITY IN THE PERMISSION CULTURE: HOW STUDENTS USE COPYRIGHTED TEXTS

Scholarly discussions about why copyright laws should be loosened are often cast in grand terms: culture refreshes itself faster when texts are easily accessible;[6] corporations will have less of a stranglehold on culture if their profit is not tied to copyright; strict IP rules breed bad attitudes about authorship and writing. But I would suggest that these claims are a bit abstract, and that teachers and students are often unconvinced that all that much can be gained if students have full access to any copyrighted text that they desire during the composition process. A pragmatic teacher of multimodal composition who is concerned about copyright may simply direct her students to the many online sources of public domain images and music, like Creative Commons or Flickr'. My second research question—Are copyrighted texts important to students' multimodal composition processes and if so, how?—aimed to gather information about whether there really are compelling reasons for students to have access to famous, copyrighted texts. The comments students had about how and why they use copyrighted texts group together into two general findings. First, there *are* compelling compositional reasons for students to use copyrighted texts. Second, referencing culturally important texts is not just important to students' composing processes, but it is also important to their identities.

Even before computers were built with the storage space and network connections with the bandwidth to handle downloading and editing copyrighted images, audio, and video, theorists of writing, rhetoric, and creativity dreamt of the radical compositional possibilities that would exist when writing was done with bits and bytes, rather than with words alone. For example, in *The Electronic Word* (1993), Richard Lanham spoke of the "full range of expressivity" available to composers who could work with media besides just the printed word (77). The availability of digital texts lets people compose with raw materials that they cannot create; even musical dunces like myself can make an audio medley, using the raw materials we find on the web. Lanham's dream is, however, dependent on a creative environment where culture is free for the taking, or what Lessig calls "free culture." In opposition to free culture is what Lessig calls the "permission culture," the culture that copyright law is creating: "Technology means that you can now do amazing things easily," states Lessig, "but you can't easily do them legally" (105).

Citation and parody are typically how we imagine students using copyrighted texts, but digital technologies make other behaviors possible. The combination of digital texts and the availability of editing software lets composers break apart and recompose texts into something totally new— not simply into recognizable parts used in derivative works. Consider this story, about one student in our class, Justin, who in the process of composing his photo essay, went searching for a handwriting font in PowerPoint's drop-down font menu. He didn't look for long, as nothing there met his fancy. Justin then took out a sheet of paper; unfortunately, he only had graph paper with a busy blue-squared background, but he didn't bother hunting for a plain white sheet. He wrote the line of text that he wanted in his photo essay on the graph paper, then pulled a digital camera out of his backpack and took a picture of the graph paper. Next, Justin uploaded the photo to his computer, opened Photoshop, used the histogram to wash out the white background and blue lines, making the background transparent; just his line of text, in his handwriting, remained. He then saved the creation as a png file, reopened PowerPoint, and laid this transparent png over his slide. Voilà: in less than five minutes, he'd made the font he wanted. As I watched Justin do this, I felt that I was seeing what Lessig described: an amazing thing done easily. Of course Justin's handwriting was not copyrighted, but this radical remaking of texts—a process that requires thought and ingenuity—could just as easily be done on a copyrighted text. Ellen, for example, said that if it were it not for a shortage of time, she hoped to do some major editing of a song she'd found: "I would've loved to be able to edit out the vocals and just use the cellos, but no software I had or could learn in so short a time was equipped to handle that." For more and more students, texts occupy a dual identity—as authored, coherent creations, but also as collections of usable elements. Remixing, the students' behavior indicates, is more than just using the coherent and recognizable parts of published texts as part of your own; it can be literally about pulling a few usable bits and bytes from an existing text.

Besides remixing, students also used copyrighted texts in other parts of their composition process. Ellen here describes how a copyrighted song was a part of her audio essay process:

> I had a hard time thinking of an idea for my sound portrait. Eventually it came down to the wire and I knew I needed an idea, so instead of thinking of stories I could tell, I put my iPod on shuffle and started listening for songs that I wanted to use. When Concrete Blonde's "Still in Hollywood" came up, I thought I could use that song and tell a story from the time I spent going to college in California. So I just started writing down some memories with that song in mind, and eventually I got a story out of it.

That Concrete Blonde song was spliced into Ellen's narrative; it was a part of her composing process from start to finish. Again and again, the composing processes that I observed, as well as the reflective cover letters that accompanied the students' major projects, expressed this essential function of *familiar, popular* texts throughout the composing process. Candice, describing in a reflective letter how she composed her video, said, "A lot of my ideas on how to use the clips and what effects I wanted to put on them came from the [copyrighted] music I wanted to use for each piece." She went on to describe how the tempo of the song she used affected her development of themes and the pace of her editing. Carson said he was "extremely proud" of the two songs he had chosen to interweave with his audio project, "since they are neither overly popular nor overly sentimental." Part of the skill in producing these multimodal texts was perceived by the students to be the editorial ability to choose music that worked with other media in their texts in compelling ways.

Most young people invest a good amount of energy into defining their identity as cultural consumers, and multimodal composition is a place where that work pays dividends. A well-selected image, song, or video clip can have a very powerful impact on an audience, particularly an audience of peers. But concerns about distribution have the potential to render this sort of cultural knowledge moot. Steve Westbrook makes this point tangible in "Visual Rhetoric in a Culture of Fear" with his discussion of how one of his student's multimodal compositions, because it used copyrighted images, was limited to classroom circulation and kept from circulating in culture at large. The larger implication is that when students are denied access to valued sites of cultural distribution because their work infringes on a copyright, they are positioned, as Westbrook states, as "*viewers of* culture," rather than as "*participants in* the continual re-creation of this culture" (466). Both students' cultural knowledge and their critical powers can be short-circuited by copyright law.

Many of our students spoke of "thinking twice" before they used a copyrighted text in their own compositions, suggesting both that they imagined a wider circulation for their multimodal texts, and that in *Free Culture* Lessig was right to ask, "how much creativity is never made because the cost of clearing rights are so high?" (104). In most cases, students thought twice, but then used the copyrighted text anyway. Consider the case of Carson, a senior English major. Carson narrowly escaped being kicked out of school for file sharing; he was twice placed on probation for excessive illegal downloading on the school's bandwidth, the second time for downloading over a terabyte of data in one day (the equivalent of about two hundred two-hour movies). Carson knew that copyright law prohibited him from using the songs, but mentioned making an early decision to limit his project's circulation to the classroom:

> I don't borrow from other people, unless I'm stealing outright, and then I don't even kid myself. The music I used in my pieces, stolen, outright. I didn't plan to get rich off it, I didn't even plan to circulate it farther than this classroom. If I thought that either one of them was good enough to

submit to some sort of contest, I would probably have to get in touch with the artists before it got too far. Who am I kidding, I wouldn't even do that. I would put it up, claim my prize, and pray like hell that neither Orbital nor Ryuichi Sakamoto ever stumbled onto the website where my work was posted. Worst case scenario, I get a cease and desist letter, take my file down, and then it lives on in underground P2P sharing.

Like that's anything new to me.

But, um, yes, stealing is wrong. Don't do it.

Looking beyond the irony and humor that make Carson's comment amusing, there is something quite distressing in it. The very compositional decisions that students are most pleased with—Carson, remember, reported being "extremely proud" of choosing the two aforementioned songs mentioned—are often made at the cost of imagining, from the start, little or no meaningful circulation of the finished text. This suggests that limiting students to composing with texts that will allow for the full circulation of the finished product may, in fact, lead them to produce texts that they are not all that interested in circulating.

STUDENTS' DISCOURSE AND METAPHORS REGARDING COPYRIGHT

The final aim of my research was to learn something about the discourse and metaphors that students had already appropriated regarding copyright. Copyright and IP theory makes much of the role that our cultural metaphors play in whether or not we accept copyright laws as fair and normal. Siva Vaidhyanathan, in the afterword of *Copyrights and Copywrongs*, for example, makes the suggestion that a rhetorical shift in the discourse around intellectual property must occur if our culture is to become less proprietary about textual ownership. For Vaidhyanathan and many others a better metaphor than intellectual creations as the real property of the author is that of intellectual work as a product of and fodder for the cultural commons. A commons framework emphasizes that any cultural or intellectual production is ultimately for the betterment of society, not just the individual author. Ideas breed new ideas, and a commons philosophy puts a premium on getting ideas swiftly into the public domain, where others can build on them.

Our students were not convinced of the property framework, but neither would I say that they articulated a commons philosophy. As they reflected on their own textual borrowing, almost all of it done thoughtfully, students often slipped into a discourse of guilt. Ben, for example, responded to the question of how dependent he had been on others' texts for his class projects with what sounds like a straightforward comment: "For the most part I've been pretty good. I did use 'Infinity Girl' by Stereolab, and music from the Donnie Darko soundtrack for my audio piece." What is notable about Ben's comment is how he brings a value judgment—"I've been pretty good"—to behavior that is, in the context of his project, an intelligent creative decision. This discourse of guilt, due in no small part to the threats of fines and jail time used by the Recording Industry Association of America to discourage file sharing, was pervasive.

Kathy, a student who had been filming a movie with a group of friends during her spare time, recognized this discourse in an interesting way. In her discussion board post, describing how she downloaded music both for her own listening pleasure and for use in video projects, Kathy wrote: "It's very hard to resist the temptation unless you're actually worried that you'll get caught." Later, when I interviewed Kathy, I read this quote back to her, and asked her why it was so hard to "resist the temptation" to illegally use others' works. Here is her response:

> KATHY: Did I write that, or did someone else write that? Are you sure I wrote that? That doesn't sound like me . . ."why is it hard to resist the temptation?" Well, the way I feel about it, I don't know how other people's ethics work, but when I use those terms like temptation, it sounds like I have hang-ups about it, but I really don't . . . like I think my personal feeling is that people kind of describe more guilt surrounding downloading than they actually have . . . I don't know why I used the word temptation there . . . I feel almost nothing, no remorse at all, except when it's an artist I care about, then I'm like she needs this money, how is she going to make music for me again? Others I don't . . . I just don't, I don't want to get in trouble for it. And maybe temptation was when I was thinking of the movies, the projects, because I was thinking more about getting caught . . . I don't want to get in trouble, which is definitely a possibility.
>
> LD: So "temptation" is a word that only exists in that frame of doing something bad . . .
>
> KATHY: Yeah, normally that word to me makes me think you're going against your conscience and that there's this tempter, and that's not really how I feel about it.

Ben and Kathy's comments reveal something complicated, yet promising. Students doing multimodal composition often use others' texts in very smart ways, but they lack a positive discourse to account for this behavior. Kathy's reflection and honesty in our later interview, however, suggest that students realize the disingenuousness of this discourse; in short, although their first impulse may be to act as if using copyrighted materials is illegal or sneaky behavior, it may be relatively easy to help them shed this discourse. Overall, it would be wise to openly discuss the various metaphors for intellectual property with students, asking them to think through how the property and the commons models fit with their behaviors as producers and consumers of texts.

Of the ten students who participated in the online discussion of copyright, only two expressed an extremely protective, pro-copyright stance. One of these students, Jack, is interesting to compare with Ellen, who had the most commons-oriented attitude toward copyright in the class. Ellen and Jack were both senior English majors, and they both reported spending the same amount of time online, about two hours each day. Ellen spent most of her time at fan fiction sites, and Jack played online video games. Like Ellen and her fan fiction experiences, Jack had also done a lot of creative work that was highly imitative, particularly songwriting, where he would often begin his composing process by borrowing the key or time signature of songs he liked and try to create similar sounding derivatives. But when asked about his attitudes toward intellectual property and authorship, particularly about whether he'd ever use Creative Commons, Jack was surprisingly protective of his work and tentative about using others' texts:

> Honestly right now I wouldn't put something I was trying to get published or looked at up on Creative Commons, because I can shop that thing around to a thousand different publishers; but if someone knows just the right place to go with it, and they take it that's theirs, they'll get it in and it's like whoops, too bad for you. So right now it honestly would make me a little bit uncomfortable to put [something up on Creative Commons] especially being someone very new, and at least trying to get his feet wet in the industry. It's definitely scary to put something up there that someone else might just be like, whish—take it—and you don't get any credit. So yeah, it does make me leery to be honest.

One important difference between Jack and Ellen is that Jack, as an aspiring comic book author, participated in an economy of writing that reinforces the belief that good writing is scarce, and that the confluence of good writing with a publication opportunity is even scarcer. The publication of comics is very much embedded in the print system, where value is connected to scarcity—only the "best books" are published, and an author only sends something out to a publisher when it is complete, as good as he can get it. Jack regularly sent his scripts to small publishers, and he waited patiently, often anxiously, for the slow and mysterious wheels of the print publication system to turn. Like literary writers, Jack was thrilled when he got any feedback on his submissions, and even something as insignificant as a handwritten *Thanks!* on a rejection letter was grounds for celebration. Because the chances of success in this print publication system are so slim, Jack was understandably reluctant to let his texts too far out of his sight, because, he notes, "I don't want anyone else stealing my work and making a profit off of it, or claiming it was their idea."

Ellen, on the other hand, frequently released her own texts into the circulation system of the Web, which she portrayed as a vast space where the impetus to share is stronger than any anxiety she had about people stealing her ideas. She sent her work out into the public arena much more often than Jack, again because the Web facilitates this sort of easy publication. When I pushed her to see if she might have any anxiety about her work being stolen or misused, she said, "I would rather that people not take my stories word for word and post them off as their own. But I guess there's no way I can [know]. The Web is such a huge place. Once you put something out there, it's kind of out of your hands."

Thus, the two different systems of publication and circulation that Ellen and Jack participated in—the Web versus print—exerted a major influence on their attitudes about authors' rights and intellectual property. While Jack saw publication as the last stage in a process that was primarily solitary, and therefore believed posting his creative work to the Web was unnecessarily risking having this finished work stolen, Ellen saw the Web as both a collaborative space and as a very large and content-filled place, where the chance of someone finding her work, let alone taking it, was quite slim. While I'm not suggesting that these are the only two student attitudes related to copyright, the experiences of these students do not seem uncommon. Jack and Ellen, and their allegiance to two different systems of publication and circulation, are representative of two categories of students we are likely to have in our multimodal writing classes.

CONCLUSIONS: WHAT'S A TEACHER TO DO?

Lawrence Lessig's Creative Commons project has met with much enthusiasm because it suggests both a way to *think* about intellectual property, and a way to *act* on this thinking. In effect, the Creative Commons licensing system says, if you believe that none of us creates alone, than acknowledge your debt to others and help their creative processes by licensing your work into the commons. My suggestion for teachers of multimodal composition is to aspire to a similar combination of talk about and opportunities for action related to copyright in their classrooms.

Talking about copyright with students, particularly by seeking information about their experiences and building on those experiences, is likely to yield discussions that touch on many issues of relevance to English studies, including authors' rights, the social nature of composition, the connection between art and profit, and the role of distributors and publishers in the creative process. Hot topics, like file sharing, can be a distraction in such conversations, but not if you can move the discussion into the larger issue of what DeVoss and Porter call "the economies of writing." File sharing can also be a way to talk about the role of distributors in the creative circuit, and the dual potential of the Internet to be either a shopping mall or a living social space.

The actions related to copyright that we encourage students to take can begin on a small scale. First, requiring students to cite all texts they use in their multimodal compositions not only acknowledges the creative debt, it also tends to raise interesting questions, such as whether a Flickr photographer who posted a random photo of a tree would expect to receive credit for her photo. Second, asking students to distribute their products on the Web, and to assign a copyright license to their finished product—either a traditional full copyright or one of the various Creative Commons licenses—requires that students think about how much control they want to exert over the distribution and use of their creative work. It is tempting for teachers of multimodal composition to do just the opposite, to limit the circulation of student texts, so as to keep classroom work within hazy fair use guidelines. Fighting this urge is important.

It is easy as a teacher of multimodal composition to feel a sense of dread at the weight of irrational copyright laws and the attendant possibility of lawsuits. This dread can be compounded if one reflects on the history of copyright law, which Jessica Litman suggests in *Digital Copyright* has taken its shape not via reasoned debate, but rather by business and industry buying the ear of lawmakers to influence policy (23). The suggestions I make herein may seem like mere stones in this dreadful ocean, but helping young people to change the way they talk, think, and act regarding copyright is the best hope for a long-term cultural shift in copyright policy.

128   LISA DUSH

NOTES

1. See: Andrea Lunsford and Susan West, "Intellectual Property and Composition Studies," *College Composition and Communication* 47.3 (1996): 383–411.

2. See: Martha Woodmansee and Peter Jaszi, "The Law of Texts: Copyright in the Academy," *College English* 57.7 (1995): 769–87, and Martha Woodmansee and Peter Jaszi, eds., *The Construction of Authorship: Textual Appropriation in Law and Literature* (Durham, NC: Duke UP, 1994).

3. Laura Gurak and Johndan Johnson-Eilola, eds., *Computers and Composition* 15.2 (1998).

4. See, for example: TyAnna K. Herrington, *Controlling Voices: Intellectual Property, Humanistic Studies, and the Internet* (Carbondale, IL: Southern Illinois UP, 2001), and Siva Vaidhyanathan, *Copyrights and Copywrongs: The Rise of Intellectual Property and How It Threatens Creativity* (New York: New York UP, 2001).

5. To view these films, visit http://creativecommons.org/learnmore

6. See, for example: Lawrence Lessig, *Free Culture: The Nature and Future of Creativity* (New York: Penguin, 2004).

WORKS CITED

Anderson, Daniel. "Prosumer Approaches to New Media: Consumption and Production in Continuum." *Kairos* 8.1 (2003). 12 June 2007 <http://english.ttu.edu/kairos/8.1/binder2.html?http://www.hu.mtu.edu/kairos/CoverWeb/anderson/index.html>.

Bollier, David. "Reclaiming the Commons." *Boston Review* 27.3 (Summer 2002). 12 June 2007 <http://www.bostonreview.net/BR27.3/bollier.html>.

Copyright clause. United States Constitution, Article I, Section 8.

Creative Commons. Creative Commons. 15 June 2005 <http://creativecommons.org>.

DeVoss, Dànielle Nicole, and James E. Porter. "Why Napster Matters to Writing: Filesharing as a New Ethic of Digital Delivery." *Computers and Composition* 23.2 (2005): 178–210.

Goldstein, Paul. *Copyright's Highway: The Law and Lore of Copyright from Gutenberg to the Celestial Jukebox.* New York: Hill & Wang, 1994.

Gurak, Laura, and Johndan Johnson-Eilola, eds. *Computers and Composition* 15.2 (1998).

Herrington, TyAnna K. *Controlling Voices: Intellectual Property, Humanistic Studies, and the Internet.* Carbondale, IL: Southern Illinois UP, 2001.

Lanham, Richard A. *The Electronic Word: Democracy, Technology, and the Arts.* Chicago: U of Chicago P, 1993.

Lessig, Lawrence. *Free Culture: The Nature and Future of Creativity.* New York: Penguin, 2004.

Litman, Jessica. *Digital Copyright.* Amherst, NY: Prometheus Books, 2001.

Lunsford, Andrea, and Susan West. "Intellectual Property and Composition Studies." *College Composition and Communication* 47.3 (1996): 383–411.

Sirc, Geoffrey. "Box-Logic." *Writing New Media: Theory and Applications for Expanding the Teaching of Composition.* Ed. Anne Frances Wysocki, Johndan Johnson-Eilola, Cindy L. Selfe, and Geoffrey Sirc. Logan: Utah State UP, 2004. 111–46.

Trimbur, John. "Composition and the Circulation of Writing." *College Composition and Communication* 52.2 (2000): 188–219.

Vaidhyanathan, Siva. *Copyrights and Copywrongs: The Rise of Intellectual Property and How It Threatens Creativity.* New York: New York UP, 2001.

Westbrook, Steve. "Visual Rhetoric in a Culture of Fear: Impediments to Multimedia Production." *College English* 68.5 (2006): 457–80.

Woodmansee, Martha, and Peter Jaszi. "The Law of Texts: Copyright in the Academy." *College English* 57.7 (1995): 769–87.

Woodmansee, Martha, and Peter Jaszi, eds., *The Construction of Authorship: Textual Appropriation in Law and Literature.* Durham, NC: Duke UP, 1994.

APPENDIX A: METHODS OVERVIEW

The research data for this article was gathered in an elective writing course, called Digital Storytelling, co-taught by myself and a colleague in the English Department of a large public university. Twelve students enrolled in the course, and ten successfully completed the coursework. The students ranged in age from 19–24, and of the final study participants, seven were female, three male. All ten of these students agreed to participate in this research study, which required that they submit all class texts to me, agree to my taking notes on their composition processes, and sit for a post-course interview. The study was approved by the university's human subjects research board prior to its start.

I received a full data set from eight of the ten students, which included the following: the major assignments created for the class; cover letters submitted with the students' photo essays, audio essays, and videos; transcripts from an online (WebCT) discussion forum conducted after we discussed the Creative Commons licensing system as a class (see appendix B); and a final interview transcript. I used the students' individual projects and their responses in the copyright posting to structure a number of specific final interview questions for each, but several questions related to my interest in copyright and authorship were asked of all interviewees (see appendix C).

Data analysis for this study was performed at two important stages: first, prior to writing the final interview questions, and second, after the final interviews. The first round of analysis aimed to identify all student comments in the data collected up to that point that related to my three research questions: 1. Do students have any pre-existing knowledge of and experience with copyright law, and if so, of what sort? 2. Are copyrighted texts important to students' multimodal composition processes and if so, how? and, 3. What discourse and metaphors do students default to when they speak about their composing behaviors with copyrighted texts? Questions tailored to specific students were then added to the final interview protocol.

APPENDIX B: PROMPT PROVIDED FOR STUDENTS' WEBCT DISCUSSION BOARD CHAT ON COPYRIGHT

I. First, skim through a few of these websites . . .

<http://www.archive.org/> The Internet Archive—source for lots of Open Source footage.

<http://www.npr.org/templates/story/story.php?storyId=4582190> Archive of NPR radio story (aired 4/9) on a guy who dubbed a new soundtrack over the Harry Potter movie.

<http://www.illegal-art.org/index.html> Illegal Art—an organization that collects some interesting examples of copyright infringement.

<http://www.illegal-art.org/audio/index.html> The audio page of Illegal Art—can download the Grey Album and some other illegal audio here.

<http://legacy.randomfoo.net/oscon/2002/lessig/> Flash presentation by Lawrence Lessig, important copyright lawyer and guy behind Creative Commons.

<http://www.opsound.org/opsound.html> Open Sound—a site that collects Open Source Music.

<http://www.djspooky.com/index2.html> DJ Spooky's home page. Spooky did an interesting remix of a public domain movie.

II. Write for about 15–20 minutes on the following questions, and/or anything else that seems relevant to legal and ethical issues surrounding using published texts. You can either answer the questions one at a time, or write a response that hits on the most important aspects of the question for you.

What do you know about copyright and the legal rules for copying and using others' works?

In your life as a consumer and producer of texts, in what ways do you ignore, flaunt, or grapple with legal and ethical issues connected to borrowing or stealing others' texts?

For what reasons do you think texts SHOULD be copyright protected?

For what reasons do you think texts SHOULD NOT be copyright protected?

In your own experiences composing digital texts in this class, how dependent upon others' works have you been? Have there been moments when borrowing/altering others' work has raised ethical questions for you? Make reference to specific assignments and moments here . . .

APPENDIX C: FINAL INTERVIEW PROTOCOLS

Questions Asked of All Students

Name

Major

Age

Briefly describe your technical aptitude and experience—do you spend a lot of time on computers? Do you know a lot of software? What websites do you frequent?

Briefly describe your creative interests—do you like to write creatively? What other creative work/activities do you do?

Tell us about how much time you spend "consuming texts" on an average day . . . How much music do you listen to; how often do you watch movies/TV; reading . . .

What do you remember from the day that we looked at the Creative Commons website and discussed copyright?

> Was that the first time you'd talked about the ethics of using others' images/music/text in a classroom setting?
>
> Have you discussed the ethics of file sharing ever, either in a classroom or with friends?
>
> After that discussion, were you any more aware of legal or ethical issues as you downloaded things, either for the projects in this class or otherwise?
>
> Do you use Creative Commons?
>
> Would you post something of yours there?

There's this notion of the "Romantic," inspired author—the genius who labors in solitude to create great art. Emily Dickinson in her room all her life, Wordsworth getting inspired by nature and such. I'm wondering if you subscribe to this notion of writing; that is, do you think writers succeed primarily because of their internal inspiration and solitary labor?

> If no, did you ever believe this?
>
> What, either in school (good peer review experiences, collaborative work, etc.), or in informal settings (friends that you brainstorm with, etc.), shifted your thinking to a belief that writing was a more social practice?
>
> In what ways, when you write (when I say writing here, I mean all kinds—both writing creative written texts, composing sound or video works), do you use other people to help you at various stages of the process? These other people might be peers, or strangers on the Web, or famous people whose texts (written, musical, etc), you use during your process.

Did you find yourself listening to music or looking at images differently during the course . . . wondering, hey, I might be able to use this in a video or an audio piece (I mean here at times when you weren't specifically looking for texts for a project) . . . I'm wondering, now that you know editing software, if you find yourself thinking more about making movies or audio pieces out of texts that already exist.

People who debate copyright and how much control creators should have over the music, text, or art they create use one of two very different metaphors to describe their position. The first is the "property" metaphor, where artistic or intellectual labor is treated like real property—the creator has sole rights over her productions and any unauthorized use is punishable like theft. A rationale here is that an artist's capital is her ideas, and that if these can't be protected, no one would create. The other metaphor is the "intellectual commons" metaphor, which says that no creator creates a work without the help of other texts, that we all need the inspiration, sometimes even the content, of other texts to make our own texts. Thus, texts should have limited restrictions on them, so that they might get swiftly into the commons for others to draw on them. I'm wondering which of these metaphors seems more sensible to you and why.

Sample of Additional, Student-Specific Questions (Ellen)

What is fanart? Fanvids?

What drew/draws you to the fan culture? Why has your involvement lasted for "many years"?

Could fan writers be adverse to press because they don't want their underground community to move above ground, to preserve the pure "undergroundness" (community/exclusive nature) of it?

I'm thinking about what you said about Anne Rice, freaking over fanfic. Do you buy the argument, sometimes expressed by famous writers who don't allow derivative works, that reading fan fiction might color readers' reactions to the original authors' book? For example, do the worlds you read about in fan fiction appear in your head when you read new books by the authors they're based on?

This is a question related to your process . . . based on the pictures in your video . . . I'm wondering about how much editing is an assumed part of your process; that is, when you're taking pictures, do you just assume you'll Photoshop them later? Was there ever a time when you didn't do this?

CHAPTER 7

Ideas Toward a
Fair Use Heuristic

Visual Rhetoric and Composition

MARTINE COURANT RIFE

Visual artists, above all, need a fair use rule that is both flexible
enough and spacious enough to permit them a considerable degree
of appropriation.

— Stephen E. Weil, "Fair Use and the Visual Arts"

In composition studies we should develop a theory of use at the intersection
of copyright and visual rhetoric. Aristotle's concept of *heuristic*, as defined by
Enos and Lauer, offers a generative starting point for this development. While
our scholarship has focused on copyright issues, and has also focused on visual
rhetoric, very little has been written on the intersection of these two important disciplinary areas. John Logie's *Peers, Pirates, and Persuasion: Rhetoric in the
Peer-to-Peer Debates* and Steve Westbrook's "Visual Rhetoric in a Culture of
Fear: Impediments to Multimedia Composition" make important starts at this
intersection, but the topic is overall undeveloped in the field. Mary E. Hocks
develops a heuristic for composing informed by visual rhetoric, but does not
include a discussion of copyright considerations in her three-part analysis.

Likewise, Anne Frances Wysocki outlines implications for teaching and writing in new media that incorporate the visual, but does not include a discussion of legal implications, nor do any of the essays in Carolyn Handa's popular and useful 2004 collection, *Visual Rhetoric in a Digital World*.

In tandem with the growing interest in visual rhetoric is a newfound focus on copyright and composition. In 1997–1998, special issues of *Kairos* and *Computers and Composition* focused on copyright and composition. One of the earliest discussions of copyright and composition appeared in Andrea Lunsford and Lisa Ede's piece exploring collaborative authorship. The authors provided a segue for others in composition to explicitly discuss the implications of fair use and copyright in the teaching of writing. In 1995 Martha Woodmansee, an English professor, and Peter Jaszi, a law professor, wrote an article published in *College English*, "The Law of Texts: Copyright in the Academy." Here they argued for reunification of legal and literary studies, and for opening of conversations. The conversation was continued in the special 1997 issue of *Kairos*, which featured pieces on copyright and composition by TyAnna Herrington and Johndan Johnson-Eilola, among others. Interest and inquiry within composition studies on fair use, copyright, and the relevance of these doctrines to the teaching of writing was further expressed in the special issue of *Computers and Composition*, edited by Gurak and Johnson-Eilola. In this issue, Shirk and Smith, Logie, Walker, and Herrington explicitly referenced and discussed fair use and its implications for composition studies.

Continuing the thread from this special issue of *Computers and Composition*, in 2000, the CCCC-IP Caucus, published its three-page fair use statement, "Use Your Fair Use: Strategies Toward Action," in *College Composition and Communication*. Recent media coverage of the peer-to-peer file sharing cases, along with the fact that hundreds of schools, individuals (including students), and peer-to-peer software distributors have been sued,[1] has understandably rekindled our disciplinary interest. Pieces have appeared by DeVoss and Porter, Porter and Rife, Rife ("Why *Kairos*"), and Logie (*Peers*), focusing on teaching composition and peer-to-peer file sharing issues. While Logie (*Peers*) discusses rhetorical turns taken as peer-to-peer file sharing services and other stakeholders developed ethos through the visual, as yet only Westbrook explicitly connects the dots between visual rhetoric and copyright as these issues impact the teaching of writing. It is from this disciplinary space opened by Westbrook that my chapter begins.

From the standpoint of a composition teacher and scholar, Westbrook examines fair use and the lack of certainty regarding fair use determinations. He argues that copyright law is shaping practice whether we acknowledge it or not. In his research, he uses a case study involving a student whose visual piece was unable to be published since the requisite permissions were denied by the copyright holder. Pointing to the missing student piece in his article, Westbrook writes, "the problem of copyright affects us and our writing students personally on the level of daily practice and, to some degree, underwrites the fundamental norms of our enterprise [. . .]. In brief: copyright law is our problem because it has the power to silence our students and us" (477–78). The author reminds us not to underestimate the power of fear and fear's ability to "silence" writers.

Westbrook makes an important move in his piece where he brings together considerations of visual rhetoric and copyright in a very pragmatic context. The issues he raises are worthy of further exploration, and Enos and Lauer's notion of an Aristotelian heuristic is helpful in developing a start for visual rhetoricians, as well as composition teachers and their students, to critically consider how copyright and fair use should, or might, shape the use of the visual in collages, montages, mashups, and remixes: "Aristotle used the term heuristic to capture the way meaning is cocreated between rhetor and audience [. . .] through this process of interaction, participatory meaning is shared [. . .] [heuristic provides an] operation between rhetor and audience in constructing probable knowledge" (Enos and Lauer 79).

In this chapter I use rhetoric in two ways. First, in a rhetorical analysis, I investigate moves made in court opinions by examining how judges construct probable knowledge in making fair use determinations. Based on a four-factor analysis, judge-authors carefully weigh the factors rather than use the factors as determinate. Second, I use Aristotle's concept of *heuristic* in order to develop a small start for the reader to continue creating probable knowledge when determining whether a use of the visual is likely a fair use. Concentrating not on "inventing techniques to articulate to others," but instead on describing implicitly a *techné* "enabling the rhetor and audience to cocreate meaning" (80), Enos and Lauer explain Aristotle's claims to two kinds of heuristics via proofs, atechnic (inartistic) proofs—those already in existence—and entechnic (artistic) proofs—those that are invented and are the rhetor's *techné*. With respect to a fair use analysis, the four factors of Section 107 can be considered a topoi, or inartistic proof because one uses the preexisting analytical framework by applying it to an existing fact situation. On the other hand, while I attempt explanation of the "inartistic proof" by analyzing how courts have conducted such analyses with the existing four-factor heuristic, at the chapter's end, I also offer a method by which the reader could build a heuristic more along the line of an artistic proof, a heuristic that would be more locally applicable to those in composition studies. Ultimately, the chapter hopes to offer "[a] meaningful rhetorical process" because a fair use analysis in the context of visual rhetoric "begins in a moment of converging forces, a situation in which members of the polis face an irresolute but pressing problem that calls for new meaning and thus compels or occasions a search to develop ever more probable courses of action or explanation" (Enos and Lauer 84).

FAIR USE AND THE CHANCE OF POSITIVE OUTCOMES

Under U.S. law, any work that is original and fixed is automatically copyright protected. Registration is not needed. With respect to copyrighted work, under Section 106 the copyright owner has the exclusive right to reproduce, distribute, perform/display, and make derivative works subject to fair use as set forth in Section 107.[2] Section 107 provides a four-part test, or "four factors" that courts use when determining when a use is "fair" and therefore not copyright infringing. It defines fair use as "reproduction in copies [. . .] or by any other means [. . .] [for uses] such as criticism, comment, news reporting, teaching (including multiple copies for classroom use), scholarship, or research." The first factor of the four examines the "purpose and character of the use," often focusing on whether such use is of a commercial nature or is for nonprofit educational purposes. The second factor looks at the nature of the copyrighted work; nonfiction has less protection than "creative" work. The third factor calculates the amount and substantiality of the portion used in relation to the copyrighted work as a whole, and the fourth considers the effect of the use upon the potential market, often focusing on whether the unauthorized user has impinged on the copyright holder's ability to profit from derivative works (17 U.S.C. Sec. 107).

Fair use analyses are appropriate only when a use is unauthorized, that is, without the copyright holder's permission or without license such as that provided by Creative Commons. Works in the public domain or otherwise not protected by copyright, such as government works and unoriginal works, don't need to be "fair uses" since fair use is triggered only when the use in question is an unauthorized use of a copyrighted work (see Rife, "The Fair Use").

Protected works include notes, web pages, software, computer code, emails, reports, patterns, tutorials, instructions, manuals, visuals, video, audio, and all other "fixed" media. Most material circulating on the Internet is copyright protected. The average cost of defending a copyright infringement lawsuit is just under one million dollars, yet the risk of litigation for educators is low if not nonexistent (Fisher and McGeveran). David Nimmer, a leading intellectual property scholar, conducted a study on copyright cases decided between 1994 and 2002,[3] and found that 90 percent of the time, if three of the four factors are found in favor of fair use, fair use will be found. One cannot generalize his findings, though, because he did not randomly select the sixty cases he examined, nor did he analyze all reported decisions. Overall, of the sixty cases he examined, twenty-four upheld fair use and thirty-six denied it (269–77). Nimmer also analyzed percentage correspondences between each of the four factors and a favorable determination, with correspondences ranging from 42 percent correspondence to factor two, and 57 percent correspondence to factor four, in the context of overall favorable findings. He states that across all four factors, there is a 51 percent correspondence to a favorable legal outcome. Since such calculations can be made in a given context (i.e., legal opinions can be created), reliance on the fair use doctrine is alive and well in for-profit environments. The everyday activities of the Internet rely on fair use. Search engines send out "spiders" that crawl the Web, copying increasingly vast amounts of data that is stored in the search engines' databases. This copying is completed without direct permission of website owners. "In other words, the billions of dollars of market capital represented by the search engine companies are based primarily on the fair use doctrine" (Band). While the cost of violating a copyright holder's rights is high if one is challenged, some relief is offered to writers and/or composers of media via the fair use doctrine.

SPECIAL CONSIDERATIONS FOR THE USE OF VISUALS

As Westbrook and Weil point out, the use of visuals and/or the creation of the visual, raises considerations and issues that are not necessarily present when using another's copyrighted alphabetic texts. Westbrook states that in composition pedagogy, teachers did not necessarily have to engage in the same kind of copyright considerations when their students used or quoted other authors' alphabetic text as they do in the current digital literacy climate and accompanying concentration on visual rhetoric (and subsequent use of the visual). Ironically, in a peer-reviewed *College English* article, Westbrook uses the case of a student-created parody of a Maybelline ad to illustrate his point. Unable to get permissions from the Maybelline advertisement copyright holder for use of the visual incorporated in his student's parody, Westbrook describes with alphabetic text the visual parody—in the space of one robust paragraph. The irony and inadequacy of describing a visual parody with text is central to Weil's argument: "images cannot be adequately defined at all, either by words or by other images" (839). Weil posits that traditional fair use analyses are inadequate for use of the visual, in part because unlike alphabetic text, the visual cannot be adequately described, summarized, paraphrased, or quoted. Instead, one who is critiquing, explaining, or using a visual for research/educational purposes is all but compelled to use the *whole* visual, thus mitigating a finding under the third factor in favor of fair use.

Another reason traditional fair use analyses seem inadequate for the visual is because visual works, unlike alphabetic text, have traditionally incorporated other visual works in their entirety—it is at the essence of the medium to do this. Weil, an emeritus senior scholar in the Smithsonian Institution's Center for Education and Museum Studies, lists examples from the Hirshhorn Museum and Sculpture Garden at the Smithsonian's exhibit *Regarding Beauty*. Artists included Jannis Kounellis, Michelangelo Pistoletto, Yasumasa Morimura, and Cindy Sherman. Upon entering the exhibit, the first six works of art all incorporated other works of art such as "casts of antique sculpture, a series of portraits from the Renaissance, Manet's painting of *Olympia* in its entirety" (836). Other visual work enumerated by Weil, exemplifying how the visual inherently incorporates existing visual works, were the work of Andy Warhol, Nam June Paik's *Video Flag* displaying almost one hundred TV monitors, each showing snippets of newscasts, documentaries, advertisements, and movies: "Outside the museum, in shimmering stainless steel, stood Jeff Koons' six-foot-high *Kiepenkerl*, a work cast directly from a twentieth-century replica of a nineteenth-century bronze sculpture depicting a local tenant farmer that once stood in a square in Munster, Germany" (836). Before the Internet presented a vast array of "the visual," artists incorporated "nature" into their work because that was the material they had to work with. As asserted by California-based collective Negativland, artists are now presented with an entirely new kind of human environment. However, the law that will eventually shape visual art and scholarly work in the current century is yet to be configured. Because of this, composition teachers may have time to shape this law, both by practice, and through research and scholarship.

REVIEW OF KEY CASES INVOLVING COPYRIGHT AND THE VISUAL

The four key cases reviewed here include *Mattel Inc. v. Walking Mountain Productions aka Tom Forsythe* (2003, Ninth Circuit), *Kelly v. Arriba Soft Corp.* (2003, Ninth Circuit), *Video Pipeline, Inc. v. Buena Vista Home Entertainment, Inc.* (2003, Third Circuit), and *Bill Graham Archives v. Dorling Kindersley* (2006,

Second Circuit). Mattel, Kelly, and Graham found in favor of fair use, while Video Pipeline found against fair use. In each case the court reviewed the four factors, creating what Enos and Lauer might define as an inartistic proof; the court decisions when taken as a whole might inform composition teachers and scholars in constructing probable knowledge under a more organic approach, or an artistic proof, regarding fair use and visual rhetorical issues. By reviewing these cases, I hope to inform the field so that it might develop a *techné* for doing these same kinds of analyses.

Mattel v. Walking Mountain

In the two Ninth Circuit cases, *Mattel v. Walking Mountain* and *Kelly v. Arriba Soft*, the court found in favor of fair use. In both cases, the court referred to the spirit of copyright law. The *Mattel* opinion acknowledges that copyright law is applied with the knowledge that "science and art generally rely on works that came before them and rarely spring forth in a vacuum [. . .] few, if any, things [. . .] are strictly new and original throughout. Every book in literature, science and art, borrows, and must necessarily borrow" (18177). In *Mattel*, artist Tom Forsythe, aka Walking Mountain Productions, was sued by Mattel for copyright and trademark infringement of Mattel's Barbie. Forsythe, a political activist of sorts, used naked Barbie dolls in pictures (made into postcards, business cards, and a website) stating his purpose was to critique the objectification of women in our society. Barbie stood as an ultimate icon and the "most enduring of those products that feed on the insecurities of our beauty- and perfection-obsessed consumer culture." He created about seventy-eight visuals of Barbie, many of which showed Barbie threatened by kitchen appliances. Examples of his work include an image of a nude Barbie doll stuffed in an empty champagne glass; four naked Barbies rolled in tortilla shells, covered in salsa, set in a stainless steel pan ready for oven baking; Barbies stuffed into blenders; and so on. He made a total of about $4,000.00 profit on the venture, half of which came from Mattel's purchase of items for purposes of litigation.

Regarding the first factor, purpose and character of the use, the key determination turned on whether or not the use was parodic, since the court noted that in the Ninth Circuit, parodic works are protected under fair use as long as it is reasonably certain that the parodic nature of a work can be easily discerned. In refutation of this, Mattel presented random persons at a shopping mall with Forsythe's pictures and asked them to note the image's meaning. Most shoppers were not able to do this. However, the court stated that it would not consider Mattel's shopping mall evidence, since whether or not a work is parodic is not a matter of public opinion, but is instead a matter of law. Interestingly, I have frequently use Forsythe's picture in PowerPoints in my writing classroom in order to help students think critically—and they too struggle with identifying and interpreting exactly what critique Forsythe captures in his pictures; however, my students have difficultly articulating the parodic nature of *any* visual parody presented to them until we read and discuss these issues. They understand that the visuals are humorous, but exactly what the political or cultural critique means is a matter of rather sophisticated interpretation. In this regard, it was smart for the court to ignore Mattel's shopping evidence both because it is unlikely that a member of the general public is thinking in a way sophisticated enough to discern "parody" at a moment's notice, and one surely cannot argue that Mattel's shopping mall survey was done with any scientific or reliable methodology (although the court ignored this point). The court decided that the parodic nature of Forsythe's visuals was reasonably apparent, and such use weighed in favor of fair use on the first factor.[4]

On the second factor, nature of the copyrighted material, the court recognized that Barbie was a creative endeavor and, as such, weighed this factor slightly against fair use. On the third factor, amount and substantiality of the portion used, the court found this weighed in favor of Forsythe, even though he used the entire doll in his images. The important point here for the court was that Forsythe radically changed Barbie in the images he depicted—she was completely out of her traditional context as the all-American girl, parts of her were sometimes obscured, and in contradiction to Mattel's arguments, the court stated that Forsythe could not have used a lesser portion of Barbie and accomplished the same end results. In the words of the court, "Mattel's argument that Forsythe could have used a lesser portion of the Barbie doll is completely without merit and would lead to absurd results. We do not require parodic works to take the absolute minimum amount of the copyrighted work possible" (18185).

On the fourth factor, effect on potential market, the court stated that since Forsythe's images depicted Barbie in highly sexualized positions, and in parody, it was very unlikely Mattel would ever develop a market for the use of Barbie in this fashion. The court also dismissed Mattel's argument that such depiction lessened the value of Barbie, claiming this assertion was without merit. According to the court, the fourth factor did not consider lessening the value of a copyrighted work because of critique. Adding to its analysis of this factor, the court went on:

Finally, the public benefit in allowing artistic creativity and social criticism to flourish is great. The fair use exception recognizes this important limitation on the rights of the owners of copyrights. No doubt, Mattel would be less likely to grant a license to an artist that intends to create art that criticizes and reflects negatively on Barbie's image. It is not in the public's interest to allow Mattel complete control over the kinds of artistic works that use Barbie as a reference for criticism and comment. (18188)

Ultimately, the court found fair use in this case because three of the four factors weighed in favor of Forsythe's use.

Kelly v. Arriba Soft

In *Kelly v. Arriba Soft*, the court found that a search engine's use of lower-resolution thumbnail images was a fair use of artist Leslie Kelly's full-size images. (Arriba also used full-sized images in an in-line linking context). Kelly is a photographer who takes pictures of the West. His pictures are posted on his website. Arriba runs a for-profit search engine that uses thumbnails for users to locate material on the Web. Its software crawls the Web and obtains images that are then used in the search engine. When Kelly learned that Arriba had used his images as thumbnails, he asked Arriba to remove the images, and Arriba did. Arriba also blocked its crawlers from obtaining further images from Kelly's website. Subsequently, Arriba received a complaint for copyright infringement from Kelly because Arriba had additional thumbnails obtained by its crawlers from third-party websites in use on its search engine. Arriba subsequently removed those images as well.

Weighing the four factors, the court found that because Arriba operated a commercial search engine and used the images in this fashion, the first factor weighed slightly against fair use. The mitigating fact was that Arriba's use changed and transformed the images, making them smaller and lower resolution. The images served a completely different function than Kelly's photographs since Arriba used the thumbnails for indexing rather than for artistic purposes. A user, according to the court, would be unlikely to use the images for artistic purposes because of their poor resolution. The court also noted that Arriba's use of the images was in the spirit of the copyright act because this use enhanced the public's ability to locate information on the Internet—thus promoting public exchange and creativity. On the second factor, nature of the copyrighted work, the court admitted that Kelly's work was creative, but because the work was already posted on the Internet by Kelly, this only weighed slightly against fair use.

On the third factor, amount and substantiality of the portion used, the court again stated that even though Arriba used entire images, this did not weigh against fair use because there was no other way to guide users to the correct location. If Arriba had only used part of the images, users could have become confused, thus lessening the value of the visual search engine.

On the final factor, effect on the potential market, the court explained how Kelly obtained fees from advertisers and from selling items marketed on his website. Arriba's search engine led users to Kelly's website. While the court did not go so far as to assert that Arriba enhanced Kelly's market, it did state that because of the low resolution of the thumbnails, Arriba did not impinge on Kelly's market for the photographs, and did not otherwise compete with Kelly's existing markets: "In addition, we note that in the unique context of photographic images, the quality of the reproduction may matter more than in other fields of creative endeavor. The appearance of photographic images accounts for virtually their entire aesthetic value" (23n37). It was important to the court that Arriba did not sell images, but simply operated as a search engine. The court thus found Arriba's use of the thumbnails to be a fair use; however, the court did not decide whether Arriba's use of larger images in online linking was "fair" because, it said, neither party had raised the issue.

Video Pipeline v. Buena Vista

Video Pipeline v. Buena Vista was argued before the Third Circuit Court of Appeals on January 21, 2003, and the opinion filed August 26, 2003. The facts were that Video Pipeline and Disney entered into an agreement whereby Video Pipeline marketed Disney movie trailers. Video Pipeline was in the business of compiling movie trailers into videotape and distributing those for commercial gain to home video retailers. The home video retailers then displayed the compiled movie trailers in their stores in order to encourage customers to purchase movies. Video Pipeline entered in contracts with many entertainment companies and had been doing business with Disney since 1988. During those years, Disney had given Video Pipeline over five hundred trailers. In 1997, Video Pipeline took its business to the Web, providing trailers through its website. Retailers such as Amazon.com, Best Buy, and Yahoo paid the company a fee based on megabytes viewed, where Web customers could click on a link through the retailers' website and view the streaming trailers. Customers were unable to download the trailers due to their streaming nature. Video Pipeline maintained trailers in a database accessible through VideoPipeline.net, but also maintained a website where people could research movies: VideoDetective.com. The Detective website allowed users to search based on a variety of search terms, and also linked to retailer websites where users could purchase movies. VideoDetective.com also ran contests where users who correctly guessed the title to a movie after watching the trailer could win prizes.

After Video Pipeline began its Web operation, Disney requested that the company remove the Disney trailers because the parties' contract did not allow for such use. Video Pipeline complied. Subsequently, in 2000, Video Pipeline filed for declaratory relief in the District Court of New Jersey, requesting a declaration that use of the Disney trailers was not a copyright violation. Meanwhile, Video Pipeline created its own clip previews of Disney movies to use on its Web applications. The clips differed from Disney trailers because they were only visual and did not include sound, voiceover, editing, or narration as did the Disney trailers; however, the Video Pipeline clips opened with a display of Miramax or Disney trademark, then a short preview from the beginning of the movie, closing with the title. Video offered these clips online just as it had with the Disney trailers. Simultaneously, Disney provided its authorized trailers on its own website for "stickiness," a term used to describe the strategy of attracting and keeping customers on a website.

In the lower district court, an injunction preventing Video Pipeline from showing the Disney clips was entered, and Video Pipeline appealed. The issue before the Third Circuit was whether or not Video Pipeline's creation and use of the movie clips was a fair use under Section 107. After noting that each of the four factors must be carefully balanced and weighed, the court found with respect to the first factor, purpose and character of the use, the use was commercial since Video Pipeline received a fee for users' rights to view the clips. However, the court said this alone did not determine the outcome of the first factor. The other consideration was whether Video Pipeline's use was different than either the movie trailers or the movies (both being copyrighted), and in this case the court found it was not. The clips were not transformative: "Whatever informational or promotional character and purpose the trailers possess, so do the clip previews" (10). While Video Pipeline argued that its use was similar to the use of thumbnails in *Kelly v. Arriba*, simply a use of indexing and referring to the entire copyrighted work, the court stated that Video Pipeline's use was not similar to Arriba's because in *Kelly*, the thumbnails were used to refer users to full-sized images, which were legally availably elsewhere on the Internet. VideoPipeline.net, unlike *Kelly v. Arriba Soft*, indexed and displayed unauthorized copies of copyrighted works, according to the court. Finally, the court agreed with the District Court and found the first factor to weigh against fair use because the two-minute clips created by Video Pipeline did not add significantly to Disney's original expression. The court also distinguished Video Pipeline's clips from a traditional movie review, in that a movie review, by critiquing and commenting on the movie, adds expression, meaning, and message to an original work. Here, the clips simply duplicated what was already present in the original expression.

Citing *Campbell v. Acuff*,[5] the court noted that with respect to the second factor, nature of the copyrighted work, it is generally accepted that "some works are closer to the core of intended copyright protection than others" (12). Citing *Harper & Row*[6] as well, the court noted that factual work receives less protection than creative or fictional work. It listed movies such as *Pretty Woman, Fantasia*, and *Beauty and the Beast* as examples of creative work. While Video Pipeline argued that this factor weighed in favor of fair use because Disney had already released the movies to the public, the court stated that whether a work is published or unpublished is a consideration under factor two, but not determinative. Because the Disney movies were considered by the court to be creative, this factor was found to weigh against fair use (upholding the district court finding).

The third factor requires the court to examine the amount and substantiality of the portion used in relation to the whole, and unlike the district court, the Third Circuit found that this factor weighed in favor of fair use. The court agreed with Video Pipeline that quantitatively, the use of two or three minutes of the original movie was proportionately small; it nonetheless revealed significant aspects of the film such as characters, plot, and tone. But, the clips were only taken from the first couple scenes of the movies, and did not reveal the endings. Therefore, the court decided that since the clips did not reveal the "heart" of the movies, this factor weighed in favor of fair use.

Again relying on *Campbell*, the court examined the fourth factor, the effect on potential market of the copyright holder. Quoting *Campbell*, the court stated that it had to take into account not only the harm to the original, "but also harm to the market for derivative works" (14). Video Pipeline argued that this factor weighed in favor of fair use because no one would ever pay to see a movie trailer—although Disney had produced its own movie trailers. But the court stated that Video Pipeline's view of market value was too narrow since it only considered direct profits. Disney had a deal with Apple Computers that allowed mutually beneficial cross-linking. The court thus held that Video Pipeline's clips could compete directly with Disney's trailers, and thus this factor weighed against a finding of fair use. Noting that three of the four factors weighed against Video Pipeline's "fair use," the court upheld the District Court injunction preventing Video Pipeline from show-ing its clips.

Bill Graham Archives v. Dorling Kindersley

On May 9, 2006, in *Bill Graham Archives v. Dorling Kindersley*, the Second Circuit upheld the lower court's decision, finding the use of several Grate-ful Dead poster images appearing in a band biography was a "fair use." In the case, the publisher Dorling Kindersley used, without permission, seven images of Grateful Dead concert posters or tickets in the book *Grateful Dead: The Illustrated Trip* (2003).[7] Prior to the book's publication, the publisher had unsuccessfully attempted to negotiate permissions with the copyright holder, Bill Graham Archives. Due to what the publisher perceived as an unreason-able licensing fee, permission agreements were never reached. Nonetheless, the publisher used the seven images in the book, incorporating them into remixed compositions, consisting of collages mixed with graphic art and tex-tual explanations and commentary. Over two thousand total images were used in the book, only seven of which came from the Graham Archives collection. After the book's publication, Bill Graham Archives brought suit for copyright infringement and requested an injunction from further publication.

With respect to the first factor, the use of the Grateful Dead images was transformative since the images were used in a timeline and for historical purposes rather than for the posters' original purposes of concert promotion. Notably, *Illustrated Trip* was a biography, while the posters were for concert promotion. According to the court, this created a strong presumption in favor of fair use. In educational contexts, we often hear statements that if a use is nonprofit, then it will be presumed to be a fair use. In this case, how-ever, the court made clear that if a use is different in nature to the intended use of the original material, that too may create a strong presumption in favor of fair use.

As a counterargument, BGA argued that placing the images along a time-line was not transformative, and that, additionally, each image should have had some kind of commentary or criticism in order to be a fair use. The court denied this, noting that a thirty-year biography of the Grateful Dead served very different purposes than those of the original posters—concert promo-tion. The court also noted that biographical use of copyrighted material is fre-quently supported as a fair use because it allows for commentary, research, and

criticism, as stated in the preamble of Section 107, language introducing the
four fair use factors. "Remix" wasn't used in the opinion as a term; however,
the court noted that "to further this collage effect, the images are displayed at
angles and the original graphical artwork is designed to blend with the images
and text [. . .]. DK's layout ensure that the images . . . are employed only to
enrich the presentation of the cultural history of the Grateful Dead, not to
exploit the copyright artwork for commercial gain" (12). Still discussing the
first factor, the court listed the exact size of the seven images, and noted that
DK's images amounted to less than one-twentieth of the original size (even
though entire images were used). Here, the court also noted the percentage of
total copyrighted material used within a subsequent text was not determinative, citing *Harper* and *Salinger*, neither of which found fair use. In *Harper*, the
infringing material was only 13 percent of the entire copyrighted piece, while
in *Salinger*, 40 percent of the subsequent work consisted of Salinger's quoted
or paraphrased letters. On the issue of DK's commercial use of the images, the
court noted that BGA's images were not used to promote the book, and the
images' use was incidental to the commercial biographical value of the book.

With respect to the second, third, and fourth factors (which together took
up less than half the opinion, since, as should be obvious, many of these last
three factors were addressed when the court examined "purpose and character"), the Second Circuit agreed with the lower court that the "nature of
the copyrighted work" factor weighed against fair use, since the posters were
creative in nature. However, the court found this factor of limited use since
the posters were not used to exploit their creative nature, but were instead
used for historical purposes. On the third factor, "amount and substantiality
of the portion used," the court admitted that entire images were used. Yet,
the court decided that entire images had to be used in this instance in order
to communicate the history of the band. Reducing the images, was deemed
sufficient to overcome the presumption against fair use.

And finally, on the fourth factor, the court stated that Dorling's use did
not harm the potential market because no actual market harm was sustained,
and, in this case, the court would not find market harm based on "hypotheti-
cal loss" of revenue. The court stated that even though licensing was available,
DK could still operate under fair use. Here, the court notes that the book was
not commercially successful, but if it had been, it may even have increased the
potential market for the posters. Nonetheless, the present use did not supersede
the market for the copyrighted work, nor did it serve as a substitute. Citing
Campbell, the court stated that "a publisher's willingness to pay license fees for
reproduction of images does not establish that the publisher may not, in the

alternative, make fair use of those images" (21). In other words, the availability of licensing does not necessarily preclude fair use protections under the statute. The court therefore found in favor of fair use on this factor as well—thus stating that in balancing the four factors, DK's use of the images was a fair use.

CONCLUSIONS: TOWARD A FAIR USE HEURISTIC

Each of these courts carefully considered the four factors of the fair use doctrine in a rather formal fashion, aligning with what Enos and Lauer might describe as an inartistic proof. But moving beyond this, can one use the methodology of the artistic proof to extrapolate a more refined heuristic that might be applicable to educational contexts?

Obviously, since critical elements of a fair use analysis consider the nature of the use (commercial versus educational), and whether the use of a copyrighted work negatively impacts the potential market for the copyright holder, "fair use" applies differently to writers in for-profit environments than it does to writers in academia. Still, whether or not a use is nonprofit or for-profit is only one consideration that courts make in deciding these kinds of cases. This fact should be clarified in the context of disciplinary misunderstandings that generalize to the extent any educational use is automatically fair. (Rife and Hart-Davidson found some indication of this belief in a recent study.)

Going beyond the four-factor test, we might find something fruitful in these four opinions when taken as a whole. All of the opinions uphold the concept that one should use others' materials thoughtfully and sparingly, but that using entire images is not necessarily prohibited as long as the images are substantially transformed through that use. Images are adequately transformed when they are remixed with graphic art, text, and additional images as in *Graham*, used for social criticism as in *Forsythe*, or used to help viewers find additional information, as in *Kelly*. In each of these cases, the copyrighted work was appropriated for use in very different contexts than those envisioned by the copyright holder. All opinions pointed to the importance of taking care when using another's *creative* work. Writers might develop a tacit awareness of the kind of works they intend to appropriate—incorporating someone's visual metaphor is less likely to be a fair use than incorporating someone's straightforward depiction of an artifact or event. On the issue of permissions, *Graham* was the strongest of the opinions in its reiteration that there is no requirement to ask permission every time. In that case, permission had been offered, but at an unreasonable price. In *Forsythe*, the court decided that because of the parodic nature of the work, Mattel would have been unlikely to give

permissions anyway. Permissions were not considered germane in either the
Video Pipeline or *Kelly* cases. Permissions were beside the point. Thus, I think
that in light of the importance that those of us in education, including our
students, have access to the materials making up our current human-visual
environment, we should not ask permissions every time. In his book, Logie,
who incorporated for comment and illustration several visuals, clearly states
his position in the appendix: "While I have done my best to identify and
acknowledge the copyright holders for these images, I have determined not
to seek permission for these obviously fair uses" (149).

Another key point to extract from these opinions is that the more synthesis
that takes places after the appropriation, the more likely a use is to be determined a "fair use." Video Pipeline did nothing to transform the Disney clips,
not even simple editing, narration, nor any kind of commentary or review. In
Graham, the copyrighted images were juxtaposed with text, commentary, and
other images, forming what we would call a remix. Forsythe's use of Barbie
was likewise well synthesized. Even though Forsythe, Arriba Soft, and Graham
used entire images, those images were so distorted and transformed from the
original, that they created something "new." In these three cases, the use of the
images was at odds with the intended use imagined by the copyright holder—
another weight in favor of fair use. According to these opinions, one might
plausibly argue that the more synthesis a remix accomplishes, the more likely
any uses of copyrighted material it contains will be deemed fair uses. This
seems much like what we have been wishing our students would do, regardless
of the medium within which they are working: we want them to take multiple viewpoints and perspectives and synthesize those. We want them to insert
themselves into larger conversations via analysis and synthesis. We want them
to develop their own theories of the world. It seems to me those old adages
encouraging students to make their work their own still applies, even more so
when it comes to incorporating the visual. In this digital-visual age, we have
even more compelling reasons for stressing synthesis and ownership of student
work in light of the application of copyright law to our everyday practices.

We might, through the *techné* of the artistic proof, generalize and extract
some basic guidelines from these four opinions for use in composition and
composition pedagogy. This heuristic might be summarized as follows:

Fair Use Heuristic for Use of the Visual

1. As to individuals or organizations who insist you ask *permission every
   time: this is simply not required under the fair use doctrine* (with the caveat that

if you are working with a publisher who insists on permissions, you may have little room for negotiation.)

2. If you are going to use another's copyrighted image, use as little as possible (either in size, amount, or pixels) in order to accomplish your own writerly goals, but do not be afraid to *use what you need to make your point.*

3. *Always work to synthesize.* Remixing another's materials with bits and pieces you have created yourself, as well as more than one outside author's work, will make your use more likely to be a fair use.

4. If you, yourself, are making something purely "creative" (a digital poem, movie, art), and using another's material that is also "creative," your use is less likely to be considered fair. But *if you are taking a position on an issue, or creating a history or documentary meant to comment and criticize an issue or events, your use may be more likely to be fair, even if the copyrighted materials you remix are creative.*

5. Remember the old adage: *Make sure what you create is "your own" work.* This means shaping and fashioning your final piece, so that you take ownership of it and make a statement different than the copyright holder.

6. If you move your work from educational, nonprofit contexts into commercial environments, you will certainly have to reevaluate the fairness of your use. *There is some evidence that the tipping point in court decisions is three out of four factors.* If your use changes such that the scales tip against you, you could end up in an uncomfortable position.

7. *Don't underestimate the power of good faith.* The court found for Arriba Soft. Remember, the company took down the images when asked to do so but was sued anyway. Arriba Soft was "good." In contrast, Video Pipeline could be deemed a "bad" party because it instituted the litigation by requesting declaratory relief that it was not infringing—a dangerous and tricky move. Unless you are a political trailblazer, like Forsythe (who also had the financial backing of the ACLU), you might want to heed warnings to cease and desist, or risk an expensive lawsuit. Careful balancing of the costs and benefits here is important.

As stated earlier, according to Fisher and McGeveran, educators are not being sued in the visual-use contexts discussed in this chapter. While Cornell University is rumored to be the first to control digital/electronic content by way of an official policy, I have yet to witness a case where a student was sued for using a visual in his or her digital portfolio or parody, or where a teacher was sued for using student writing in his or her academic journal article, such as the context in Westbrook's piece. Of course, it *could* happen. But since the relatively new technology of the Web and our disciplinary interest in visual rhetoric have not yet caused legal restrictions on use to solidify, we still have a space to shape law by practice. Understanding these issues along with our students is a good starting point. I think the more we learn about fair use and its application to visual rhetoric, especially through our very clever rhetorical lenses, the less likely fear of infringement will silence any of us.

NOTES

1. See Katherine M. Lieb's piece, listed in the works cited, for a full comparative discussion between legal events in the music industry and those in the visual images industry.

2. Section 106, Title 17 of the U.S. Code, the copyright law, outlines the basic rights provided to a copyright holder. However, several other sections of the code speak to very specific uses that are outside the normal purview of composition teachers—for example, there's a special section on archiving for librarians. It's worth mentioning here that there's also a special section, Section 106A for a "work of visual art," but it has extremely limited application and I will therefore not discuss this section of the law in detail. Application is limited because "work of visual art" is defined in Section 101, the definition section of the law, as a "painting, drawing, print, or sculpture, existing in a single copy" or limited to two hundred or fewer copies, and each copy must be consecutively numbered by the author and signed. Therefore, content on the Internet will not fall under this definition. The coverage of Section 106A is commonly known as VARA (Visual Artists Rights Act). It gives a right to only the authors of "works of visual arts" and is not transferable to copyright holders even if the artist transfers his or her copyrights in a piece of art. The purpose for VARA is mainly political in that the United States enacted it in order to have some argument that it is in compliance with international intellectual property treatises that require "moral rights." Moral rights are legal rights that require attribution, right of publication, and right to integrity in work. The United States does not have "moral rights" in its legal regime in this sense. The U.S. ethic of plagiarism is similar to other countries' legal regimes of "moral rights."

3. His idea was to generally survey the top sixty cases that occurred after the last Supreme Court opinion on fair use, *Campbell v. Acuff*, 1994. Nimmer's article was published in 2003, so his data does not include cases after 2002.

4. The section of the Mattel opinion where the court discusses the first factor also contains an excellent definition and analysis of "parody."

5. *Campbell* involved the use of Roy Orbison's song "Pretty Woman" by 2 Live Crew. In that supreme court case, the court discussed fair use in detail, but ultimately sent the case back to the lower court for a determination of whether there was impact on the copyright holder's market.

6. *Harper & Row* was another supreme court case that decided fair use. In the case, *Nation* scooped Harper & Row by publishing a tiny excerpt from President Gerald Ford's memoirs before the Harper & Row publication came out. The court balanced the four factors and found that in this case, the use was not fair.

7. My discussion in this section on the *Graham* case is condensed and excerpted in part from an informal Web piece I wrote through the IP Caucus's annual case reviews, "Remix as 'Fair Use': Grateful Dead Posters' Re-publication Held to Be a Transformative, Fair Use," listed in the works cited.

WORKS CITED

Band, Jonathan. The Google Print Library Project: A Copyright Analysis. 2005. 30 May 2007 <http://www.policybandwidth.com/doc/googleprint.pdf>.

Bill Graham Archives v. Dorling Kindersley Limited, et al. USCA (Second Circuit.2006). <http://fairuse.stanford.edu/primary_materials/cases/GrahamKindersley.pdf>.

Campbell v. Acuff-Rose Music, Inc. 510 U.S. 569, 583–585. (1994). <http://supct.law. cornell.edu/supct/html/92–1292.ZS.html>.

CCCC-IP Caucus. "Use Your Fair Use: Strategies Toward Action." *College Composition and Communication* 51.3 (2000): 485–88.

Copyright Law of the United States. 2003. 17 May 2007 <http://www.copyright. gov/title17/>.

"Cornell University and Publishers Announce New Copyright Guidelines Governing Use of Digital Course Materials." Cornell University Press Relations Office. 19 Sept. 2006. 15 May 2007 <http://pressoffice.cornell.edu/Sept06/AAPCopyright.shtml>.

DeVoss, Dànielle Nicole, and James E. Porter. "Why Napster Matters to Writing: Filesharing as a New Ethic of Digital Delivery." *Computers and Composition* 23.2 (2005): 178–210.

Enos, Richard Leo, and Janice M. Lauer. "The Meaning of Heuristic in Aristotle's Rhetoric and Its Implications for Contemporary Rhetorical Theory." *A Rhetoric of Doing: Essays on Written Discourse in Honor of James L. Kinneavy.* Ed. Stephen P. Witte, Neil Nakadate, Roger D. Cherry. Carbondale: Southern Illinois UP, 1992. 37–44.

Fisher, William W., and William McGeveran. "The Digital Learning Challenge: Obstacles to Educational Uses of Copyright Material in the Digital Age." A Foundational White Paper. The Berkman Center for Internet & Society at Harvard Law School. Research Publication No. 2006–09. (Aug. 2006.). 18 Nov. 2006 <http://cyber.law.harvard.edu/home/research_publication_series>.

Gurak, Laura J., and Johndan Johnson-Eilola, eds. Intellectual Property. Special issue of *Computers and Composition* 15.2 (1998).

Handa, Carolyn. Visual Rhetoric in a Digital World: A Critical Sourcebook. Boston: Bedford/St. Martin's, 2004.

Harper & Row, Publishers, Inc. v. Nation Enters. 471 U.S. 539, 589–90. (1985). <http://caselaw.lp.findlaw.com/scripts/getcase.pl?court=US&vol=471&invol=539>.

Herrington, TyAnna K. "The Interdependency of Fair Use and the First Amendment." *Computers and Composition* 15. 2 (1998): 125–43.

———. "The Unseen 'Other' of Intellectual Property Law or Intellectual Property Is Not Property: Debunking the Myths of IP Law." *Kairos.* Spring 1997. 27 Mar. 2007 <http://kairos.technorehtoric.net/3.1/coverweb/ty/kip.html>.

Hocks, Mary E. "Understanding Visual Rhetoric in Digital Writing Environments." *College Composition and Communication* 54.4 (2003): 629–656.

Hunter, Robert, Stephan Peters, Chuck Wills, and Dennis McNally. *Grateful Dead: The Illustrated Trip.* London: DK Adult, 2003.

Johnson-Eilola, Johndan. "Intellectual Property: Questions and Answers." *Kairos* 3.1 (1997). 30 May 2007<http://www.kairos.technorhetoric.net/3.1/coverweb/johndan.html>.

Kelly v. Arriba Soft Corp. 336 F. 3d 811 (Ninth Circuit 2003).

Lieb, Katherine M. "Can the Television and Movie Industries Avoid the Copyright Battles of the Recording Industry? Fair Use and Visual Works on the Internet." *Washington University Journal of Law and Policy* 17 (2005): 233–58.

Logie, John. "Champing at the Bits: Computers, Copyright, and the Composition Classroom. *Computers and Composition* 15 (1998): 201–14.

———. *Peers, Pirates, and Persuasion.* West Lafayette, IN: Parlor Press, 2006.

Lunsford, Andrea, and Lisa Ede. "Collaborative Authorship and the Teaching of Writing." *The Construction of Authorship: Textual Appropriation in Law and Literature.* Ed. Martha Woodmansee and Peter Jaszi. Durham and London: Duke UP (1994). 417–38.

Negativland. "Fair Use." n.d. 14 May 2007. <http://www.negativland.com/fairuse.html>.

Nimmer, David. "'Fairest of Them All' and Other Fairy Tales of Fair Use." *Law and Contemporary Problems* 66 (2003): 263–87.

Porter, James E., and Martine Courant Rife. *MGM v. Grokster*: implications for educators and writing teachers. WIDEpaper Series. Paper #1. 28 June 2005. 17 May 2007 <http://www.wide.msu.edu/widepapers/grokster/>. Republished in NCTE-CCCC online <http://www.ncte.org/cccc/gov/committees/ip/125704.htm>.

Rife, Martine Courant. "Remix as 'Fair Use': Grateful Dead Posters' Re-publication Held to Be a Transformative, Fair Use." *Major Intellectual Property Developments of 2006.* (2007). <http://www.ncte.org/cccc/gov/committees/ip/>.

———. "The Fair Use Doctrine: History, Application, and Implications for (New Media) Writing Teachers." *Computers and Composition.* 24.2 (2007): 105–226.

————. "Why *Kairos* Matters to Writing: A Reflection on Our Intellectual Property Conversation During the Last Ten Years." *Kairos* Tenth Anniversary Issue, 11.1 (2006) <http://english.ttu.edu/KAIROS/ 11.1/ binder.html?topoi/rife/index.html>.

Rife, Martine Courant, and William Hart-Davidson. "Digital Composing and Fair Use: Exploring Knowledge and Understanding of Fair Use Among Teachers and Students in a University Professional Writing Program." Pilot study report. SSRN Working Paper Series (1996). <http://papers.ssrn.com/sol3/papers.cfm?abstract_id=918822>.

Salinger v. Random House, Inc. 811 F.2d 90 (Second Circuit). (1987) <http://www.law.cornell.edu/copyright/cases/811_F2d_90.htm>.

Shirk, Henrietta Nickels, and Howard Taylor Smith. "Emerging Fair Use Guidelines for Multimedia: Implications for the Writing Classroom." *Computers and Composition* 15 (1998): 229–41.

Video Pipeline, Inc. v. Buena Vista Home Entertainment, Inc. 342 F. 3d 191 (Third Circuit 2003), cert. denied, 124 S.Ct. 1410 (2004).

Walker, Janice R. (1998). "Copyrights and Conversations: Intellectual Property in the Classroom." *Computers and Composition* 15 (1998): 243–51.

Weil, Stephen E. "Fair Use and the Visual Arts, or Please Leave Some Room for Robin Hood." *Ohio State Law Journal* 62 (2001): 835–47.

Westbrook, Steve. "Visual Rhetoric in a Culture of Fear: Impediments to Multimedia Production. *College English* 68.5 (2006): 457–80.

Woodmansee, Martha, and Peter Jaszi. "The Law of Texts: Copyright in the Academy." *College English* 57 (1995): 769–87.

Wysocki, Anne Frances. "The Multiple Media of Texts: How Onscreen and Paper Texts Incorporate Words, Images, and Other Media." *What Writing Does and How It Does It: An Introduction to Analyzing Texts and Textual Practices*. Ed. Charles Bazerman and Paul Prior. New Jersey: Lawrence Erlbaum Associates, 2004. 123–63.

CHAPTER 8

Blogging Down

Copyright Law and Blogs in the Classroom

TYANNA HERRINGTON

Composition instructors continue to take advantage of developments in technology to provide their students with means and motivation to improve communication. A current trend is to use weblogs, popularly called blogs, as a genre for student writing development. Regardless of the potential benefit of classroom blogging, the opportunity for global accessibility of blogs, coupled with student authorship, creates a need for instructor awareness of intellectual property law and its relationship to student blog writing.

It is fitting that the Constitution's intellectual property clause (Copyright Clause) supports learning as its highest goal. The driving policy behind the provision presents a means for intellectual development and progress in a democratic, egalitarian society by establishing a limited monopoly in intellectual products to allow society to use information, build on that knowledge, and benefit from it. The constitutional provision is designed to make this possible by generating an incentive in authors to create new intellectual products. The policy of the intellectual property clause supports educational advancement and, by relationship to the rest of the Constitution, democratic dialog and free speech. The policy makes clear that the heart of intellectual property law is the heart of the democratic process.[1]

Regardless of the policy behind the intellectual property clause, most conflicts between parties are focused on areas of law rather than policy. Federal statutory law provides explicit treatment of intellectual products in areas of legal conflict and classifies protection for intellectual work in patents, trade secret, trademark, and copyright. Since student blogs would be protected by copyright; copyright law is the focus of the following discussion. Where constitutional intellectual property policy supports learning, the law of intellectual property provides structure for treating conflicts that arise between or among parties making claims to intellectual products. Students who develop blogs, whether in or out of a classroom, are creators of copyrighted works that could be the subject of intellectual property conflicts treated by law. Considering both statutory and case law, this chapter considers the legal and ethical decisions that instructors must face when requiring students to create blogs as part of their classroom responsibilities.

This chapter is separated into four sections: section 1 explains related issues in the statutes in intellectual property law and provides analysis of their application to student blogs; section 2 treats existing case law and analysis of issues related to student copyright control; section 3 offers synthetic discussion of issues regarding copyright and blogs; and section 4 concludes with suggested directions that composition instructors might consider when supporting student blogging for classroom activities.

THE STATUTORY LAW

1976 Copyright Act's Directives for Copyright Acquisition and Control

Sections 101–205 of the Copyright Act of 1976, still controlling law today, delineate who can retain a copyright and how copyrights are treated. Section 102 sets out that authors can retain copyrights in:

1. literary works;

2. musical works, including any accompanying words;

3. dramatic works, including any accompanying music;

4. pantomimes and choreographic works;

5. pictorial, graphic, and sculptural works;

6. motion pictures and other audiovisual works;

7. sound recordings; and

8. architectural works.

Authors are individuals who create expressions, including those noted herein, and students can certainly claim copyrights for their authored works, regardless of their status as students. As I explain later in detail in the section on work-for-hire, student status is not the same as employee status, under which conditions a student would create work that could be controlled by the university. So student-authored works, even those created within a classroom, are copyrighted and controlled by student authors.

It is also important to note that Section 102(b) extends only to originally authored works and prohibits copyrights in "any idea, procedure, process, system, method of operation, concept, principle, or discovery, regardless of the form in which it is described, explained, illustrated, or embodied in such work." Copyright thus protects only the expressions of ideas, rather than the ideas themselves, and instructors who use blogs in classroom work may need to explain to students the differences between plagiarism and copyright violation. A student who uses someone else's idea could plagiarize without violating copyright, since copyright protects only the expression of an idea rather than the idea itself.

Copyright and Blogs

Most blogs are textual at their base and would be considered literary works, but they might also communicate information through music or images and could be copyrighted on this basis as well. Students can certainly retain a copyright in blogs they create. Under Section 201, copyrights are provided to authors of creative products. Authorship can exist in an individually created work, a joint work in which more than one author contributes to a work, or in a corporate entity under the work-for-hire doctrine. And since the enactment of the Copyright Act of 1976, creators are not required to file for copyrights in order to acquire them. Section 101 states that "a work is 'created' when it is fixed in a copy or phonorecord for the first time" and although a copyright holder gains benefits from registering the copyright, registration is not required.

Section 106 lists the rights of the copyright holder. Students who create blogs potentially develop material in which they might claim copyright control, thus it can be useful to understand the nature of authorship in copyright for creating that control. Section 106 provides a basis for investigating student rights regarding their copyrighted blogs. Copyright holders, including student holders of blogged material, have the right to copy the work, distribute it, create derivative works from it (works extended from the original), or display it. They also have the right to prevent others from doing so. But students' copyrighted blogs, just like all copyrighted works, are subject to the fair use exception to their rights. Blogs and other intellectual products are also subject to uses that would otherwise be prohibited, as long as those uses support the policy intent in the Constitution's intellectual property provision to advance learning or, the overall goal of free speech and the Bill of Rights, to support democracy.[2]

Normally, a blog's textual content would be copyrighted as the author's creation, and any music, images, or other expressions contained in the blog would be copyrighted in their own right. If a student created each part of the blog, the music, images, video clips, and other work, then he or she would retain a copyright to each expression separately as well as to the blog as a whole. But it is conceivable that different kinds of blog content could be sufficiently merged into one expression, where it would be impossible to separate the content into different pieces of communication. In this case the blog, including its text, music, and images, would be copyrighted as a single work, and its various portions—melded together—could not be treated as individual copyrighted works and separated from the work as a whole.

This situation becomes much more complex when a student creates an original text in a blog that includes images, music, and other content authored by another creator. Unless the student used another author's materials validly, with a license, supported by the fair use doctrine (explained later in this chapter), a First Amendment claim, or some other legally supported treatment, he or she would likely be in violation of that author's copyright by these additions, even while the copyright to the blog text would be held by the student. More complex is the situation where all the copyrighted expressions in a blog become so sufficiently merged that a student's work could not be severed from the works of others. In this case, the blog as a whole could be considered a copyright violation.

A joint work exists where more than one creator contributes to a work; in the absence of a contract making a specific, intended arrangement clear, each contributor would retain an equal share in the work as a whole and have equal say in whether, how, and to whom license to the work could be given. Instructors who ask students to create blogs that provide open space for responses from others should consider the potential that their students might participate in joint work development and would be wise to explain this to students before they begin their work.

Fair Use

There are situations where a student or other user can make nonviolative use of copyrighted work, just as others can do the same with theirs. The fair use doctrine in Section 107 of the Copyright Act allows a range of these valid uses without the need to obtain a license from the creator. Users can make copies and disseminate work in order to quote, criticize, comment, report the news, educate, research, express an idea in parody, and pursue scholarship. But these uses must be tempered; where a work's marketability is hampered or where amount and substantiality of use is extreme, for example, a user may be inhibited. Students may attempt to make fair use of materials included in their blogs and instructors may attempt to claim fair use in students' copyrighted blogs. Instructors should prepare their students to make valid fair uses of materials that go into blogs, as well as maintaining awareness of their own uses of materials, especially when they are student generated.

There are no absolute lines to be drawn for determining what is or is not a fair use. Instead, users can only make determinations based on a scale of what may be more or less likely to be supported use of copyrighted work. So, for example, in a case where a blogger copies a paragraph-long quotation from a book, about which he or she makes critical comments regarding the content of the quote, using an insubstantial amount of the work without affecting the marketability of the original work, the use would likely be supported by fair use. If any one of those elements changed, the use would be less likely to be supported. In contrast, with a case where a blogger uses an image as a splash background simply to decorate a blog, making it easily available to copy and download and makes no critical comment about the work, the use would be very likely be insupportable as fair use.

Instructors must be concerned, too, about their own uses of student work in blogs. Because students working to create classroom assignments are not categorized as employees creating works for hire, neither instructors nor their universities retain the rights to student copyrights to use for their own purposes. But instructors can use student material validly if fair use claims are well supported.

Work for Hire

Work for hire is a legal fiction of corporate authorship treated in the Copyright Act of 1976 (Section 101). Under the work for hire doctrine, a corporate entity—or noncorporate organization, for that matter—can claim copyright in a work created by an employee if the employee created the work within the scope of his or her duties. To determine whether a creation is a work for hire, both these conditions have to be met. To decide whether a creator is an employee for purposes of work for hire, the claimant must look to these thirteen elements from agency partnership law:

- The hiring party's right to control the manner and means for creating the product. The greater the control, the more likely the creator is to be an employee.

- The level of skill required from the creator. The greater the level of skill of the hired party, the less likely he or she is to be an employee.

- Where a hiring party provides instruments and tools to create the intellectual product, the court will find support for determination of a work for hire.

- If the hired party worked at the hiring party's place of business rather than his or her own, this element will lead to a more likely finding of work for hire.

- The longer the duration of the relationship between the two parties, the greater the possibility of a work for hire.

- When the hiring party assigns additional projects to the hired party, he or she displays more control and is more likely working in the status of employer for purposes of work for hire.

- The more discretion the hired party has over when and how long to work, the more likely he or she is an independent contractor and can maintain control over the work.

- Hired parties who are paid by the hour, week, or month rather than by the job are more likely to be employees.

- When a hired party has a role in hiring and paying assistants, he or she may be legally determined to be a independent contractor.

- If the work created was something usually within the realm of the hiring party's business, this element could help make a showing that the work was not for hire.

- When a hiring party is not in business at all, it is harder for him or her to claim to be an employer.

- Hiring parties who pay benefits to hired parties are more likely than not to be employers.

- Hired parties who are taxed through the hiring party's business are more likely to be employees. (Brinson and Radcliffe quoted in Herrington, "Who Owns," 136–37)

No single one of these elements can lead to a determination of employee status, but the combination of all of them together helps courts make a decision. But work for hire status derives not only from the assessment that the creator is an employee; it must also be determined that the created product was within the range of duties that the author was hired to complete. Without either one of these decisions, there can be no work for hire status.

Students who produce materials within classrooms are not working as employees for their professors or universities, and work for hire does not apply to the work of student creators when they develop creative products in their capacity as students. Students' copyrights of their work remain their own and are not legally controlled by their professors, so it is an important caution to educators that they should not to attempt to apply the work for hire doctrine to student work.

Clearly, students' classroom-based materials are not works for hire, but there has been some discussion regarding an assumption that students provide implied licenses to the work they develop within their classrooms; I discuss this area of law in the following section in an overall analysis regarding student-generated materials for classroom use.

CASE LAW

Case law regarding student copyrights is slim but includes *Choe v. Fordham U School of Law*, which treats a student author's claims of control over the intellectual product that he created for his university's law journal while he was a student; *Seshadri v. Kasraian*, in which a professor filed a suit against a former graduate student for copyright violation; *Burr v. Kulas, et al.*, in which a PhD candidate sued her dissertation advisor for loss of the degree, theft of intellectual property, and theft of personal manuscripts for personal gain; *Levine v. Oxford Press*, which centers on a graduate student's claim that an author misappropriated research from her dissertation; and *Woods Hole Oceanic Institution v. Joseph E. Goldman*, a case concerned with a research institution's application of the work for hire doctrine.[3] These cases provide no bright line treatment of student copyright issues but are useful as a jumping off point to explain potential applications of the law.

In an interesting twist, *Choe v. Fordham U School of Law* treats a case in which a law student, Jerry Choe, sues the *Fordham International Law Journal* for the editors' "mangling" of his legal comment (a form of law article) in the law journal. Choe's claims, among others, include a "moral rights" claim to his creative work. His suit was filed on the basis of an argument that the editors changed his work so much that it could no longer be called his own.

In *S.R. Seshadri v. Masoud Kasraian*, a graduate student, Masoud Kasraian, was sued for copyright violation by his professor, S. R. Seshadri. Kasraian published an article, "Double-Grating Thin-Film Devices Based on Second-Order Bragg Interaction," as a single author after his professor, with whom he had jointly authored the work, had previously withdrawn the initial journal submission from the *Journal of Applied Physics*. Upon the initial journal submission, both Kasraian and Seshadri signed copyright release forms to the journal and provided their names (the student's listed first) as authors of the article. After the submission, Seshadri uncovered what he claimed were mistakes in the work and withdrew the article for publication. Some time later, when Kasraian resubmitted the work in his own name and told his professor that he included acknowledgment and a thank-you to him, Seshadri demanded that his name be removed from the work and that Kasraian not use any of the words or ideas he contributed to the work. Although the court noted that Seshadri might have legal recourse in areas other than copyright, it supported Kasraian's status as a joint author of the work and dismissed Seshadri's copyright infringement claim.

In *Burr v. Kulas, et al.*, in which a doctoral student, Burr, sued her academic advisor, Lemon, and department director, Kulas, for copyright infringement, the court treated the case of a student's right to control the copyright in her work. Burr had been pursuing work on her dissertation, which examined the impact of North Dakota's educational regulations on Native American populations. As part of her work, Burr created a questionnaire, which she used to gather information for her research. After Burr was hospitalized for kidney failure and was absent from work while undergoing a kidney transplant, a department faculty member instructed the department secretary to enter Burr's office, copy the questionnaire, and return it without Burr's authorization. Her faculty advisor and members of the department used the questionnaire for their own purposes. The case treated a complicated set of legal determinations regarding the Lanham Act and severance of liability of the university (based on sovereign immunity) from individual liability of Burr's advisor and other faculty members involved in the violation. Kulas, Lemon, and other members of the department forwarded these complex legal defenses in the attempt to stop the legal proceedings in this case by asking for summary judgment, but, to date, their initial success at summary judgment has been appealed and overturned, and the court has found that Burr has a valid right to pursue her claim of infringement.

In *Levine v. Oxford Press*, a graduate student, Levine, pursued an unsuccessful suit for copyright infringement of her unpublished doctoral thesis entitled *The Other Kropotkin*. Levine wrote her dissertation at Stanford University and claimed that Todes, a professor at Johns Hopkins University who published his book, *Darwin Without Malthus*, through the defendant, Oxford University Press, had misappropriated her copyrighted work. The court had no reservations about supporting Levine's claim in a copyright to her dissertation, but held for the defendant after finding the probability that Todes copied Levine's work too tenuous to provide credence to the suit.

Woods Hole Oceanic Institution v. Joseph E. Goldman illustrates the circumstances in which a student's work can be a work for hire. In this case, the student, Goldman, signed an agreement to work for Woods Hole, a research institute, while a student, but with an explicit contract that stated that his work would be in the capacity of an employee of the institution and within the realm of control of his employer. Goldman worked in the capacity of a work-study student to contribute to a documentary developed to chronicle research regarding atmosphere and the ocean in the North Atlantic. In this case, although Goldman was learning in the process of working for Woods Hole, he was hired explicitly for the purpose of helping to develop the documentary and had contractually agreed to work as an employee. The court found that he was clearly working for the institute as an employee and that the work he did was within the scope of his duties there; thus, his work was considered a work for hire.

SYNTHETIC ANALYSIS OF INTELLECTUAL PROPERTY LAW APPLIED TO STUDENT BLOGS

My research rendered no case law on student copyright and blogs, and I found only one off-point case, *Grendysa v. Evesham*, that mentioned blogs in an academic setting, in which a teacher was accused of downloading blogs regarding Internet pornography within his classroom. Where the aforementioned cases are not directly instructive about how the intellectual property law treats students' creative products in the classroom setting, they do provide some guidance for treating students' copyrighted work. Their totality indicates that students do retain their copyrights as joint authors with their professors (*Seshadri v. Kasraian*) or as sole authors (*Burr v. Kulas*) unless they work in the capacity of an employee under the conditions of work for hire (*Woods Hole v. Goldman*) or the claim has too tenuous a basis for pursuit (*Levine v. Oxford Press*).

The following analysis examines ways that students' intellectual products may be treated in the classroom by considering the nature of blogs and how they may be dealt with under copyright law. After this initial exploration, I take a close look at the fiduciary responsibilities of instructors to their students, and then, by following a focused treatment of legal issues in the potential for implied licenses, I examine copyright violation in online databases such as the Turnitin site.

The Nature of Blogs

The first step in determining how the intellectual property law applies to a product is to examine the nature of the creative work. In our case, the second is to understand how it is treated in the classroom. (For purposes of discussion here, I examine the structure of a blog as a single-author work, assuming that an instructor would ask a student to create a closed document for purposes of fulfilling a class assignment). A blog, like any other post-1978 copyrighted work, is copyrighted when it becomes fixed in a tangible means expression, whether the holder registered the work or not. The Copyright Act of 1976, enacted in 1978, makes this clear.

The copyright law applies to digital products just as it does to hard copy work, even though the character of digital products makes determining how the work should be treated more difficult. By its nature, a blog is a digital product, and in most cases, blogs are published on the Web and accessible to viewers and users worldwide. The digital nature of a blog published to the Web makes it easy to view, copy, and disseminate. Under usual circumstances, bloggers intend to publish their work on the Web with the specific purpose of making their materials accessible and they assume the risk that users may copy and redistribute their work. A blogger whose work is copied from the Web could make a copyright claim against a user who copied and disseminated his or her work, however difficult it might be to pursue. The blogger would have to weigh the risk of violation against the desire to blog publicly and make a decision accordingly.

Students whose instructors demand that they create blogs published to the Web also make their work accessible and at risk for copyright violation. The legal risks are the same for students as for any other bloggers, but in contrast to bloggers who make their own choices about creating public access to their materials, students may have fewer choices. This issue of choice goes beyond the legal issues involved in treating copyrighted work, so I examine the nonlegal issues surrounding this activity in the following section, "Instructor Care: Ethical Relationship to Students."

Bloggers who use others' images, sound files, design structures, or other enhancements have the potential to violate copyright in placing these files onto their blog sites. They are responsible for defending their choices and for handling court-determined violations that occur. Students would also be responsible for copyright violations, but plaintiffs pursuing copyright claims might also direct legal action against the university as a "deep pocket" defendant, both as a secondary source of relief and also in a potentially supported claim that, through the instructor, the university controlled students' actions and could be held responsible.

In any case, a classroom setting in which an instructor controls students' choices regarding their work is rife with possibilities for ethical abuse of student work. Instructors' unique relationship to students creates a situation in which they should take particular care in how they treat student work, especially if they expect students to publish their work to public forums. The relationship between students and professors and the treatment of intellectual products within that relationship is the subject of the following section.

Instructor Care: Ethical Relationship to Students

Instructors are in a special position of control in relation to their students because they determine students' grades and sometimes even their futures, when grades, progress in classes, and completion of work within a semester is important for scholarships, start times for employment, or other life benefits. In this special relationship to students, instructors have a fiduciary—heightened—duty of care.[4] Professors who require blogs in their classrooms should be aware that the ramifications of this kind of requirement may lead to different consequences than requiring hard copy versions of student-created products.

Physically controlling a copy of a work is not the same as making a copy, so to retain a hard copy of a student draft, or even a digital document of the student's work, does not violate copyright. Simple receipt of a work is not the same as copying the work or distributing it. Controlling a tangible work, such as a book or paper, allows the holder to lend the work, move it physically from one location or another, post it in a physical location, or destroy it, among other possible physical actions. But the holder (with the exception of fair use possibilities) must not copy it, create derivative works from it, or use it in a way that amounts to copying and distributing the work.

Even though a holder of a tangible work has a relatively great amount of freedom for treating the work in its physical form, a professor who has control over students' work, even in physical form, has an added ethical duty of care. Instructors who have power over their students' creative choices—and sometimes over their students' futures—must treat student work in a way that does no harm.

Beyond this special duty of care with physical documents, when instructors begin to consider how they might "display" or "transfer" student documents in online settings, their limitations become more severe. To post a physical document on the Internet would require an instructor first to scan it, which is making a copy, and to copy the work violates the student's copyright. Then to distribute a copied work by placing on the Internet—publishing it—violates the copyright further.

An instructor might have the students themselves post their work on the Internet. In this case, there would be no copyright violation, but the potential for ethical abuse would exist were a professor to demand that students publish work they might not want to publish. If the publication site were restricted only to those who share the classroom setting, the possibility for ethical problems decreases. And where students willingly agree to add clauses to their work to provide licenses for others to use or copy their work, instructors could be more comfortable about working with student copyrights. In any case, ethical violations still occur when instructors coerce their students to subject their copyrighted work to potential abuse or to sign agreements. Not only could these agreements be invalid as "adhesion clauses," over which the student has no power to negotiate, but in either case, instructors would violate the duty of care that their positions of power create.

Some instructors might argue that demands for students to create and publish original work on a public website is a condition of taking the course and that students have a choice to attend or not. It is common that some courses require tasks that others do not and "course shopping" is widespread among students who want to choose the best courses for their purposes. But there are many cases where a professor's course may be the only one available or where the time in which the course is scheduled is the only one possible for filling a student's schedule. In these situations, agreements to take the course would come with an "adhesion clause," unsupportable in contract law, that makes an agreement nonnegotiable and, thus, puts the student in a position in which he or she is powerless to make valid choices. Again, the law notwithstanding, instructors have a duty of care not to harm their students or coerce them to put their copyrights at risk.

Implied License

Although unsupported in direct statements under the copyright law, an argument can be made that implied licenses ensue in situations where content creators participate in digital forums in which copying their work is a condition for use of the forum itself. For example, posting to an email distribution list requires the reader to make a digital copy of a work in order to view it and respond to it; as part of participation on a discussion board, it is common to copy posted comments in email responses and an "implied license" can go far enough to allow this as well. Whether works are in digital form on the Internet or in hard copy, the fair use doctrine allows a user to copy them for critical comment. But a distinction exists in an "implied license" where it goes beyond fair use to assert a license to users, notwithstanding the existence or nonexistence of a fair use exemption to a copyright claim.

Blogging provides some inherent distinctions from email, in that, arguably, even though bloggers create an implied license for readers to view their blog content, there is no implied license to copy and distribute their work. Fair use is still applicable, however, regardless of copyright claims in the work. So students' copyrights to their blog content would still ensue in publicly accessible webbed spaces, but protecting their work would be more difficult since it would be open to all who access their blog sites.

Some claim that an implied license exists when students submit their work to educators with the expectation that it must be used and evaluated as part of what occurs in a classroom setting. Turnitin.com has attempted to justify the use of student work for its own commercial purposes by referring to a number of cases (see *Foad Consulting Group v. Musil Govan Azzalino, et al., Lulirama, Ltd., Inc. v. Axcess Broadcast Services, Inc., Effects Associates v. Cohen,* and *I.A.E., Inc. v. Shaver*), but note that none provide supporting evidence to allow noninfringing use of student work, particularly for commercial purposes. However supportable an argument for implied license may be for instructors' use of student work within closed classroom settings when limited to evaluation and use of work for classroom interaction, there is no legal support in copyright statutes either for an "implied license" or, with the exception of fair use when applicable, for allowing instructors either to copy or distribute copies of student work.

Turnitin and Other Student Work Databases

Controversy is growing over the legality and ethicality of demanding that students submit their work to antiplagiarism mechanisms in the forms of database sites such as the Turnitin structure. The Turnitin database, a commercial entity, profits from students' work when some institutions and instructors require their students to submit their work as a means to curb plagiarism. The database uses a digital mechanism to compare students' submissions to find instances of copied materials. Recent responses have increased since students from McLean High School in Fairfax County, Virginia, protested against their school's use of Turnitin (Glod).

Although the McLean High School students may have valid arguments that educators who use database plagiarism checkers are treating them as guilty before they are proven to be so, the more pointed legal issues involve copyright violations. Educators who provide students' copyrighted work to commercial entities that profit from students' work without their permission violate students' copyrights. And use of these commercial databases is arguably not even valid for student blog creation. The nature of blogs is such that instructors are unlikely to fear the potential for plagiarism. Bloggers create content much like they would a diary, adding comments to topics that they begin earlier or creating content regarding new topics on a regular basis. But if instructors fear plagiarism enough to demand that their students submit work to plagiarism databases or if their institutional policy requires these demands, both instructors and their institutions could be found liable for copyright violations.

University or Other Institutional Policies
Regarding Treatment of Student Work

Many instructors begin educating themselves on how they might treat their students' work by reading and understanding their institutions' copyright policies. These policies range in content from those that claim the rights to all students' work to others that note that students' retain their copyrights, even in the work they create for class.

Regardless of the force they might have within their own campuses, institutional policies do not substitute for the law. Instead, they are external to the law and merely reflect institutions' desires for how student work should be treated, or provide interpretations of how they believe the law should be applied. Unfortunately for students, many university policies are designed to further institutions' rather than their students' interests (Astala 32).

Reconciling institutional policy with law and ethics can be difficult when faculty members find themselves at odds with the policies set in their workplaces. In the case of intellectual property conflict, an institution may not provide legal support to a faculty member who does not follow institutional policy. But if that institutional policy violates legal or ethical standards, notwithstanding the desires of those who created the policy, a faculty member can be put in a compromised position to follow mandates within the workplace. Unfortunately, there are no easy solutions for dealing with conflicts in this area, but I provide suggestions in the conclusion of this chapter.

SUGGESTIONS FOR INSTRUCTORS' CLASSROOM TREATMENT OF STUDENT BLOGS

Instructors would most likely find it helpful to base their treatment of students' classroom work both on awareness that students retain copyrights in their work and on cognizance of their own ethical duties, which are heightened by their fiduciary relationship to students.

Where it is reasonable to expect students to submit class work for evaluation and as a basis for supporting the learning process through in-class interaction, instructors should be aware that there are potential legal consequences for copying and distributing student work outside the classroom setting. Difficulty arises when the traditional classroom setting becomes superseded by a technological construct that allows student work to be placed in locations that are accessible to those outside the classroom. Just as an instructor could be found to violate a student's copyright by copying and distributing a hard copy document outside the classroom, the same consequences could follow by copying and distributing a digital document; and when materials are placed in open forums such as the Web, not only is distribution of student work broad, but this action makes the work more vulnerable to copying and distribution by those outside the classroom.

Even a nontraditional, digital classroom can be controlled so that it is provided only to students and professors within a particular class construct with the aid of limiting features. Instructors can arrange to protect entry into their digital class space by password, so that it is closed to those who have not registered for the class. Students and their instructors could interact in a closed digital space much like they do in a traditional classroom where there would be no need to copy and distribute student work, and thus, students would be better protected from the potential that their copyrights would be infringed.

But, of course, in the case where instructors ask students to produce blogs as part of their class assignments, the issues become complicated. Part of the pedagogical motivation for using blogs as classroom assignments is to provide students with experiences in which they write for real readers. By implication, these readers come from outside a classroom space, where students' blogs would be posted to the Web. Students would produce their own original documents to post to blog sites rather than instructors making copies of student work for distribution, so claims of copyright violation would not be supportable. However, educators would still be faced with ethical decisions about the power they hold to force students to post their blogs outside a classroom venue. So even where copyright violation is not likely, in the case where students post or distribute their own work, instructors should be aware that their power to control grades can have a negative impact on student choice.

Instructors can help minimize the potential that they might, even unwittingly, coerce their students to treat their intellectual products in undesirable ways. Digital classrooms could be established in formats that provide students with choices for submitting their intellectual products for class use. For example, students might click on a radio button on a class submission site that allows them to choose that their work only be used within the closed classroom space, digital or otherwise. Or they might choose a button that shows that they wish their work to be used during the course in open forums, but only with the intention of supporting course activity. Alternatively, they might opt to allow use of their work for any university purpose. As long as students are truly free to make these choices, the potential for ethical misuse of their work can be curtailed.

A particularly difficult problem that educators might face is when institutional policy conflicts with their intentions to protect student work from copyright infringement or ethical mistreatment. For example, instructors may find themselves in a compromised position when institutional policy requires them to submit students' work to plagiarism detection databases such as Turnitin or to internal databases for institutional use.

Instructors who realize that submitting students' work to these kinds of databases infringes on student copyrights may wish to ignore policy. But, of course, they must consider the difficulty of going against the instructions of their employers. The most extreme option is simply to disregard institutional policy in favor of protecting students' work and bear the burden of the consequences. But instructors could also make a case for change or for justification of their choices in treating student work by providing their institutions with well-supported written explanations for why these kinds of databases can infringe students' copyrights. Attempts to persuade administrators to make different institutional choices could lead to a change in policy and serve the institution well. Ultimately, individual instructors must make the choices that support their beliefs and teaching philosophies, even as they balance employers' mandates, and these choices can be nothing but the responsibility of the individual.

Educators have always been accountable for treating student work ethically and legally, but with the advancement of technology and its use in the classroom, negotiating methods to do so becomes more difficult. Where potential pedagogical benefits of new teaching methods can be great, it is often well worth the effort to maneuver through the intricacies of intellectual property law to meet the challenges of a new world of learning, both for students and their instructors. I hope that educators will not be daunted by the difficulty in understanding and meeting the requirements of ethics and intellectual property law while making choices for treating work in their classrooms, but instead move forward with developed awareness of the legal and ethical ramifications of what the new world of teaching holds in store, and in doing so, deepen their own and their students' learning experiences as they move through the process.

NOTES

1. For a more extensive discussion of policy and intellectual property not within the realm of the narrow focus of this chapter, see Herrington, *Controlling Voices*.

2. See Patterson and Birch and Herrington, "Interdependency," listed in the following works cited section.

3. See also similar cases in *Chou v. Univ. of Chicago*, *Johnson v. Schmitz*, and *Rainey v. Wayne St. Univ.*

4. See the specific, detailed treatment of law and educator fiduciary duty in Astala, and Scharffs and Welch.

WORKS CITED

Astala, Melissa. "Wronged by a Professor? Breach of Fiduciary Duty as a Remedy in Intellectual Property Infringement Cases." *Houston Business and Tax Law Journal* 3.31 (2003): 31–65.

Burr v. Kulas. 532 N.W.2d 388. N.D., 1995. 1 June1995. 22 Nov. 2006 <https://www.ndcourts.com/court/opinions/960384.htm>.

Copyright. United States Copyright Office. Library of Congress. 12 Oct. 2006 <http://www.copyright.gov>.

Copyright Clause. U.S. Constitution. Article I, Section 8, Clause 8.

Choe v. Fordham U School of Law. 920 F.Supp. 44 (S.D.N.Y. 1995) aff'd 81 F.3d. 319 (Second Circuit 1996).

Chou v. Univ. of Chicago. 254 F.3d at 1347, 1361 (Federal Circuit 2001).

Effects Associates v. Cohen, 908 F.2d 555 (Ninth Circuit 1990), cert. denied, 121 S.Ct. 173 (2000).

Foad Consulting Group v. Musil Govan Azzalino, et al., 270 F3d. 821 (Ninth Circuit 2001).

Glod, Maria. "Students Rebel Against Database Designed to Thwart Plagiarists." *Washington Post* 22 Sept. 2006. 12 Mar. 2007 <http://www.washingtonpost.com/wpdyn/content/article/2006/09/21/AR2006092101800.html>.

Grendysa v. Evesham Township Board of Education. F.Supp.2d, 2005 WL 2416983. D.N.J., 2005.

Herrington, TyAnna K. *Controlling Voices: Intellectual Property, Humanistic Studies, and the Internet.* Carbondale: Southern Illinois UP, 2001.

———. "The Interdependency of Fair Use and the First Amendment." *Computers and Composition* 15.2 (1998): 125–43.

———. "Who Owns My Work? The State of Work for Hire for Academics in Technical Communication" *JBTC* 13.2 (1999): 125–53.

———. "Work for Hire for Nonacademic Creators." *JBTC* 13.4 (1999): 401–26.

I.A.E., Inc. v. Shaver, 74 F.3d 768, 772 (Seventh Circuit 1996).

Johnson v. Schmitz. 119 F. Supp. 2d 90, 91 (D. Conn. 2000).

Levine v. Oxford Press. F. Supp., 1993 WL 377630. N.D.Cal.,1993. 13 Sept. 1993.

Lulirama, Ltd., Inc. v. Axcess Broadcast Services, Inc., 128 F.3d 872, 879 (Fifth Circuit 1997).

Patterson, L. Ray, and Stanley F. Birch Jr. "Copyright and Free Speech Rights." *Journal of Intellectual Property Law* 4 (1996): 1–23.

Rainey v. Wayne St. Univ. 26. F. Supp. 2d 963, 966 (E.D. Mich. 1998).

Scharffs, Brett G., and John W. Welch, "An Analytic Framework for Understanding and Evaluating the Fiduciary Duties of Educators." *Brigham Young University Education and Law Journal* 159 (2005): 159–229.

S. R. Seshadri v. Masoud Kasraian, et al., No. 97–1610 (Seventh Circuit U.S. Court of Appeals).

Woods Hole Institute v. Joseph E. Goldman. F. Supp., 1985 WL 5968 (S.D.N.Y.), 228 U.S.P.Q. 874. United States District Court, S.D. New York.

Work for Hire. Copyright Act of 1976, U.S.C. 17. § 101.

PART III

Concluding Polemics

Changing the Future of
Composition and Copyright

CHAPTER 9

The (Re)Birth of the Composer

JOHN LOGIE

In a May 28, 2003, entry on the "Eschaton" weblog titled "Venturing Out from the Batcave," Duncan Black—then posting under the pseudonym "Atrios"—composed the following sentence: "After exchanging the secret handshake, swearing our allegiance to Stalin and Mao, and burning some candles at the altar of the Holy Clenis™ [ed. note: this is an in-jokey reference to President Bill Clinton], we settled down to a nice meal. I revealed my secret identity—as a Philadelphia gym teacher." Who was blogging thus? Was it the superhero implied by the invocations of the Batcave and the characterization of the pseudonym as a "secret identity"? Was it Duncan Black, who has never, in fact, been a gym teacher (though he did reside in Philadelphia). Is there an "Atrios" that can fairly be distinguished from Duncan Black? Liberal polity? We can offer only partial answers, for the good reason that Internet discourse is a networked, composite space where text is superficially detached from the humans who produce it—and yet the identities of the bodies composing these texts still matter greatly, despite the immateriality of most new media.

Once the composer is (re)born, the claim to decipher a text is no longer an exercise in futility. To give a text a composer is to impose limitations on that text, but this does not furnish it with a final authorized meaning. Such a conception suits rhetorical criticism very well, which has long concerned itself with the important task of understanding the speaker's complex interrelationships with both audience and text: when the composer is recognized, the text is increasingly accessible—an opportunity for the rhetorical critic. Hence there is no surprise in the fact that, historically, the reign of the Author has also been characterized bya narrow conception of literary criticism, nor again in the fact that criticism (at least rhetorical criticism) is today more compelling owing to the Author's comparative instability. In the richness of twenty-first-century compositions, everything is embedded, everything is coded; the structure can be decoded, "parsed" (like computer code) at every point and at every level because there is/was a composer or composers; composition regularly posits meaning regularly to repurpose it, prompting a chaotic aggregation of meanings. In precisely this way composition—by accumulating public, published expressions of ideas, interpretations, and claims—constitutes what may be called an antitheological activity, an activity that is truly revolutionary because prompting a multiplicity of composers to articulate a multiplicity of (com)positions is, in the end, to challenge God and his hypostases—reason, science, law.

To return to Atrios's sentence. One composer (whether understood as Atrios, Duncan Black, or even Batman) can fairly be said to have written it: its source, its voice is a critical element in the true scene of twenty-first-century composition. A text is made of multiple compositions, drawn from many previous composers, and entering into dynamic relationships with contemporaneous compositions. There is no one place where this multiplicity is stabilized, but the composer remains a central node in the network of voices and meanings, and more central, in many cases than (as was hitherto said) the reader. The composer is the node wherein all of the quotations that make up a composition met, mingled, and morphed. To the extent that texts have unity (or not), the composer is a critical participant in this determination. The composer has an undeniable history, biography, psychology: she is simply that someone who bears primary (but not exclusive) responsibility for the invention, arrangement, style, and/or delivery of the composition. That is why it is absurd to hear contemporary composition condemned in the name of a humanism that hypocritically promises to offer isolated, stable, authentic voices. Classic criticism has obscured the networked composer in order to celebrate the Author: for that criticism, there is no other person in literature than the one who authors. We are no longer willing to be the dupes of the "authorization" game, wherein students are promised insight into their own "authentic" selves even as their compositions are being repositioned as chattel. We know that to give composition its future, it is necessary to revise the myth. The death of the Author must be requited by the (re)birth of the composer.

The preceding paragraphs are a point-by-point parodic revision of the first and final paragraphs of Roland Barthes' germinal 1967 essay, "The Death of the Author."

Why?

Because despite the intervening forty years, Barthes' essay remains the most focused and influential critique of the Romantic construction of authorship. Barthes' essay offered a new understanding of the processes of textual production and reception, grounded in his argument that it is not the author who should determine the meaning of a text. Nor should the text itself be considered determinative (as the so-called New Critics argued in the decades immediately prior to Barthes' essay). Rather, Barthes argued, it is the reader in whom the multilayered and multivocal possibilities of a text stabilize into meaning. And yet, in his determination to terminate and bury the flawed Romantic Author, Barthes failed to fully articulate the reader as a viable alternative to the Author, ultimately abandoning the site of textual production altogether. Thus, Barthes' concluding call for the purported death of the Author to be requited by the birth of the reader presents us with a model wherein texts are meaningfully delimited only by their ultimate recipients. The now-deceased sources of these texts are offered no opportunity to participate in meaning-making. Barthes effectively denies the Author even the opportunity to audibly spin in his grave.

Since the publication of "The Death of the Author," many scholars have taken up Barthes' work, often pairing it with Michel Foucault's contemporaneous response, "What Is an Author?" These essays can now fairly be described as the foundational texts in an ongoing critique of Romantic authorship and its consequences. Not least among these consequences are U.S. and European copyright laws, which, to varying degrees, depend on the maintenance of an author as the primary step in transforming creative work into fungible property. In short, copyright law depends upon the author functioning chiefly (and usually momentarily) as the owner of a text on the verge of entering the traditional revenue streams afforded by print publication. In the past decade, a wave of legal, rhetorical, and literary scholarship has argued that contemporary U.S. copyright is at odds with the more nuanced understandings of authorship available in the wake of Barthes' and Foucault's critiques.

As the title of this chapter suggests, I believe Barthes' attempted murder created too large a vacuum. Others have noted this vacuum and suggested that it is best remedied by revitalizing the Author. The title of Sean Burke's 1992 book, *The Death and Return of the Author*, is emblematic of a broader argument, made by many scholars and critics, that the Author remains indispensable for textual criticism. Functionally, the Author might not be immortal, but he is at least as resilient as Count Dracula (who has "died" onscreen in well over one hundred films). Unlike Burke, I believe that the Romantic Author richly deserved the stake Barthes drove into his heart. Indeed, my argument suggests that twenty-first-century composers are routinely composing wholly valid and persuasive texts without necessarily invoking the conventional claims of authorship and the attendant claims of ownership policed by copyright laws.

These claims were thrown into sharp relief by Martha Woodmansee's immensely valuable scholarship on the history and cultural significance of the Romantic construction of authorship. Woodmansee points up three key elements that characterize this construction.

First, the Author is expected to be *solitary*. This expectation is embedded in the traditional portrait of the (implicitly male) genius writing by candlelight in a garret, well removed from the rough and tumble of daily life. The isolation of the Author is understood to be a necessary step in preparing the genius to channel his muse, or the divine, or, in Wordsworth's memorable description of his own composing process, the "spontaneous overflow of powerful feelings from emotion recollected in tranquillity." As Karen Burke LeFevre writes:

> Romanticism holds that the writer is inspired from within [. . .]. In the romantic tradition, the inspired writer is apart from others and wants to keep it that way, either to prevent himself and his creations from being corrupted by society, or to maintain a necessary madness (in the style of Poe) that is thought to be, at least in part, the source of art. (17)

Thus, the Romantic Author is abstracted from society (except, presumably, for those occasions when he is gathering powerful feelings from his interactions with others).

Second, the Author is expected to be originary. The Author's obligation to deliver something heretofore unseen is precisely what distinguishes him from the broader array of working writers. While there are (and were) many working writers who transmit words from point to point without ever establishing novelty claims for their work products, the mantle of authorship is limited to those who overtly aspire to delivering writings that are sui generis.

Finally, the Author is expected to be *proprietary*. At minimum, the Author must retain an ownership interest in his works long enough for the rights to those works to be sold. Woodmansee identifies the late sixteenth- / early seventeenth-century German philosopher Johann Gottlieb Fichte as offering the conceptual basis for the transformation from writer to possessive author:

> In his central concept of the "form" taken by a thought—that which it is impossible for another person to appropriate—Fichte [. . .] establishes the grounds upon which the writer could lay claim to ownership of his work—could lay claim, that is, to authorship. ("Genius" 52)

In his 1993 book *Authors and Owners*, Mark Rose takes Woodmansee a step further, arguing, "the distinguishing characteristic of the modern author [. . .] is proprietorship; the author is conceived as the originator and therefore the owner of a special kind of commodity, the work"(1). Importantly, both Woodmansee and Rose identify proprietary authorship as a recent and historically contingent development, driven in part by the increasing affordability of codex books and the rise of a literate reading public in seventeenth- and eighteenth-century Europe.

Understanding the Romantic construction of authorship as having been driven, in part, by the development of specific literacy technologies invites the obvious question—how might the seismic shifts in our current literacy technologies inform our understanding of discursive production? In a 2002 article titled "Theorizing Cyberspace: The Idea of Voice Applied to the Internet Discourse, " Ananda Mitra and Eric Watts engage in a lengthy discussion of the production of discourse in Internet spaces without ever referencing authorship as such, or, indeed, any of the signature elements that have characterized authorship since the rise of the Romantics. Indeed, the discursive agents described by Mitra and Watts are not solitary in any meaningful sense of the term. Whatever originary and proprietary impulses these discursive agents might have appear to be sublimated to the more pressing questions of how best to establish a stable virtual locus, which appears to be more soapbox than residence (thereby shifting the scene of discursive production to a public space like the agora or town square, and away from the home as emblematic private property):

[W]e define cyberspace as a discursive space produced by the creative work of people whose spatial locations are ambiguous and provisional. The notion of a discursive space is related to the way in which specific discourses can create unique spaces and communities that are built around the texts that are voiced in that space. Using the notions of discourse and community as suggested in Foucault's (1972) "discursive formation," Fish's (1980) "interpretive community," and Bizzell's (1982) "discourse community," it is possible to argue that these "communities" and "spaces" are produced around the discourses of the agents who are voicing themselves. In making this conceptual connection, several ideas are related because the notions of voice, agency, discourse, and space can now be combined to claim that cyberspace is created when voices gain the agency to speak in, and to, the virtual public. Using their voices these agents create cyberspace where speaking agents can comfortably dwell, and create their ethos or "dwelling space," which they inhabit and from where they can address the public sphere. (486)

Mitra and Watts's lengthy examination of Internet discursive practices appears to reflect a burgeoning shift in the vocabulary used to describe the production of texts. In this passage Mitra and Watts retrieve and repurpose three key concepts from textual, literary, and rhetorical critics, but they nevertheless are able to wholly sidestep the traditional vocabulary of author and work (though Foucault, Fish, and Bizzell do not avoid this terminology, especially in the articles cited here). Mitra and Watts's article appears to reflect the possibility of truly transformative approaches to discourse within Internet spaces.

Then again, there is also considerable evidence to suggest that the opportunities for alternative constructions in virtual spaces are largely circumscribed by the established understandings of authorship and rhetorical agency that scholars bring to cyberspace. In her 2005 book, *Composition in Convergence: The Impact of New Media on Writing Assessment*, Diane Penrod outlines a series of opportunities for improved composition pedagogy that materialize when one engages seriously with twenty-first-century digital technologies. It is clear from the text as a whole that she and I share a tremendous enthusiasm for these technologies and their attendant possibilities. But my heart sinks when Penrod closes an early chapter by stating: "convergence [defined as "the merging of writing technology and assessment"] can and will transform writing assessment practices as well as offer the students the respect they deserve as authors who own their own words" (86).

Texts like Penrod's leave little doubt that the title of "author" still carries a significant amount of rhetorical power. And many of my colleagues in rhetoric and composition studies quite reasonably hope to offer access to this power to their students. I will confess that have repeatedly been startled to hear or read colleagues whom I had assumed to share my distaste for the baggage embedded in the Romantic construction nevertheless endorse "authorship" as the ultimate goal of composition pedagogy.

For example, based on passages like this I presumed that the distinguished composition historian and critic Sharon Crowley shared my own desire for an end to the reign of the Author.

> In order to exalt the role of a sovereign author in composing, modernism posited that language exactly represented the ideas in a composer's mind—that it was, in other words, subservient to the author's wishes and the author's control. Modernism denied that language is larger than any of its individual users, that it has meaning only insofar as it has a history and a current community of users. This denial awarded authors sovereignty over their thought processes and the language they used, so that the contents of mind could be viewed as an accurate representation of reality. ("Modern" 43)

Elsewhere in the same article, Crowley momentarily settles on my preferred term for the nonauthorial producer of discourse writing, "A rhetorical attitude toward composition emphasizes copiousness, abundance, plenitude, aggregation, so that a composer will have something to say whenever an occasion arises" (43). I absolutely agree with and endorse these arguments and find Crowley's phrasing powerful and cogent. And this left me confused when, during Crowley's response to Karlyn Kohrs Campbell's plenary lecture at the inaugural meeting of the Alliance of Rhetoric Societies, Crowley said the following:

> One of the great difficulties in teaching first-year composition or public speaking, it seems to me, is that students in these courses do not view themselves as authors. And yet, even though they may deny the possibility of authorship to themselves, they are agents nonetheless, both individually and collectively, in the production of classroom talk and writing that reproduces exclusionary hegemonic discourses. One paradoxical task facing the teacher of writing or public speaking is to make students aware of the discursive agency that works through them, and

of its possible effects on others, while at the same time helping them to grasp the art or craft that can lead to their assumption of authorship. ("Response")

I wish to hasten to point out that Crowley's arguments are not necessarily directly contradictory. Is is both possible and reasonable to argue that the Author-as-sovereign is a deeply flawed and troubling construction while still recognizing that, for the foreseeable future, that's where power will be residing. Thus, we might well do our students a disservice if we fail to alert them to the value of seizing the mantle of traditional authorship.

But I think we can do better.

And I think a key step toward circumscribing the functional power of the Author lies in shifting our vocabulary in order to refuse to reinscribe his reign in the composition classroom. Indeed, scholars within composition studies have been searching for decades for a vocabulary that might serve to undercut the Author's hegemony. Susan Miller's 1989 book, *Rescuing the Subject: A Critical Introduction to Rhetoric and the Writer*, offers a memorably withering dismissal of traditional authorship:

> [A] reformed vision of how specifically written discourse originates can rescue a concept of the "subject" or "author" of writing from its currently precarious theoretical and philosophical place. We can, that is, explain historically why it remains feasible to investigate the human "writer" without necessarily surrounding that person with the now easily deniable claptrap of inspired, unitary "authorship" that contemporary theorists in other fields have so thoroughly deconstructed. (3)

But Miller also acknowledges that her colleagues had yet to offer a viable alternative to the Romantic construction of authorship. She writes:

> [Composition studies has not] fully conceived of the literate person as a "writer," who may or may not be an "author," a source of writing whose full participation in culture depends on an active yet ambivalent relation to all written texts. (3)

My sense is that the "writer" Miller offers here is too limited and vague a figure to effectively challenge the Author.

I argue here that the figure of the composer, if stabilized and clarified, might offer a more compelling counterweight to the traditional author.

Of course, "composer" is by no means a new term for scholars of rhetoric and composition. Many have used "composer" as a functional substitute for "author," but few have spelled out why, specifically, the resonances embedded within "composer" are to be preferred to the solitary, originary, and proprietary model of the Romantic construction of authorship.

We can now sketch an emerging portrait of a twenty-first-century composer that might well rival the Author, both in terms of inherent appeal and ability to manifest persuasive, powerful texts. To the extent that twenty-first-century composers, almost by default, are using networked computers as their preferred tools for composition, they ought never be understood as solitary. Twenty-first-century composers are large and contain multitudes, but so too do their preferred composing tools. The window of a typical twenty-first-century composer's word processor is routinely supplanted by windows for email, Web browsing, and chat. All of these diminish the degree to which one can ever approximate the isolation that characterizes portraits of the Romantic Author. Of course, even that Author's isolation was a mirage.

Twenty-first-century composers also contend with the nagging awareness that a staggering archive of already-written texts is close at hand. At times, the availability of these texts via a mouse click or two serves as a reminder of an intimidating tradition that has the potential to stifle the individual talent. For the moment, the comprehensiveness of this archive is dramatically limited by the strictures of copyright laws, but we can envision a time when this will change.

Print-focused copyright laws now constitute the chief obstacle to the development of an electronic library rivaling Jorge Luis Borges' "Library of Babel." This is not an exaggeration. The raw computing power of contemporary desktop and laptop computers greatly exceeds what is needed for the transmission and display of scanned textual materials. Current estimates are that one-fifth of the world's population has high-speed access to the Internet. As this number rises, so too will the amount of excess bandwidth (e.g., the bandwidth devoted to supporting "always on" high-speed connections for home users who typically do not consume that bandwidth without interruption throughout an entire day). This "spare" computing power and bandwidth could provide the infrastructure needed to deliver a nearly complete archive of the works published to date. The value of this library would be greatly enhanced were the texts not merely visible, but fully searchable and indexed.

The presence of such an archive would necessarily transform the politics of what we now term *originality*. Proverbs have repeatedly delivered the message at the heart of the famous passage in Ecclesiastes that reads:

> What has been will be again, what has been done will be done again;
> *there is nothing new under the sun.* Is there anything of which one can say,
> "Look! This is something new"? It was here already, long ago; it was
> here before our time.(Ecclesiastes 1:9–10)

But our proverbial understanding of this notion will, in the not-too-distant
future, be paired with the technological means to verify the degree to which
our putatively "original" contributions to the great heap of human discourse have already been largely anticipated and prefigured by others' work.
Twenty-first-century composers will, over time, learn to refrain from claiming originality as they recognize the degree to which even their most aggressively distinctive compositions have antecedents, analogs, and echoes, all of
which will be accessible in the space of a few mouse clicks.

Nor will or should twenty-first-century composers embrace the proprietary models associated with the Romantic construction of authorship. Too
often, copyright has functioned primarily as a means of separating texts from
their composers. The print-based publication economy benefited from limiting the complex question of textual ownership. In short, while scholars of
literature, rhetoric, and composition have long acknowledged the rich inter-
weaving of voices in any specific text, publishers needed a signatory. Further,
they needed that signatory's ownership claim over a text to be, if not absolute,
so profound as to insulate them from the prospect of an unexpected obligation to compensate additional contributors. In short, the economics of print
publication prompted a structure in which publishers could state "All Rights
Reserved" and then enforce many of those rights. To the extent that this bargain produced fair compensation for composers, it was arguably reasonable for
its time. That time has passed. The comparatively frictionless "publication"
afforded by the Internet has allowed composers to aggressively revisit the politics of textual ownership. And the Internet also offers a remarkably efficient
mechanism for staging and circulating alternatives to traditional print-based
copyright. The most successful of these is, without question, the Creative
Commons project, which provides both structure and support for those composers and copyright holders who wish to unbundle the array of rights now
embedded within the familiar © symbol. A typical Creative Commons license
might welcome subsequent reuse of the composer's work, including commercial exploitation of the work, so long as the composer was acknowledged by
name for her contributions to the new work. By finding mechanisms to, in
effect, give their work away, Creative Commons composers are opting out
of the traditional proprietary models of copyright. This does not necessarily

imply that these composers are not pursuing credit or even compensation for their compositions. Rather, it suggests that what counts as adequate compensation moves well beyond the direct, monetary compensation offered by traditional publishers.

This rather brief review of the practices of some twenty-first-century composers points up the degree to which the Romantic construction is now counterbalanced by composing models that reject the solitary, originary, and proprietary aspects of traditional authorship.

Where the Author was typically portrayed as solitary, twenty-first-century composers are clearly *networked*, both in terms of their participation in social networks and in terms of their use of machines that are routinely interrupted and permeated by other voices scattered throughout the various networks that constitute the Internet. Where the Author was originary, twenty-first-century composers are more commonly *responsive*. While a particular circumstance may call for a putatively novel response, it may also call for a strategic response that rearranges existing information. For example, a credible blog post might be largely if not wholly unoriginal (e.g., a quote) but if it appropriately responds to a particular contemporary circumstance (e.g., a blog quoting FDR's speech on Pearl Harbor in the immediate aftermath of the 9/11 attacks) it will likely be acknowledged as successful. This, in turn, limits the composer's ownership claims. While the traditional Author labored in order to own and, with a little luck, sell, the fruits of his labors, the typical composer is not so directly or so obviously out for a buck. That said, composers are typically conscious of the exchange value of their efforts, and many see themselves as happily contributing to an expanding and diverse dialogue—or polylogue, more properly. Among twenty-first-century composers, we can observe bloggers pursuing a model I describe as "social/capital/istic." While bloggers are a varied lot, stretching from opportunists hoping to cash in on the next Internet boom to gentle, giving souls who wish to share their innermost thoughts and haikus, almost all of them recognize that blogs hold some promise of social capital. The connections established through blogs are now, routinely, the basis for personal and professional friendships. The power of blogs is attributable to the genre's leveraging of the medium to facilitate interconnected compositions, in which an initial text is linked to and critiqued, and the critique is, in turn, linked to and critiqued. If we are forced to concede that the Author did not die, we do well to acknowledge that he has a younger sister, and that her networked, responsive, and social/capital/istic orientations happily counter most of what people tended to dislike about the Author in the first place.

One reasonable objection to the use of *composer* as a replacement for *author* is that the term is, in common usage, inextricably tied to its associations with specifically musical composition. While this is a fair objection, there are also considerable advantages to this connection. Chief among these is the long-standing recognition that the art of musical composition does not necessarily require an aggressive claim of originality. Since the development of viable notation and recording methods, musical composers have, to varying degrees, acknowledged their dependancies on previous works. For example, in 1873, Johannes Brahms composed "Variations on a Theme by Joseph Haydn." While musicologists now argue that the core theme of the piece might not actually be drawn from Haydn, the final measures contain a brief quotation of a cello line from Haydn's Clock Symphony. Brahms presented this new work, acknowledging it as dependent upon the work of one of his musical forebears without shame or embarrassment. And indeed, musicians have long tended to announce themselves as participating in a fluid economy of influence, appropriation, and reinvention. This sentiment is perhaps best encapsulated by Igor Stravinsky, who famously said, "A good composer does not borrow, he steals."

Stravinsky's quote appears to have been based upon T. S. Eliot having said, "Immature poets imitate; mature poets steal." Eliot, in turn, was likely quoting Pablo Picasso's "Good artists borrow. Great artists steal." For Picasso, of course, this was much more than a generalized statement regarding artistic behavior. It was also an expression of the specifics of some of his artistic practices. Picasso's collage technique was grounded in his directly appropriating scraps of others' works (newspaper clippings, for example) and embedding them into his own paintings. Along with Georges Braque, Picasso articulated an artistic strategy that reverberated throughout the arts. Indeed, collage is arguably the signature art form of the twentieth century. As each medium gained access to affordable copying technology, collage practices became more and more popular. Collage techniques have repeatedly moved from the margins to mainstream creative practice.

Students tend to arrive in our classrooms with a baseline understanding of the broad arc of American popular music, and indeed, their awareness of the rich and complex array of composing practices across musical genres is an excellent starting point for a broader discussion of what it might mean to act as a twenty-first-century composer. Cultural critic Siva Vaidhyanathan briefly outlines this complexity in his 2001 book, *Copyrights and Copywrongs: The Rise of Intellectual Property and How It Threatens Creativity*. He writes:

> Tracing influence through something as organic and dynamic as American music is never simple. Blues-based music is often the product of

common and standard chord structures and patterns. Relying on or referring to a particular influence can be as important as any "original" contribution to a work. A composer might employ a familiar riff within a new composition as a signal that the new song is part of one specific tradition within the vast multifaceted canon of American music. As Willie Dixon wrote: "When you're a writer, you don't have time to listen to everybody else's thing. You get their things mixed up with your ideas and the next thing you know, you're doing something that sounds like somebody else." Because repetition and revision are such central tropes in American music, rewarding and encouraging originality is a troublesome project in the music industry. (120)

And indeed, encouraging originality is a troublesome project in composition pedagogy. To the extent that writing teachers still offer assignments that represent little more than paraphrases of Langston Hughes's assignment in "Theme for English B," ("Go home and write / a page tonight. / And let that page come out of you—/ Then, it will be true.") they are participating in a ritualized pageant of "authenticity." Hughes was neither the first nor the last to wonder, in response to such an assignment, "I wonder if it's that simple?" (52) And indeed, generations of students have responded to such assignments by crafting texts and personae that satisfy the assignment's embedded call for authenticity, without feeling a special obligation to yoke their words to historical or empirical truth. Composition lore is rich in episodes where the "best" response to an assignment of this type is revealed to be a fabrication. A teaching space in which students were encouraged to compose rather than "author" texts would carry with it an implied opportunity to develop creative and strategic responses to the assignment without necessarily fully embracing the obligations of full ownership and full originality. Vaidhyanathan points to "repetition and revision" as central tropes in American music. They are also central tropes in American composition pedagogy.

The paperback edition of Vaidhyanathan's book features a portrait of the tool that, more so than any other (with the possible exception of the personal computer) has introduced the broad public to the techniques of collage, appropriation, and remixing that are commonplace among twenty-first-century composers—the DJ's turntable. The cover depicts the turntable in action, with a mixmaster's left hand poised to scratch a vinyl record, and the right hand on a fader. Since the early 1980s, listeners to American popular music have become accustomed to musical compositions that blend fragments of existing works with new melodies, freestyle raps, genre-bending collisions of sound. The turntable is now complemented by digital sampling—in which sounds are easily extracted from their initial contexts, and revised, repurposed, and recontextualized in ways that are chiefly limited by the creative impulses of the composer. Noted producer and turntablist DJ Shadow describes his composing process as follows: "Cutting and pasting is the essence of what hip-hop culture is all about for me. It's about drawing from what's around you, and subverting it and decontextualizing it" (qtd. in Rule 55). This is the power that we should be offering to students in the composition classroom. The strategies of cutting, pasting, extracting, subverting, and decontextualizing extant works are (or will be) at least as important as the Author's supposed sparkings of original genius. We should be leveraging our students' understandings of the astonishing complexity of contemporary musical compositions in order to build a transdisciplinary, multimedia composer who might well leave the Author looking comparatively isolated and limited.

The strategies that DJ Shadow employs for musical composition are all increasingly common strategies for textual and visual composers. Indeed students' increasing comfort with the multimedia tool kits typically included in the purchase price of a contemporary computer are already producing striking juxtapositions of richly varied texts. Part of the reason why we ought to prefer "composer" to "writer" is that twenty-first-century composition is about much more that the arrangement of alphabetic characters and punctuation. Electronic texts are proving every bit as malleable as the musical compositions that DJs and samplers have been slicing, dicing, and remixing. Now that a standard word processor offers the opportunity to seamlessly embed video clips, we would do well to recognize that conventional practices of citation and quotation are, well, so twentieth century (or even nineteenth). Our students are ready to do more than "author" texts. Indeed, while the Author is effectively yoked to the first rhetorical canon of Invention, the composer is comparatively free to roam, and the core claims for the value of a particular composition might well stem from its style, its arrangement, or its delivery, even in the absence of an invented, foundational "original thought."

In the end, this chapter recapitulates some of the more valuable theoretical interventions of the past few decades in order to remind us of the value of the term *composer* that is already used fairly regularly by scholars in rhetoric and composition. At best, it offers a focused rationale for a familiar but pointed rejection of the term *author* in favor of a more specific iteration of *composer*. Indeed, upon reflection, this chapter does not appear to offer much in the way of new information. Then again, perhaps it doesn't have to, given that I understand myself as a composer, rather than an author of this text. As such, I am comfortable with having ceded significant space to the voices of others within these pages. I am not threatened by my own dependencies, seeing them instead as the rough equivalent of samples embedded in my latest remix project.

Now, it's your turn.

WORKS CITED

Barthes, Roland. "The Death of the Author." Trans. Richard Howard. *The Rustle of Language.*1st ed. New York: Hill and Wang, 1986.

Crowley, Sharon. "Response to Karlyn Kohrs Campbell, 'Agency.'" Rhetoric Society of America. 2003. 19 May 2007 <http://www.rhetoricsociety.org/ARS/pdf/croleyars.pdf>.

———. "Modern Rhetoric and Memory." *Rhetorical Memory and Delivery: Classic Concepts for Contemporary Composition and Communication.* Ed. John Frederick Reynolds. Hillsdale, NJ: Erlbaum, 1993. 31–44.

Hughes, Langston. "Theme for English B." *The Collected Works of Langston Hughes,* vol. 3. Ed. Arnold Rampersad. Columbia: U of Missouri P, 2001. 52–53.

LeFevre, Karen Burke. *Invention as a Social Act.* Carbondale: Southern Illinois UP, 1987.

Miller, Susan. *Rescuing the Subject: A Critical Introduction to Rhetoric and the Writer.* Carbondale: Southern Illinois UP, 1989.

Mitra, Ananda, and Eric Watts. "Theorizing Cyberspace: The Idea of Voice Applied to the Internet Discourse." *New Media & Society* 4.4 (2002): 479–98.

Penrod, Diane. *Composition in Convergence: The Impact of New Media on Writing.* Hillsdale, NJ: Lawrence Erlbaum, 2005.

Rose, Mark. *Authors and Owners: The Invention of Copyright.* Cambridge, MA: Harvard UP, 1993.

Rule, Greg. "DJ Shadow + Akai MPC = History" *Keyboard* (Oct. 1997): 51–56.

Vaidhyanathan, Siva. *Copyrights and Copywrongs: The Rise of Intellectual Property and How It Threatens Creativity.* New York: New York UP, 2001.

Woodmansee, Martha. *The Author, Art, and the Market: Rereading the History of Aesthetics.* New York: Columbia UP, 1994.

———. "The Genius and the Copyright." In *The Author, Art, and the Market: Rereading the History of Aesthetics.* New York: Columbia UP, 1994. 35–55.

Woodmansee, Martha, and Peter Jaszi. *The Construction of Authorship: Textual Appropriation in Law and Literature.* Durham: Duke UP, 1994.

CHAPTER 10

Own Your Rights

Know When Your University
Can Claim Ownership of Your Work

JEFFREY R. GALIN

Some legal scholars argue that universities own everything that faculty produce. For example, in *Copyright Law on Campus*, Marc Lindsey writes that the only legally effective way "an employee can retain his own copyright of works created on the job is by" an explicit assignment of the employer's copyright to the employee in writing (4). The American Association of University Professors' Statement on Copyright argues conversely such ownership under the work for hire theory is inappropriate because it would vest in the institution "the powers, for example, to decide where the work is to be published, to edit and otherwise revise it, to prepare derivative works based thereon (such as translations, abridgments, and literary, musical, or artistic variations), and indeed to censor and forbid dissemination of the work altogether" (2). The statement argues further that "[s]uch powers, so deeply inconsistent with fundamental principles of academic freedom, cannot rest with the institution." Lindsey relies on a literal reading of the law, while the AAUP statement relies on the theoretical grounds of the Constitution and common law.

The implications of this debate are broad ranging for faculty and university policy-makers alike. Universities typically use the logic of the Bayh-Dole Act to claim all patentable or licensable products, not just those receiving federal research dollars. Increasingly, universities are combining the logic of Bayh-Dole with the work for hire clause of copyright law to claim ownership of marketable faculty works as well. While classroom materials and published writings have traditionally been considered the exclusive intellectual property of their creators, universities are making increasing claims to faculty works such as course materials, particularly online, faculty-produced texts that utilize grant, corporate, or campus resources, specially assigned works, and other works with commercial potential, including artistic works. As universities fall under greater financial pressures and administrations seek new revenue streams to support university research, the pressures for ownership and control of faculty work are only going to increase. As a result, it is more imperative than ever before that faculty understand how copyright law and campus policies affect their work and how faculty can play a role in shaping these policies.

From my experiences as a former chair of the CCCC Caucus on Intellectual Property (CCCC-IP), codrafter of IP policies at two different universities, and member of the union bargaining team for IP, I provide in this chapter some basic explanations of copyright in higher education,[1] an analysis of the economies of knowledge and status and how they distinguish ownership of university works from works in a market economy, and a rationale for determining who owns faculty works and why we should care. I draw from actual case studies to identify terms and concepts that faculty need to understand, such as traditional works of scholarship, work made for hire, appreciable university support, university-supported works, conflicts of interest and commitment, grant-sponsored works, institutional works, specific assignments, and ownership and use of student writing. Since IP policies differ from university to university, I also identify subtle differences in language that can lead to substantially different outcomes for faculty and their copyright concerns. I conclude by providing strategies for clarifying these complexities and differences in order to encourage faculty to take proactive roles on their own campuses.

FACULTY OWNERSHIP OF SCHOLARSHIP AND SOFTWARE

Most faculty members have probably not read their university's intellectual property policy concerning copyrights, either out of a lack of awareness or an assumption that this policy does not apply to them. However, faculty should become familiar with the content of this policy so that they may understand its scope and actively protect their rights *before* potential conflict develops. In fact, faculty may find it instructive to print out a copy of their institution's policy and review it while reading this chapter. The most common concerns emerge when faculty receive grants or use specialized resources for scholarly work or curricular development, have special assignments to develop new programs, find themselves in workplace disputes over use of course materials or collaborations gone wrong, or publish scholarly works that compromise patentable products. At times, mentorship relationships between graduate students and thesis advisors can lead to problems in student support of faculty work or competitive rights to publish research results. Faculty may find to their dismay that their institution has reserved perpetual rights to use or archive their works for teaching and research purposes. Some universities go so far as to claim rights to all intellectual property created by faculty but release some rights back to the creators. Still other institutions "unbundle" the rights of copyright to ensure that both the faculty member and the institution benefit mutually from faculty works.

While IP policies differ from campus to campus, it is possible to identify clusters of commonality. The following case studies demonstrate the aforementioned range of concerns listed and provide opportunities to discuss common practices. Case 1 explores questions of copyright ownership concerning scholarly works and a copyrighted work that may also be patentable. Case 2 presents a complex dispute over ownership of course materials that grows out of a hostile work environment. These cases are highly contextual, as are all copyright disputes in higher education. Nonetheless, they provide opportunities to understand the majority of faculty concerns of ownership of their own works in higher education; they also offer information that may help individual readers advocate for change in their own campus's IP policy.

CASE 1

As director of Writing Across the Curriculum (WAC), you have decided to develop an assessment protocol for determining the success of WAC courses on campus. You write a research proposal with the director of University Assessment on campus and your WAC coordinator and get approval from your campus Human Subjects Review Board to develop an interface for student submission of surveys and writing samples and for readers to rate the collected data. A university employee helps to code the interface. A graduate assistant and secretarial assistant help "clean" and format the data. During the development phase of the interface, both the director of University Assessment and the WAC coordinator take jobs at other universities. The former would like to implement the system at his new institution. Before the latter is replaced with a new coordinator, you, as the lead designer, register the completed prototype with the Office of Technology Transfer.

After a year of use and incremental changes, you, the former director of Assessment, and the new WAC coordinator present the results of your research at a conference of program administrators. The audience is as interested in the interface as they are in the results of your study. Your design team decides to write a book on the study and to market the interface. After a complex collaborative drafting process, you are able to find a publisher for your volume that will also produce the interface commercially. The volume includes fifteen screen snaps of the interface that were produced by Media Resources on your campus and graphs and tables that were developed by the Office of Institutional Effectiveness in a specialized software, SPSS. You would like to use the proceeds from the book and interface sales to fund the assessment program for WAC but are unsure if you have a right to do so. How do you determine what rights each of the former and current development team have to the published work, the assessment interface, and the proceeds therefrom?

Most faculty would likely assume that they have a right to control the products of their scholarly efforts and therefore own copyright of the works in question. After all, the mission of universities is to create and disseminate new knowledge. Furthermore, our chairs and deans almost never tell us what or where to publish, what materials to use, or how to develop assessment procedures. In this particular case, no one even asked the WAC director to develop an assessment program. Furthermore, it is highly unlikely that a dean would request an English professor to design a piece of software for any purpose, because such work is typically outside of the scope of normal work for humanities professors. To determine ownership in a scenario like this one, most faculty would turn to their campus IP policy and authorities on campus who could provide the necessary information about university policies and procedures concerning copyright ownership. In such a case, faculty could be wrong to assume they retain ownership but may find that early contact with the Office of Technology Transfer has paved the way for using proceeds as desired.

Case 1 offers a practical example of copyright ownership resulting from collaborative research relationships that typically form at universities. It raises questions concerning traditional works of scholarship, patentable works (such as software), works made for hire, institutional works, specific assignments, substantial use of university resources, creator's rights in university-owned works, use of proceeds to fund university programs, and ownership and use of student writing.

FUNDAMENTAL PRINCIPLES OF
INTELLECTUAL PROPERTY POLICIES (IPPS)

In order to understand the issues represented by case 1, we need to turn to the specific language of intellectual property policies and the underlying principles of copyright law. Typically, faculty members would only look at their own university's policy to clarify such concerns. However, for the sake of comparison, I draw upon IPPs from two institutions—the University of Utah and Florida Atlantic University—to demonstrate how differently this case would be resolved depending on the specific policy that governs faculty works. Such a discussion also provides a context for advocating for change at institutions with overly restrictive policies.

The simple answers to the questions raised in case 1 are that most universities will probably release the book and retain the interface. I turn to policy and statute to offer reasons for these responses. The University of Utah's policy, entitled "Ownership of Copyrightable Works and Related Works," introduces the aforementioned questions of ownership and control, as well as a few statutory features of copyright ownership.

> The purpose of this policy on ownership of copyrightable Works is to outline the respective rights that all members of the University community—faculty, students and staff—have in such Works created during the course of affiliation with the University. This policy preserves the practice of allowing faculty to own the copyrights to traditional scholarly works, and at the same time seeks to protect the interests of the university in works that are created with the substantial use of university resources (see section III). Although this policy provides guidelines for determining copyright ownership, faculty are strongly encouraged to clarify issues of ownership and revenue sharing by specific written agreements with the Technology Transfer Office at the outset of the project or otherwise as soon as practicable. (1)

This opening demonstrates the tension universities face between their principle missions to "create and disseminate knowledge" and their desires to protect university interests in works to which they have committed substantial resources. This tension parallels the constitutional language out of which the separate bodies of intellectual property law, patent and copyright, emerged in the late 1700s. The U.S. Constitution explains that copyright's purpose is to "promote the Progress of Science and useful Arts, by securing for limited Times to Authors and Inventors the exclusive Right to their respective Writings and Discoveries" (U.S. Constitution, Article I, Section 8., Clause 8). The "progress of science and the useful arts" can only occur when there is both incentive to create and a limited period of time during which creators exert exclusive control over the duplication, distribution, and performance of their works. (U.S. Constitution, Article II, Section 4)

This balance, however, does not imply that faculty should own their works. The letter of copyright law actually implies the opposite. Ashley Packard explains that "faculty writings should belong to universities under the copyright law's work-for-hire provision" (2). Even though copyright vests to the creator at the moment that something is recorded in tangible and reproducible form, the work for hire clause of Section 101 of the Copyright Act of 1976 asserts that any work that is created by an employee within the scope of employment is owned by the employer.[2] It stipulates further that the only way an employee can own such works is if both employee and employer sign an explicit written agreement that alters the default work for hire clause. Many scholars, like Marc Lindsey, have interpreted these statutes to mean that faculty members are employees who create works made for hire when they publish and produce teaching materials; therefore, their works belong to the university.[3]

Other scholars have argued that a "teacher exception" has survived the 1976 revision of the Copyright Act of 1909 even though no reference to the exception exists in the newer statute. These scholars draw on case law, common custom and practices of universities, a common law exception prior to 1976, and dicta from court cases where issues of teacher exception emerge but are not directly addressed in case rulings. Melville Nimmer, a leading authority in the copyright field, refers to two common law cases, *Sherrill v. Grieves*[4] and *Williams v. Weisser*,[5] for creating the academic exception to the work for hire doctrine. Todd Borrow explains that in "both of these cases, the courts 'considered the work made for hire concept with respect to professors but did not find works made for hire, in a large part due to policy and custom'" (3). He explains further that "[i]n the United States, these two cases alone comprise the judicial 'authority prior to the 1976 Act for the existence of an exception from the work made for hire doctrine for professors.'" Speaking of the scanty authority for this exception, Judge Richard Posner writes in the dicta of *Hays v. Sony Corp. of America* that

> it was scanty not because the merit of the exception was doubted, but because, on the contrary, virtually no one questioned that the academic author was entitled to copyright his writings. Although college and university teachers do academic writing as part of their employment responsibilities and use their employer's paper, copier, secretarial staff and (often) computer facilities in that writing, the universal assumption and practice was that (in the absence of an explicit agreement as to who had the right to copyright) the right to copyright such writing belonged to the teacher rather than to the college or university. (Quoted in Packard 5)

Posner drew upon criteria from earlier law that better defined the work for hire concept, noting the lack of university supervision of academics' writing. He notes further that even though the "literalist of statutory interpretation" concludes that the exception has been abolished, Posner concludes that the exception has survived because of the

> havoc that such a [contrary] conclusion would wreak in the settled practices of academic institutions, the lack of fit between the policy of the work-for-hire doctrine and the conditions of academic production, and the absence of any indication that Congress meant to abolish the teacher exemption [. . .]. (5–6)

There are several strong articles by legal scholars that trace the case law history of this debate,[6] work that I will not repeat in this chapter. Instead, I cite intellectual property policies because they represent the "policy and custom" that define university intentions for copyright ownership. Furthermore, most faculty can only turn to their campus intellectual property policies for guidance because the legal status of the exceptions for scholarly work have not been decided definitively in case law or represented in statute. For the time being, it is enough to realize that the majority of intellectual property policies today acknowledge the faculty exception for scholarly works, notwithstanding the debates over work for hire doctrine, and that the vast majority of conflicts at universities are settled based on readings of the policy rather than in the courts.

Utah's policy follows a trend recorded in 2001 by Seventh Circuit Judge Richard Posner, whom Packard cites in "Copyright or Copy Wrong: An Analysis of University Claims to Faculty Work": 42 percent of seventy university policies under study recognized the academic tradition of faculty ownership of what most call "Traditional Works of Scholarship" (Kromrey 5). This figure represents an update and almost doubling of the number of policies that recognize the faculty exemption. Nearly a decade before, Posner found only 26 percent of policies included such an acknowledgment at that time. My own informal review of twenty-five IPPs suggests that the figure has risen to 92 percent since 2001.

The body of Utah's policy states under the "General Rules of Ownership" for faculty that the university's principal mission "is the creation and dissemination of knowledge." Without addressing whether the university might own works, the policy immediately

> transfers to the Creators any copyrights that it may own in a traditional scholarly Work created by University faculty members that result from teaching, research, scholarly or artistic endeavors, regardless of the medium in which the Work is expressed, unless the Work was developed with substantial use of University resources and commercial use is made of the Work. (3)

Such a blanket transfer is common among universities but not universal. Even though Utah's policy reserves the right of the university to develop commercial works that have been created with "substantial use of University resources," it stipulates that such opportunities require the university to "obtain the prior, written consent of the faculty Creator, normally at the beginning of the project when the resources were provided." It stipulates further, that "[i]f the Creator intends to make commercial use of the work, then disclosure must be made as required under section IV.A., "Commercialization and Revenue Sharing" (5). Typically "disclosure" means that a faculty member must submit a form with the Office of Technology Transfer on campus to announce the work and enable the campus IP committee to determine ownership rights.

Conversely, Utah's policy asserts that "[w]orks created by University staff and student-employees within the scope of their University employment are considered to be works made for hire, and thus are Works as to which the University is the owner and controls all legal rights in the Work" ("General Rules of Ownership" 2–3). It states further that works created by these groups that are "*outside* the scope of their University employment are not covered by this policy and are considered to be owned by the Creators," unless substantial resources are used in their creation. In essence, Utah's policy exempts most faculty works from the work for hire clause, while most staff and student-employee works are governed by the clause. Utah's policy represents an example of a carefully crafted document that enables both faculty and the university to determine ownership rights without much difficulty. To determine ownership of both the scholarly work and the interface in case 1 using the University of Utah's policy, we must ask five primary questions: 1. How are the employees in case 1 classified under the policy? 2. Is the work within the scope of employment for the university staff and student-employees? 3. Did this work utilize substantial university support? 4. Is the work also patentable? 5. And, finally, is the work commercialized?

All of the primary collaborators in case 1 contributed to the scholarly work and are considered coauthors. The WAC director is the only creator who is both a tenure-track faculty member and administrator; however, writing scholarly works is not considered within the scope of university employment for any of the other university staff who are involved.

To answer whether the work used substantial university resources, we must ask what constitutes substantial university support and who makes this determination? The policy includes a full page describing substantial use and how the decision is made. Of the five criteria for substantial use, only one—"Exception 2"—might impact the scholarly book, the use of special resources. This criterion concerns works that use university facilities "not available to the general public and beyond the level of facilities and services" that are typically available to faculty (e.g., office space, libraries, limited secretarial and support staff, ordinary use of computers or phones or other university facilities or equipment) (4). Exception 2 could vest copyright ownership of the book with the university because camera-ready screen captures were made by Media Resources, and the Office of Institutional Effectiveness processed all of the data and created the graphs. While some faculty on campus have regular access to SPSS, the expensive software package is not typically used by humanities professors. Notwithstanding the use of these additional resources, it is highly unlikely that the Office of Technology Transfer (OTT) would recommend university ownership of the work because the resources used were not significant, and assuming control of the copyright would contradict the university's stated mission to maximize the development and distribution of new knowledge. Furthermore, the potential of financial return is so small that the university would likely not bother asserting its rights.

Finally, the incentive for the team to publish the results of their work would be subverted if the university chose to assert its rights. Nonetheless, the university may elect to recover costs of these resources from the royalties as a matter of course. Such reasoning is typical of the OTT's decision-making process, especially when the OTT consults regularly on such issues with an Intellectual Property Committee, deans, chairs, or equivalent supervisors of creators. Even if the university would not likely claim ownership, the creators would have to disclose the book to the OTT before signing any publishing contracts.

Under the Board of Regents' union contract at Florida Atlantic University (FAU), where this case is actually set, the decision is even easier. Article 18 of this document states that "[w]orks created with University Support are the property of the University, unless they are Traditional Works of Scholarship or Instructional Works" ("Intellectual Property" 52). As a Traditional Work of Scholarship, the book is unquestionably "the property of the Creator," irrespective of university support. If they have not signed all of their rights to the publisher, all three coauthors, WAC director, WAC coordinator, and former director of assessment have equal rights to the book because they have all contributed to it equally. Each contributor retains the rights to reproduce the work, publish other works based on the original, sell or transfer the work to others, or publicly perform or display the work (U.S. Constitution, Article XVII, Section 106).

The assessment interface is another story altogether. In the case of this work, even the WAC director, who is also a faculty member, might be classified as an administrator and therefore subject to the works for hire clause at the University of Utah. The fact, however, that he was not assigned to develop the assessment project or the interface and that the interface design might be considered outside the scope of his employment may weigh in his favor. On the other hand, work on the interface by the other design team participants would almost certainly be considered work for hire. It is worth noting here as well that the work of the student and secretarial assistant is likely to be deemed support work rather than making them equal authors who have contributed "an independently copyrightable element" (McSherry 73). While no special agreement was struck that stipulated copyright ownership, staff members spent several hundred collective working hours designing, coding, and testing the interface. These efforts make the determination of the faculty member's classification irrelevant. Couple the staff time with commercialization, and most TTOs would claim this work for the university. Finally, the work may also be patentable.

FAU's union contract makes absolutely clear that FAU would own the assessment interface. Under the definition of Inventions, Article 18 states that "[s]oftware and/or code, which can be either patented as an Invention or copyrighted as a Work, will be treated as an Invention for the purposes of assignment of rights and ownership" (18.2[b]2). Furthermore, since this work is not considered a traditional work of scholarship or instructional work, the creators must disclose it to the OTT. Even if the university chose to release the interface back to the assessment team, it would still reserve a royalty-free right to use the work "for educational or research purposes" (18.5[b]). Unless FAU released the work back to the assessment team, no one on the team would have a right to use it, modify it, make copies of it, or present it in any public forum without the express permission of the university. In order for the former assessment director to use it at his new institution, he would have to have a signed agreement with FAU. Furthermore, even though the WAC director developed the design and has saved the original design notes to demonstrate ownership, he may not be allowed to display representations of the design at the administrator's conference or in the book without the express written permission of the university. Even though the policy states that "Employees shall control their personal correspondence and notes," it states further that "Employees shall serve as the University's agent for purposes of maintaining and controlling laboratory notebooks, raw data, and other working papers, all of which are the property of the university" (18.4[c]). The implications could not be clearer. The interface, the design notes, and the data collected for the WAC assessment process are owned by the university.

This final point brings us to our last two issues concerning case 1: distribution of proceeds and ownership and control of student work that serves as data for the assessment study. At most institutions, IPPs include a revenue sharing formula that establishes what percentages go directly to the university, departments, centers, and the creator. These percentages can be negotiated in advance if a project director has the foresight and justification to do so. Concerning student work at FAU, Article 18 defines a Creator as "an employee as defined in this collective bargaining agreement who creates a Work or creates or discovers an Invention" (18.2[e]). Students are not covered and therefore retain ownership of all works they create. When they sign a consent form to participate in the study, however, they commit to submitting a survey and a first and second draft of a near, end-of-term paper. By signing this consent form, they allow the principal investigators to use their works to assess the WAC program for the "life of the study plus five years." After that time, the materials are destroyed. Since all collected data is "kept confidential on a secure FAU server" and "results will be reported in aggregate form," students need not be concerned about misuse of their works (Galin, Consent Form).

Case 1 has provided opportunities to lay out copyright basics, definitions for several key terms, and an example of how an Office of Technology Transfer would handle a collaboratively produced scholarly work that used substantial university resources and an assessment interface that would likely be deemed a work made for hire. Case 2 provides an opportunity to examine ownership of teaching materials that are produced by a course coordinator, whose responsibility it is to develop and distribute these materials. It also explores how a stressful hostile environment both leads to and complicates ownership rights.

CASE 2

You are a non–tenure-track associate professor of Clinical Pathology and Pathology course director at your university's College of Medicine. You have received so many teaching awards that you were made ineligible for most future awards so that others might have a chance. In May, after you have finalized the fall schedule for all teaching sessions within the Introductory Pathology course, a former colleague, who had been denied tenure in your department and who was returning from a leave of absence, asked your dean to return to teaching nine pathology lectures in the course that you coordinate. The dean asks you to change the schedule to accommodate this person, even though her current contract has her directing the Animal Care Facility for 100 percent of her time. She is a veterinarian, not a board certified pathologist. Reluctantly, after numerous meetings between you and your dean, you reassign seven of the nine requested lectures to your former colleague, even though previously scheduled faculty had already developed their teaching materials.

Meanwhile, your chair resigns and another chair is appointed but remains for only two days, so your Dean names himself acting chair of your department. He unilaterally changes the remaining course schedule less than two weeks prior to the start of classes. That same day, you resign as course director because you feel that you are being undermined and forced from your position. Your dean appoints the veterinarian to your director position. You write the dean that you will clear out your office before school starts the following week, and you go that night to remove some of your most valuable personal teaching materials. Two days later, you find out that you are no longer scheduled to teach your

seventeen hours of lecture and six three-hour labs. That same day, the
new appointee and department secretary enter your office without your
permission and go through over eleven years of teaching materials in
your office—files, your desk, and your computer—to gather materials
for the upcoming classes. Immediately afterward, the dean sends you a
note saying that some unauthorized person has entered your office and
removed university property (presumably a reference to the visit you
told him you were making to your own office). In addition, he states
that he has copied all of your computer data for security purposes. He
has the locks changed to your office, your department, and the lab in
which you have taught for many years. Large portions of materials you
created, along with materials that were given to you by a former colleague, are distributed to students without your permission, many under
the new director's name.

   After months of struggle that include the dean removing the newly
appointed Pathology chair and reinstating himself to that position, a
faculty senate report censoring the dean, and a meeting at which the
dean states your best interests would be served by finding a job elsewhere and that your "leaving would also be best for the institution,"
you file for copyright on your pathology teaching materials and later file
a copyright lawsuit against the former course director and dean. You
resign your position as associate professor and take a position at another
medical school.

   Who has rights to use the course materials, in what contexts, and
based on what arguments of use? How does a hostile work environment
affect the claims to ownership?

   There is no simple answer to these questions. Once a case like this goes
to court, the judge and jury must make the decisions. Interestingly, *Bosch v.
Ball-Kell* has been decided, but the case summary has not been made public
because the plaintiffs have moved to have the decision vacated and requested
a new trial because of improper jury findings and bad jury instructions. For
the sake of clarity, I have left out many significant elements of the actual case,
including a charge of intentional infliction of emotional distress that was
dismissed (perhaps inappropriately), numerous claims and counterclaims by
both plaintiffs and the defense, and direct analysis of court findings because
they are not publicly available. Furthermore, the aforementioned details
are drawn primarily from a faculty senate report that was not allowed into
evidence in the actual court case because it concerned the dean's behavior,

which was not at issue in the copyright case. The information is essential, however, for the purposes of this chapter to demonstrate how institutional disputes emerge and magnify into cases for the courts. I do refer in several places to documents provided by the plaintiff, whom I have had the good fortune of meeting. I leave the legal decisions to the courts but provide here an institutional analysis that unpacks the issues this case raises for faculty to make pre-court decisions.

Few copyright disputes in higher education ever make it to federal court, where all copyright cases are heard. In fact, since the enactment of the Copyright Act of 1976, only a handful of such cases have ever been decided.[7] The majority are resolved at the institution based on the specifics of the case at hand and readings of the intellectual property policy and related documents. But before we return to policy language, it is necessary to tease out some of the issues from this scenario.

This case represents the kind of dispute that none of us would ever expect to occur. Yet, its underlying principles represent the most likely problem faculty will face in higher education: university claims of ownership for teaching materials. In addition, it dramatizes how complex copyright concerns can become when situated in highly volatile institutional relationships. It also provides a case study for determining the scope of the works made for hire clause in the Copyright Act of 1976. Perhaps most important of all, it demonstrates how important copyright ownership determinations can be in institutions of higher education.

As in case 1, the central issues involve the works made for hire doctrine and the traditional exemption for scholarly works, but there are additional practical matters that complicate things further. For example, when a legal crisis emerges just two weeks before the term is to begin, does the university have a right to use copyrighted materials without permission of the creator because of the negative impact it may have on academic programs? When there is a hostile environment created by a dean, does a faculty member have a right to take absolute control over teaching materials? Finally, if a dean has authority to seize control of a department by installing himself as chair, does his direct supervisory role change rights to ownership of teaching materials?

We can only begin to answer these questions if we turn to the IPP that was in place at the institution where the case developed: the University of Illinois (UI). A close reading of the policy reveals why this case ended up in court. Unlike policies at a range of other institutions, the UI policy is ambiguous concerning teaching materials other than class notes. While it nods at an acknowledgment of the academic exception, it struggles to maintain the typical balance. We can see this struggle in the objectives of the document. More importantly, we could have predicted this struggle by realizing an important distinction that emerges in a comparison with the University of Utah's policy. Utah separates patent and copyright policies into two related but distinct documents; UI combines all intellectual property into a single document. It becomes immediately clear upon reading the purpose and objectives of the UI document that it was written primarily to address patentable and licensable inventions. Works appear to be addressed as an afterthought.

The opening statement of the UI policy claims that the purpose of the IPP "is to provide the necessary protections and incentives to encourage both the discovery and development of new knowledge and its transfer for the public benefit." This language echoes the constitutional directive that underlies copyright and patent law. The second clause, however, emphasizes the financial goals of the policy, which often lead to unbalanced definitions of "public benefit." The policy continues, "a secondary purpose is to enhance the generation of revenue for the University and the creators" (Article III, Section 1). This stated focus on financial returns stands in stark contrast with the stated purpose of the Utah copyright policy, which seeks to "outline the respective rights that all members of the University community [. . .] have in such Works created" while affiliated with the university. The very next statement of the Illinois policy introduces the practice of faculty owning copyrights to "traditional scholarly works" unless substantial university resources have been used to create them. In the four primary policy objectives that follow, it becomes clear that this financial focus concerns patents rather than works:

(i) To optimize the environment and incentives for research and for the creation of new knowledge at the University;

(ii) To ensure that the educational mission of the University is not compromised;

(iii) To bring technology into practical use for the public benefit as quickly and effectively as possible; and

(iv) To protect the interest of the people of Illinois through a due recovery by the University of its investment in research.

Interestingly, there is no mention here of works, copyright law, academic tradition, or the complexities of assigning ownership that govern other policies that I mention later. The first two objectives work in concert and lead to the second two. Universities have always sought to create new knowledge.

The Bayh–Dole Act changed university responsibilities when the Patent and Trademark Act Amendments of 1980 "created a uniform patent policy among the many federal agencies that fund research, enabling small businesses and non-profit organizations, including universities, to retain title to inventions made under federally-funded research programs" ("Bayh-Dole Act"). This legislation gives universities the right to claim ownership of patents developed with federal funding and a responsibility to commercialize as many as possible by transferring them to the private sector. According to Howard W. Bremer in "The First Two Decades of the Bayh-Dole Act as Public Policy," the Bayh-Dole Act has contributed about forty-one billion dollars to the U.S. economy over the past twenty years by facilitating technology transfer from universities of patents and licenses that would not likely have reached the market otherwise. At the same time, however, legislation created a new gold rush mentality for potential revenue that could distract universities from their central missions of creating and disseminating new knowledge and training future generations of American citizens. The first two objectives of UI's policy acknowledge this tension by optimizing the environment and incentives for creating new knowledge without compromising the educational mission of the university.

If there was any doubt that objectives one and two derive from the Bayh-Dole Act rather than copyright law, objectives three and four confirm this affiliation. Typically, there is not much money to be made in faculty works. Nor is it likely that most works will produce the kind of technology that objective three desires to bring "into practical use for the public benefit." There are times when universities invest in faculty works; however, the vast majority of such cases involve specialized labs in the sciences out of which most inventions emerge.

These objectives help us interpret the intent of the policy and anticipate possible difficulties, but they are not binding statements that can be used to resolve copyright disputes. For our purposes, the significant passages are the definition of traditional academic copyrightable works in section 2 (Definitions) and section 4 (Copyrights).

The policy states that traditional academic copyrightable works are

> a subset of copyrightable works created independently and at the creator's initiative for traditional academic purposes. Examples include *class notes* [emphasis added], books, theses and dissertations, educational software (also known as courseware or lessonware), articles, non-fiction, fiction, poems, musical works, dramatic works including any

accompanying music, pantomimes and choreographic works, pictorial, graphic and sculptural works, or other works of artistic imagination that are not created as an institutional initiative (as specified in Section 4[a] [2] cited later).

This definition recognizes the academic tradition of exempting certain works of scholarship from the works for hire clause of the Copyright Act; however, it is less clear than most IPPs. Had this dispute occurred at the University of Utah or Indiana University, there would have been no question that faculty owned these materials. As noted earlier, Utah makes no claims to such materials unless developed with substantial university resources and commercialized. Indiana University's IPP states unequivocally that "traditional works of scholarship" and "instructional materials" do not belong to the university (Indiana University).

Had the dispute occurred at the University of Pittsburgh, ownership would have vested with faculty as dictated by traditional exceptions, but the university would have retained "a non-exclusive, irrevocable, perpetual, royalty-free license for course material created by the faculty in the course of employment" (University of Pittsburgh II.A). The Texas A & M system also "recognizes and affirms the traditional academic freedom of its faculty and staff to publish pedagogical, scholarly or artistic works without restriction"; however, each university would "retain a royalty-free right to use the materials for educational purposes" (Texas A & M 2.1.3). While all of these policies make slightly different claims, all of them are more explicit than UI's policy.

In the University of Illinois's policy, "class notes" appear among the non-exhaustive list of examples. Since a high percentage of universities exempt all teaching materials from the works for hire clause, one might reasonably expect that class syllabi or course materials beyond class notes may also qualify as traditional academic copyrightable works in this context. Certainly, the absence of other course materials in the aforementioned definition is not in itself proof that they are not covered by this definition. At the same time, however, the definition leaves sufficient doubt that we must turn to other passages to determine the status of other class materials.

Section 4, concerning ownership of copyrights, states that "[u]nless subject to any of the exceptions specified below [. . .]creators retain all rights to traditional academic copyrightable works as defined in Section 2 (b) above. (See, however, Sections 4(b)2 below.)" Section 4(b)2 names four exceptions to creator ownership of scholarly works. Only the second of the four categories is of concern on this issue. The second exception explains that the university will own works that are created as "a specific requirement of employment or as an assigned university duty that may be specified [. . .] in a written job description or an employment agreement." The policy notes that such a statement "may define the full scope or content of the employee's university employment duties comprehensively or may be limited to terms applicable to a single copyrightable work" (Section 4(a)2). The university will also own the work if the university "provides the motivation for the preparation of the work, the topic or content of which is determined by the creator's employment duties and/or when the work is prepared at the university's expense." Similar statements appear in all of the other documents as well, but the others clearly exempt teaching materials from works made for hire.

The vague nature of the language here is frustrating because it reads like most work for hire clauses but does not help us determine clearly whether teaching materials other than class notes should be classified as "a specific requirement of employment," whether described fully or as a specific task. Nor does it help us determine whether the university can be said to have "provided the motivation for the preparation" of the teaching materials, whether such materials are determined by "the creator's employment duties," or whether the work can be considered to have been "prepared at the university's expense." To make these determinations, we must turn to the letter of employment and any other documents that represent "motivation for the preparation" of the materials. The plaintiff's letter of employment stipulates that her expected duties included "direct instruction and course coordination" ("Plaintiff's Motion for New Trial" 6). This language might be construed as a specific requirement of employment; however, we are all expected to produce syllabi and other course materials. Is a coordinator of a course held to a different standard? It is hard to say. The fact that the dean as self-appointed chair authorized the other defendant to take and use the plaintiff's teaching materials begs the question: Is the authorization by the dean who is acting as chair appropriate or legal? Should it be? In the end, only the courts can answer these questions, but a clarified IPP would be highly instructive.

Even though the case is still pending in federal court because of post-trial motions, the "Plaintiff's Motion for New Trial and to Alter or Amend Judgment" notes the court's conclusion that the plaintiff owned two of the three sets of copyrighted materials outright. Ownership of the third set is being contested, but not on grounds of works made for hire. The motion clearly states that "declaratory judgment should be entered in favor of Bosch [the plaintiff] with regard to defendant's 'work made for hire argument'" (I. Background). In the court's eyes, a course coordinator is to be treated like all other faculty concerning teaching materials absent specific language to the contrary. Once an official decision is handed down, this case may provide the most explicit case law yet in the application of the work for hire clause to faculty-created teaching materials. At the very least, the trial summary will be instructive to faculty who face similar work made for hire claims in the future.

Difficulties with definitions and policy language create the possibility of a problem, but the root of the dispute over these materials lies in the severely harassing environment that fostered the copyright infringement lawsuit in the first place. Had the dean not taken such drastic measures to wrest control of the pathology program from the curriculum director, the suit would likely never have been filed. Perhaps, more importantly, had the dean not encouraged the new curriculum director to take the plaintiff's course materials without permission and had she not distributed them to the students for several years after the initial conflict began, the lawsuit would never have been filed. Clearly, the plaintiff in this case was mistreated, and no faculty member should have to endure similar mistreatment; nevertheless, the case points to several unresolved issues worthy of examination, namely the question of whether or how the work environment should impact copyright decisions.

Indeed, there is some discord between the economies of the academic work environment and the assumptions that underlie copyright law. Corynne McSherry explains that "copyright law in general assumes that authors need and deserve monetary profit, and fosters a market economy in intellectual commodities" (75). She continues, "Few bonds of trust exist in their market, and one of the principal objects of copyright law is to make up for that lack by defining and defending the respective economic interests of property owners." She contrasts this market economy with the "gift economy" of knowledge in higher education—a "system based on the reciprocal and personalized exchange of gifts rather than the impersonal selling of private property." In this system, we write articles and chapters like this one to be published by an academic press. While some money exchanges hands over the life of the book and the editor of this collection may make several hundred dollars, the contributors do not expect to receive remuneration beyond credit toward promotion and tenure. McSherry explains that

> [g]ift exchange, ideally, is a mechanism for allocating resources toward community reproduction. Through the quality and generosity of one's giving and receiving, one demonstrates authority, spiritual favor, and especially, honor and status. (75)

Consider the relationships between graduate students and their faculty mentors who help guide these academic apprentices through the production of their theses and dissertations, or the relationship struck between students and faculty in an average course. Typically the best teachers are those who demonstrate their authority, knowledge, and generosity during and after class. McSherry only hints, however, at the underlying economy of status that drives the gift economy. Status is not achieved merely by the quality and generosity of giving and receiving.

The economy of status is highly competitive, awarding tenure to some and not to others. It establishes a pecking order among the disciplines and ranks of faculty at the university. Furthermore, it fosters specialization to such a degree that the greatest mark of faculty success is not financial, as it would be in a market economy, but scholarly status: if not scholarship, then teaching, and if not teaching, then administration. Not unlike the market economy, the economy of status fosters egocentric behavior. At its best, that behavior becomes self-defining and preserving. At other times it becomes self-serving, and at its worst self-defeating.

In case 2 it is the economy of status that underlies nearly all of the interactions among the three parties named in the copyright infringement lawsuit. Policy decisions cannot be understood outside of these academic economies without jeopardizing the fragile fabric on which they are built. For this reason, I turn briefly to offer a few historical facts that underlie this copyright dispute.

According to the former department chair who had hired both the plaintiff, Bosch, and the key defendant, Ball-Kell, in the early 1990s, Ball-Kell was hired with the hope that she would, eventually, become course director for the fall General Pathology course. He planned to give her a few years to "establish her classroom and laboratory teaching role and to make good progress in scholarly activities" toward tenure and promotion (Bartlett, Exhibit C) During her first few years, her role in the veterinary clinic grew, and she did not publish anything. A few years into her position, she made statements that "seriously offended some of the volunteer faculty (hospital pathologists who teach during the pathology curriculum)," which required "damage control" for several days on the part of the chair. The fall out from that faculty meeting eventually led to an attempt by Ball-Kell to file a grievance against the chair, which she later dropped. From that time forward, their relationship was strained. Before he retired, the chair gave all of his teaching materials to Bosch to support her role as course director of Pathology. After his retirement, Ball-Kell went up for but was denied tenure in 2000 (Bosch, Report on Complaint against Regional Dean 5). She was given a one-year terminal contract. At the end of that year, the dean changed her 30-percent role as director of the Laboratory Animal Care Facility to 100 percent with a 0 percent appointment in Pathology. She took a personal leave and decided, upon returning from leave, that she would like to resume teaching nine lectures that she taught before her position changed. She approached the dean in May of 2002 to resume teaching in August.

This bit of historical background enables us to see why Ball-Kell approached the dean to request lectures rather than Bosch, the course director. It also suggests that tensions may have existed between Bosch and Ball-Kell prior to this request. Finally, it enables us to predict that the dean's intervention could only lead to conflict because it disrupted the economy of status at multiple levels. The claims over copyright control involved no financial interests. They grew out of Bosch's investment in her teaching as a non–tenure-track associate professor. Her academic identity resided in those materials, which she understandably had a desire to control. Had the dean realized how significantly he had underestimated the relationship between teaching identity and course materials for a non–tenure-track associate professor, he might have responded differently. Ultimately, however, it was the vagueness of the University of Illinois's IPP that enabled her to file the lawsuit. And it was that same vagueness that enabled the defense to dispute her claims of copyright ownership.

CONCLUSIONS

Few if any readers of this chapter will ever file a copyright infringement suit concerning their scholarship, computer software, or teaching materials. But this chapter is not ultimately about avoiding court. It is about owning our rights, learning how to read the IPP at our own institutions in relation to those of others, knowing what to look for—when policies are weak or vague, what terms to note, what additional documents to locate—and knowing what steps we can take to secure our intellectual efforts as we navigate the economies of the academic system. As contributors to the gift economy, we have to be prepared to release some control over our works. At the same time, the university must recognize the economy of status that governs the production of new knowledge upon which faculty build their professional reputations and, collectively, the reputation of the institution.

Given the dilemma of balancing a teaching mission with respect for faculty rights, the California State and New York University systems collaborated to produce an impressive document entitled "Intellectual Property, Fair Use, and the Unbundling of Ownership Rights." It is worth noting briefly here why unbundling the rights of copyright ownership can benefit authors and universities. The document asserts that "initial ownership" of "intellectual property in traditional university settings, and the subsequent disposition of the associated ownership rights, often has been unguided—sometimes to the detriment of teaching, learning, and research." It states further that the "effectiveness of higher education requires a better understanding of how ownership rights associated with new intellectual property promote the mutual benefit of faculty, staff, and students and their learning communities" (CETUS 9). Therefore, it calls for new models for allocating intellectual rights, "based on licensing agreements which anticipate the influence of new technologies on teaching, learning, research, and creative activity in American universities" (CETUS 10). Undoubtedly, such an unbundling of ownership rights would have clarified the University of Illinois's policy.

In the hopes of preventing even one more case like case 2, I close with two specific suggestions for faculty to better understand and assert ownership rights, and I provide an appendix of fifteen factors to consider when reviewing IPP documents. First, note whether your university's IPP covers all works and inventions in a single document or splits them into separate documents. Stanford; Utah; California State University, San Bernardino; Brown; Columbia; and Pittsburgh policies all separate patents and works into different policies. It is not automatically the case that separate documents are better for faculty, although they are often more explicit. For example, Columbia University asserts ownership of "course content and/or courseware which may be created under the aegis of a school or department of the University" but recognizes faculty ownership in "non-institutional course content and courseware" (Columbia University). Such a distinction would likely have prevented the confusion in case 2 that led to a copyright lawsuit. If your university uses a single document for all IP, then it is important that you note the balance of focus on works and inventions, the clarity of defined terms, and the allocation of ownership.

Second, understand that there are multiple documents that govern ownership of works in academia. The primary document is the campus IPP as it pertains to copyrights. If there is a campus policy for patents, it too will have some reference to works that support patents and data. Perhaps of equal (if not greater) importance is the actual letter of employment. For most tenure-track faculty, such a letter outlines general research, teaching, and service expectations and may include special assignments relevant to an IP policy. Other related documents include emails in which a chair or dean clarifies new or additional assignments, or perhaps a mandate from a university committee. For example, had a comprehensive report on the assessment of WAC been mandated by the faculty senate or undergraduate dean at FAU and the nature of the report specified what graphs and charts needed to be included, the ownership of those materials would likely have been clarified. A number of additional documents may impact faculty ownership rights ranging from special policies for distance education, third-party contracts, and releases of rights like consent forms. Some institutions use memoranda of understanding to complement or clarify a policy rather than rewrite it. Finally, note whether your institution has a union contract, for it is possible that university policy may conflict with this contract, in which case, you might be able to lobby the university to change its policy to conform to the contract.

Certainly, the cases discussed earlier in this chapter and the suggestions offered herein represent a small sampling of the IP issues relevant to academia. While I may not have offered an exhaustive list of these issues, I hope to have revealed some of the key problems we face as faculty members as well as useful strategies for beginning to address these problems. As writing teachers, we may not possess the expertise of practicing lawyers; if, however, we make individual and collective efforts to become better aware of language concerns within IP policy documents, we will find ourselves in a much better position to own our rights at our home institutions, understand when we must disclose our work, and know when the university has a right to claim copyright ownership of our efforts. This knowledge may enable us not simply to avoid disputes but to better advocate for substantial and equitable changes in institutional policies and practices.

NOTES

1. I am not a lawyer and do not offer my analysis herein as legal advice.

2. Visit IUPUI's "Copyright Management Center" at http://www.copyright.iupui.edu/WorkMadeForHire.htm for full references to the works made for hire language in the Copyright Act and selected quotations from important cases on these issues for faculty works.

3. For a nuanced explanation of the works made for hire provision, see Packard (2–4).

4. *Sherrill v. Grieves*, 57 Wash. L. Rep. 286, 20 C.O. Bull. 675 (1929). Mathieu Deflem explains in "Resisting the Commodification of Education" that "the Supreme Court of the District of Columbia held that an instructor who taught for United

States Army officers held a copyright to his lectures. The instructor had written a textbook on his lectures, but prior to the book's publication, U.S. military authorities had already printed a pamphlet that incorporated the instructor's teachings. The court ruled that the teacher, not his employer, owned the copyright to his lectures because he was not obliged to reduce his lectures to writing as part of his work for the military authorities."

5. *Weinstein v. University of Illinois*, 811 F.2d 1091 (Seventh Circuit 1987) held that the faculty member at the University of Illinois retains the copyright to a research article because university policy specifically stipulates such an outcome. The decision is important because it interprets an IPP to decide ownership.

6. See Ashley Packard's " Copyright or Copy Wrong: An Analysis of University Claims to Faculty Work" and particularly references in her notes to Cooper Dreyfuss, Philip T. K. Daniel and Patrick D. Pauken, Gregory K. Laughlin, Russ VerSteeg, Todd Simon,. and Todd Borow. Also note Elizabeth Townsend's "Legal and Policy Responses to the Disappearing 'Teacher Exception,' or Copyright Ownership in the 21st Century University" and Laura Lape's "Ownership of Copyrightable Works of University Professors: The Interplay between the Copyright Act and University Copyright Policies."

7. See the list of cases cited by Mathieu Deflem in "Resisting the Commodification of Education" for a quick summary of cases concerning faculty ownership in higher education. *Bosch v. Ball-Kell* may be the next definitive case on these issues.

WORKS CITED

American Association of University Professors. Statement on Copyright. *AAUP Home Page*. 1999. 13 March, 2991 <http://www.aaup.org/spccopyr.htm>.

The Association of University Technology Managers. "Bayh-Dole Act." 5 Aug. 2007 <http://www.autm.net/aboutTT/aboutTT_bayhDoleAct.cfm>.

Bartlett, Gerald L. Exhibit C: Bartlett Letter to Committee on Academic Freedom & Tenure Re: BB Qualifications 06–20–03. Email Attachment from Bosch, Barbara. Post-trial motion. 18 July 2007.

Borrow, Todd A. "Copyright Ownership of Scholarly Works Created by University Faculty and Posted on School-Provided Web Pages." *University of Miami Business Law Review* (1998): 149–69.

Bosch, Barbara. Post-trial motion. Email to Jeffrey R. Galin. 18 July 2007.

———.FW:RE:P.S. Email Attachment to Jeffrey R. Galin. Report on Complaint against Regional Dean Donald E. Rager (Peoria) by Associate Professor of Clinical Pathology Barbara D. Bosch, by the Senate Committee on Academic Freedom and Tenure. 16 July 2007.

Bosch v. Ball-Kell 2007 WL 601721 (C.D.Ill.). *Westlaw*. U.S. District Court, C.D. Illinois. 12 July 2007.

Bremer, Howard W. "The First Two Decades of the Bayh-Dole Act as Public Policy." 1999. National Association of Universities and Land-Grant Colleges 11 Aug. 2007 <http://www.nasulgc.org/COTT/Bayh-Dohl/Bremer_speech.htm>.

CETUS (Consortium for Educational Technology for University Systems). "Intellectual Property, Fair Use, and the Unbundling of Ownership Rights." 6 Aug. 2007 <http://www.calstate.edu/AcadSen/Records/Reports/Intellectual_Prop_Final.pdf>.

Columbia University. Columbia University Copyright Policy. 3 June 2000. 12 Aug. 2007 <http://www.columbia.edu/cu/provost/docs/copyright.html>.

Crews, Kenneth. "The Law of 'Work-Made-For-Hire' Select Statutes and Cases." 14 Sept. 2001. Copyright Management Center IUPUI. 12 Aug. 2007 <http://www.copyright.iupui.edu/WorkMadeForHire.htm>.

Deflem, Mathieu. " Resisting the Commodification of Education: University Policies Against Commercial Lecture Notes Companies." 1999. *Publications—Mathieu Deflem* 12 Aug. 2007 <http://www.cas.sc.edu/socy/faculty/deflem/zteachlaw.htm>.

Florida Atlantic University. Article 18: Inventions and Works. *Florida Atlantic University Board of Trustees/United Faculty of Florida Collective Bargaining Agreement 2006–2009.* 2006. 8 Aug. 2007 <http://www.fau.edu/provost/files/CBA2006–2009.pdf>.

Galin, Jeffrey. Consent Form. 2007. Florida Atlantic University. 8 Aug. 2007 <https://swise.fau.edu/wac>.

Hays v. Sony Corp. of America. 847 F.2d 412; U.S. App. 1988.

Indiana University. Assignment and Protection of Intellectual Property. 9 May 1997. 11 Aug. 2007 <www.research.iu.edu/respol/intprop.html>.

Kromrey, Jeffrey, et al. "Intellectual Property and Online Courses: Policies at Major Research Universities." *NECC 2005 Research Paper Archives.* 2005. International Society for Technology in Education. 24 July 2007 <http://center.uoregon.edu/ISTE/uploads/NECC2005/KEY_6920072/Kromrey_IntellectualProperty NECC2005_RP.pdf>.

Lape, Laura G. "Ownership of Copyrightable Works of University Professors: The Interplay between the Copyright Act and University Copyright Policies." *Villanova Law Review* 37. 2 (April 1992): 223–71.

Lindsey, Marc. *Copyright Law on Campus.* Pullman, WA: Washington State UP, 2003.

McSherry, Corynne. Who Owns Academic Work? Battling for Control of Intellectual Property. Cambridge: Harvard UP, 2001.

Packard, Ashley. "Copyright or Copy Wrong: An Analysis of University Claims to Faculty Work." *Communication Law and Policy* 7(Summer 2002): 8 August 2007 <http://coursesite.cl.uh.edu/hsh/Packard/Copyright%20or%20 Copy%20 Wrong.pdf>.

"Plaintiff's Motion for New Trial and to Alter or Amend Judgment." Email Attachment from Bosch, Barbara. "Post-trial motion." 18 July 2007. No.03 C 1408. U.S. District Court for the Central District of Illinois Peoria Division.

Texas A & M University. "Intellectual Property Management and Commercializa-
    tion." 26 May 2006. 8 Aug. 2007 <http://otc.tamu.edu/uploads/media/A&M_
    System_Intellectual_Property_Policy_17–01.pdf>.

Townsend, Elizabeth. "Legal and Policy Responses to the Disappearing 'Teacher
    Exception,' or Copyright Ownership in the 21st Century University." *Minnesota
    Intellectual Property Review* 4.2 (2003): 209–83.

University of Illinois. Article III. Intellectual Property. *The General Rules Concern-
    ing University Organization and Procedure.* 3 Sept. 1998. 8 Aug. 2007 <http://
    web.archive.org/web/20030412175433/www.uillinois.edu/university/policies/
    general.php>.

University of Pittsburgh. University of Pittsburgh Policy 11–02–02: Copyrights. 5
    Sept. 2006. 28 May 2007 <http://www.pitt.edu/HOME/PP/policies/11/11-
    02-02.html>.

University of Utah. "Ownership of Copyrightable Works and Related Works." 14 May
    2001. 8 Aug. 2007 <http://www.admin.utah.edu/ppmanual/6/6–7.html>.

APPENDIX: FIFTEEN FACTORS TO CONSIDER
WHEN REVIEWING IPP DOCUMENTS

1. As demonstrated in case 1, it is important to read the stated purpose of the policy, as
   it often offers insight into the intent of language that is found in later statements.

2. Definitions are fundamental to all IPP documents. Often they distinguish between
   traditional works of scholarship/instructional works and institutional works.

3. Read carefully sections that pertain directly to ownership of works.

4. Note who is covered by your campus IP policy. If you work collaboratively with
   graduate students to gather data for research that inform a dissertation, students
   will typically retain ownership of their work but may share ownership with the
   faculty member of the data collected.

5. Note whether teaching is included in an academic exemption or as an exception.

6. Note statements on online delivery of materials if applicable.

7. Determine whether joint works are deemed university property or vest equally
   with their creators. Students may have rights, for instance, to publish their own
   articles based on work that you have developed collaboratively.

8. Look for passages that discuss patentability of works; for in most cases universities
   will claim ownership of works that can be patented.

9. Also, find the university's revenue sharing formula. Typically, creators receive
   between 35–50 percent of proceeds after costs are recovered.

10. Look for clauses that enable transfer of ownership and the commensurate rights
    and responsibilities of all parties.

11. Note exceptions for university ownership of scholarly works.

12. If you find clauses on extraordinary support or compensation or substantial use, make sure to know what triggers university ownership. At some institutions, any grant over $2,500 serves as a trigger. Others stipulate that all grant money triggers ownership.

13. Furthermore, know how determinations of substantial use are made. At some institutions, the provost is given this responsibility in consultation with deans and department chairs. At other schools, an Intellectual Property (or Copyright) Committee makes recommendations to the provost, vice president of research, or president. Most likely, the staff of your Office of Technology Transfer know the procedures and can help you interpret them.

14. Realize that nearly all IPPs require disclosure of certain works, especially those that will be published or sold commercially.

15. Review the Conflict of Commitment and Interest documents, which will prevent you from using university resources for your own commercial benefit and may require you to remove all references to the university's name if you are teaching outside of your home institution.

LIST OF CONTRIBUTORS

BRIAN D. BALLENTINE is an assistant professor and coordinator for the Professional Writing and Editing program at West Virginia University. Prior to completing his PhD at Case Western Reserve University, he was a senior software engineer for Philips Medical Systems, designing user interfaces for Web-based radiology applications and specializing in human–computer interaction. This past work experience ties to his current research interests, which include open source and free software, technical communication, digital literacy and hypertext theory, as well as intellectual property and authorship. In his spare time, Ballentine still enjoys coding, including working with and contributing to several open source projects.

LISA DUSH is a lecturer in the Writing Across the Curriculum program at the Massachusetts Institute of Technology. She is also the director of Storybuilders, a business that helps individuals and organizations tell stories with digital media.

JEFFREY R. GALIN is an associate professor of English and director of both the Center for Excellence in Writing and WAC at Florida Atlantic University. He has coedited *The Dialogic Classroom: Teachers Integrating Computer Technology, Pedagogy, and Research* and *Teaching/Writing in the Late Age of Print*. He has published articles in *College Composition*; *Communication, Computers and Composition*; and *Kairos*. As the IP committee chair at California State University, San Bernardino, he helped draft an IP policy for faculty works. While serving on the IP committee at FAU, he helped craft FAU's IP policy and served on the union bargaining team. He has also chaired the CCCC Caucus on Intellectual Property and continues to serve on the NCTE CCCC-IP Committee.

TYANNA HERRINGTON is an associate professor at the Georgia Institute of Technology. Her educational background (JD 1985 and PhD 1997) forms a basis for her research treating issues of power and access in law and societal discourse. Her books are in law—*Controlling Voices: Intellectual Property, Humanistic Studies, and the Internet* (2001), *A Legal Primer for Technical Communicators* (2003), and a new development, *iProp: Students' Rights and Responsibilities in Intellectual Property*—but her articles treat issues in technical communication as well, many focusing on international communication and distributed education. Herrington's Fulbright professorship to St. Petersburg, Russia, in 1999 allowed her to develop the continually expanding Global Classroom Project that supports Russian and American students' and professors' analyses of cross-cultural issues in online venues. She continues to research and teach in both intellectual property and international communication.

SOHUI LEE is a lecturer in the program in Writing and Rhetoric at Stanford University and assistant director of the Hume Writing Center. Interested in new media composition, she has published an online tutorial for students and instructors called "Rhetorical PowerPoint" with Bedford/St. Martin Press online (2007). In addition to composition, Lee studies transatlantic literary romanticism. Her publications include articles and essays in *Symbiosis: A Journal of Anglo-American Literary Relations, American Periodicals, Romanticism on the Net, Britain and the Americas: Culture, Politics, and History: A Multidisciplinary Encyclopedia* (2005), and in *Sullen Fires Across the Atlantic: Essays in Romanticism* (2006). She is currently writing a monograph on American literary nationalism and its transatlantic imagination in antebellum nationalist discourse, poetry, and narratives.

JOHN LOGIE is an associate professor of Rhetoric in the Department of Writing Studies at the University of Minnesota. His scholarship addresses questions of rhetorical invention, authorship, and textual ownership, with a particular focus on how communicative technologies—especially electronic media—intersect with and influence these questions. He is the author of *Peers, Pirates, and Persuasion: Rhetoric in the Peer-to-Peer Debates* (2006), which addresses the vexed discourse surrounding music and media copyrights on the Internet. His articles have appeared in *First Monday, Rhetoric Society Quarterly, Rhetoric Review, Computers and Composition, KB Journal, Technical Communication Quarterly*, and several edited collections. Logie has served as chair of the Intellectual Property Committee of the Conference of College Composition and Communication, and as cochair of the CCCC's Intellectual Property Caucus. He lives in Minneapolis with his wife, two daughters, a pair of cats, and an infuriatingly evasive family of moths.

CLANCY RATLIFF is an assistant professor at the University of Louisiana at Lafayette, where she also directs the first-year writing program. She is the coeditor of *Into the Blogosphere: Rhetoric, Community, and Culture of Weblogs*, the first collection of scholarly essays about blogging. She received the John Lovas Memorial Academic Weblog Award from *Kairos: A Journal of Rhetoric, Technology, and Pedagogy* in May 2006 for her weblog, CultureCat, which she has maintained since 2003 and which has been Creative Commons licensed since that time. She also received the 2006 Hugh Burns Best Dissertation Award from *Computers and Composition* for her dissertation, *"Where Are the Women?" Rhetoric and Gender in Weblog Discourse*. She has been involved in the CCCC Intellectual Property Caucus since 2004.

JESSICA REYMAN is an assistant professor of rhetoric and professional writing and director of the Institute for Professional Development at Northern Illinois University. Her research and teaching interests include technical and professional communication, digital rhetoric, and copyright and intellectual property law. She received her PhD in rhetoric and scientific and technical communication at the University of Minnesota in 2006. Reyman is the author of articles appearing in *College Composition and Communication* and *Technical Communication*, and is coeditor of the online edited collection *Into the Blogosphere: Rhetoric, Community, and Culture of Weblogs* (2004). She has also served multiple times as assistant chair of the Intellectual Property Caucus for the Conference on College Composition and Communication.

MARTINE COURANT RIFE is tenure-track writing faculty in the Communication Department at Lansing Community College and a PhD Candidate in the Rhetoric and Writing program at Michigan State University. Her research is at the intersection of technical communication, rhetorical invention, and intellectual property. Her work has most recently appeared in *Technical Communication, Computers and Composition, Kairos*, and *Teaching English in the Two-Year College*. She has an active license to practice law in Michigan. She is currently conducting a WIDE Research Center–supported national study with William Hart-Davidson titled "Is There a Chilling of Digital Communication? Exploring How Knowledge and Understanding of Fair Use Influence Web Composing."

STEVE WESTBROOK is an assistant professor of English at California State University, Fullerton, where he teaches courses in composition, creative writing, and cultural studies. His essays have appeared most recently in *College English, Language and Learning Across the Disciplines*, and *New Writing: The International Journal for the Practice and Theory of Creative Writing*.

INDEX